Six Weeks to Find a Job

Hodder & Stoughton

A MEMBER OF THE HODDER HEADLINE GROUP

Orders: please contact Bookpoint Ltd, 130 Milton Park, Abingdon, Oxon
OX14 4SB. Telephone: (44) 01235 827720, Fax: (44) 01235 400454. Lines are open
from 9.00–6.00, Monday to Saturday, with a 24 hour message answering service.
Email address: orders@bookpoint.co.uk

British Library Cataloguing in Publication Data
A catalogue record for this title is available from The British Library

ISBN 0 340 812591

First published 2003
Impression number   10 9 8 7 6 5 4 3 2 1
Year   2009 2008 2007 2006 2005 2004 2003

Copyright © 2003 Wendy Hirsh, Charles Jackson, Hilton Catt, Patricia
Scudamore, Steve Morris, Graham Willcocks, Alison Straw, Mo Shapiro, John
Sponton, Stewart Wright.

All rights reserved. No part of this publication may be reproduced or
transmitted in any form or by any means, electronic or mechanical, including
photocopy, recording, or any information storage and retrieval system,
without permission in writing from the publisher or under licence from the
Copyright Licensing Agency Limited. Further details of such licences (for
reprographic reproduction) may be obtained from the Copyright Licensing
Agency Limited, of 90 Tottenham Court Road, London W1P 9HE.

Typeset by SX Composing DTP, Rayleigh, Essex.
Printed in Great Britain for Hodder & Stoughton Educational, a division of
Hodder Headline Plc, 338 Euston Road, London NW1 3BH by
Cox & Wyman Ltd, Reading, Berkshire.

Every effort has been made to trace and acknowledge ownership of copyright.
The publishers will be glad to make suitable arrangements with any copyright
holders whom it has not been possible to contact.

chartered
management
institute

inspiring leaders

The leading organisation for professional management

As the champion of management, the Chartered Management Institute shapes and supports the managers of tomorrow. By sharing intelligent insights and setting standards in management development, the Institute helps to deliver results in a dynamic world.

Setting and raising standards

The Institute is a nationally accredited organisation, responsible for setting standards in management and recognising excellence through the award of professional qualifications.

Encouraging development, improving performance

The Institute has a vast range of development programmes, qualifications, information resources and career guidance to help managers and their organisations meet new challenges in a fast-changing environment.

Shaping opinion

With in-depth research and regular policy surveys of its 91,000 individual members and 520 corporate members, the Chartered Management Institute has a deep understanding of the key issues. Its view is informed, intelligent and respected.

For more information call 01536 204222 or visit www.managers.org.uk

CONTENTS

Week One: Planning Your Career

Introduction		11
Sunday	What do you want from work?	12
Monday	What kind of job would you enjoy?	23
Tuesday	What are you good at?	33
Wednesday	Identifying your career options	45
Thursday	Collecting information	57
Friday	Making a choice	70
Saturday	Taking the first steps	85

Week Two: Job Hunting

Introduction		101
Sunday	Understanding the modern job market	102
Monday	Availability, accessibility and application	112
Tuesday	Targeting	122
Wednesday	Attacking the visible market	132
Thursday	Attacking the invisible market	148
Friday	How to get headhunted	164
Saturday	Applying selectivity to your job search	178
Conclusion	Job hunting as a part of a career strategy	187

CONTENTS

Week Three: Writing Your CV

Introduction		193
Sunday	Thinking about you	195
Monday	Getting the basics right	206
Tuesday	Knowing you . . .	216
Wednesday	Knowing me . . .	230
Thursday	Getting down to the writing	243
Friday	Almost there	254
Saturday	Getting your CV across to the employer	268

Week Four: Succeeding at Your Interview

Introduction		277
Sunday	The interview process	278
Monday	Do your research	286
Tuesday	Know yourself	303
Wednesday	Preparing yourself for success	317
Thursday	The interview – responding skilfully	328
Friday	Your moves	336
Saturday	Putting it all together	347

CONTENTS

Week Five: Tackling Interview Questions

Introduction		359
Sunday	What's involved?	360
Monday	Are you sitting comfortably?	370
Tuesday	What have you done so far?	379
Wednesday	Who are you?	393
Thursday	How will you do the job?	409
Friday	Will you fit?	421
Saturday	Are you ready?	434

Week Six: Assessment Centres and Psychometric Tests

Introduction		450
Sunday	The Assessment Centre process	452
Monday	Competency based interviews	458
Tuesday	Preparing for Group Exercises	470
Wednesday	Preparing for psychometric tests and questionnaires	479
Thursday	Preparing for Presentation Exercises	494
Friday	Preparing for Analysis Exercises	505
Saturday	Pulling it all together	514
Appendices		521

ABOUT THE AUTHORS

Wendy Hirsh and Charles Jackson

Wendy Hirsh and Charles Jackson have written extensively about career development practice. They advise many leading employers in both the public and private sectors on developing strategies for career development and the design of career interventions.

Hilton Catt and Patricia Scudamore

Hilton Catt and Patricia Scudamore have both worked in Human Resource management, recruitment and training for over thirty years. They are now professional writers specialising in HR and career-oriented subjects.

Steve Morris and Graham Willcocks

Steve Morris is Director of the Burton Morris consultancy, an agency that has developed new ways of writing for businesses. He is also Director of the Letterhouse which specialises in letters and emails for business. Graham Willcocks is an experienced author and trainer on management, communication and interpersonal skills and runs successful workshops for top management teams. He is Director of Wesley House Consultants.

Alison Straw

Alison Straw is Head of Learning and Development at Selfridges. Her work involves developing a learning climate to improve success.

ABOUT THE AUTHORS

Mo Shapiro

Mo Shapiro is a qualified practitioner of Neuro-Linguistic Programming and partner in *IN*FORM Training and Communication, www.inform-global.com. She has an outstanding record as an emotional fitness coach, management trainer and public speaker. Mo contributes expert advice to all popular media and has co-authored *Succeeding at Interviews in a Week* and *Tackling Interview Questions in a Week*.

John Sponton and Stewart Wright

John Sponton and Stewart Wright are Directors of Informed Assessment Limited which specialises in assessment for recruitment, personal development and career management. John is a Chartered Psychologist and Stewart is an experienced assessment consultant.

Planning your career

**WENDY HIRSH
CHARLES JACKSON**

WEEK ONE

CONTENTS

Week One

Introduction		11
Sunday	What do you want from work?	12
Monday	What kind of job would you enjoy?	23
Tuesday	What are you good at?	33
Wednesday	Identifying your career options	45
Thursday	Collecting information	57
Friday	Making a choice	70
Saturday	Taking the first steps	85

INTRODUCTION

Week One

Work is an important part of our lives. We rely on it for income, but many of us also want more. We expect work to be interesting, to use our skills, and to fit in with our other commitments and interests. We often seek a sense of moving forward in our working lives. This is what many people mean by the term 'career'.

However, very few of us put much effort into planning for the kind of career we want. Thinking about where we are going at work is something we all need to do throughout our working lives.

By working through a simple series of steps and exercises, you can help yourself to be clear about what you want, what your options are, and how to move forward. If you want to use this week to go through these steps, you should begin by acquiring a notebook or folder in which to keep the information you will be generating.

Week One

SUNDAY

What do you want from work?

In taking the first steps towards a new career plan, we look at the following issues:

- your motivation for planning
- a simple framework for career planning
- what you want from work

As we set out to consider what we are doing at work and where we wish to go, there are always a number of seemingly good reasons to put it off yet again. So we have to start by confronting why we need to look at our own careers, and what the likely benefits might be.

Clearing away the barriers

The very term 'career' often seems daunting. Nowadays, careers are simply sequences of work experience. These can

Week One

SUNDAY

involve sideways moves, moves between employers and/or between different types of work, and even periods out of paid employment. More people are having 'portfolio' careers, combining several paid or unpaid work activities at the same time. However, all careers need thinking about if we are to find satisfaction in our work and non-work lives.

A barrier to career planning for many people is the lack of a clear approach to thinking their way through the many uncertainties involved in sorting out future job options. We will introduce a simple framework which can be used to guide our thinking.

Once you have looked at why you need to plan and understood the overall framework, then you are ready to move on to the first personal task: to take a long cool look at what you really want to get out of work.

The aim of these initial steps is to reduce your level of anxiety and set you free to think as widely as possible before you narrow down the field to particular jobs. Few of us are ever really lateral enough in our career planning.

Why try to plan your career?

Most of us feel from time to time that we should reconsider where we are going, but it seems safer not to think about it just yet.

Career planning is not just for the very young or the redundant. Most of us will need to rethink our careers several times in our working lives.

Such rethinking may lead to very modest changes, such as a rather different job with your current employer. Or it may

lead to a much more radical change of direction, as you realise that the essence of your line of work does not suit or satisfy you. Or it may result in no change at all, except a new appreciation of where you are going and why it feels right.

Planning as a necessity
It is important to be aware that by not planning you put yourself in real danger.

Work opportunities are changing all the time, and some jobs become obsolete or reduce in numbers as others open up. If we do not ensure our own employability by acquiring the right skills and moving into areas which offer some opportunity, then no one else will do it for us.

Gone are the days when careers were an orderly progression managed by the employer. These days change is continuous. Work often comes as projects and most employers expect individual employees to take the main responsibility for managing their own careers. This means we must look

SUNDAY

around for suitable work avenues to pursue and persuade our employers that we are ready to tackle fresh challenges.

If you are in any real doubt as to whether you should stop and think about your career direction, remember that 'failing to plan is planning to fail'. Successful people often say they have 'just been lucky'. This is true only to the extent that none of us can map out our future careers in every detail. Success, however, does depend on having some goals in mind and seeking opportunities to move towards them.

Your own reasons for reviewing your career
Now you need to clarify why you are looking at your career at this particular time. Some reasons might be:

- Not enjoying the current job (finding it boring, stressful, frustrating, etc.).
- Feeling that career progression is blocked (no obvious next step, employer does not recognise potential etc.).

- Suspicion that you are in the wrong kind of work altogether and need a more radical change.
- Fear of job loss, or wish to maintain employability.
- Trying to find a new route back into paid work (after redundancy or an educational course or a period of caring for dependants).
- A desire for other forms of work (voluntary work, work in 'retirement', self-employment, etc.).
- Wishing to find a better fit between work and non-work priorities (caring for children, less travelling, more flexible or shorter hours).

A framework for career planning

Any approach to career planning involves focusing both on yourself and on the job market. The framework used here encourages you to think first about yourself.

First consider three main questions in relation to yourself:

- What do you want from work? (work values)
- What kind of job would you enjoy? (job interests)
- What are you good at? (skills)

Then turn your attention to the *job market* and:

- look at the broad types of jobs available
- identify some possible career options
- find out about jobs with which you are not familiar, either inside your organisation or elsewhere

SUNDAY

Week One

On the firm foundation of these two types of knowledge you can then:

- make your career choice
- start to take action

A simple diagram can help you to remember these basic building blocks of career planning.

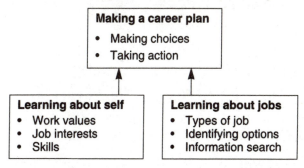

The building blocks of career planning

What do you want to get out of work?

The rest of today's programme will be devoted to starting to look at what you really want from work: your *work values*.

You may feel you work primarily to pay the bills. However, if you had to choose between two similar jobs, would you automatically take the job which paid more? Not necessarily. One job might involve a longer journey to work, the other might be in an organisation you know to be facing an uncertain future.

It is clear that what would matter most to another person might not matter most to you. Some of us are happy to take

Week One

S U N D A Y

Exercise 1: understanding your work values

Give each statement a score out of 10 using the scale below.

```
0                                        10
|_____|
```
Not important *Extremely important*
to me   *to me*

How important is it that your work: **Score**

1 Encourages accomplishment and achievement? ....

2 Offers you steady employment and security? ....

3 Provides new and different experiences? ....

4 Requires you to take personal and financial risks? ....

5 Provides good financial rewards and social status? ....

6 Benefits the community or provides a service to others? ....

7 Gives you the opportunity to use your initiative? ....

8 Is in an organisation that treats people fairly? ....

9 Is with colleagues that are easy to get along with? ....

10 Offers opportunities to direct and influence people? ....

SUNDAY — Week One

Now identify which statement has been given the highest score and rank that statement 1, find the statement with the next highest score and rank that statement 2, and so on. The order in which the values are ranked shows us the kind of rewards we want from work. Values ranked highest tell us about work settings that are likely to be attractive to us and values ranked low are likely to be unattractive to us.

Value	Work involves:	Rank
Achievement/ Challenge	Using your abilities; offering interest and challenge	....
Security/ Stability	A comfortable work environment that is not stressful	....
Variety	Meeting new people and many different projects	....
Enterprise/ Risk	Creating something new from scratch; coping with uncertainty	....
Economic Status	High salary, occupational and social standing, prestige	....
Altruism/ Service	Concern for the welfare of others	....
Autonomy	Being in control of your own work	....
Equity	Concern for fairness and equality of opportunity at work	....
Social	Friendly work environment	....
Influence	Opportunities to lead, manage and influence	....

Week One
SUNDAY

a risky career decision, because, for instance, we are confident in our own abilities, or because we think that a particular job is really worthwhile.

Start with your real priorities
Knowing the kind of work that would meet your real priorities means understanding your work values.

Start by completing Exercise 1 on the previous pages.

Where does work fit with the rest of your life?
This is another key question to think about early in the career planning process. For example, how much time do you want to devote to work? It is not just a question of whether you want to to work full time or part time, or whether you mind working shifts or at weekends. The question is about how central you want your work to be in your life. How will you achieve work/life balance?

SUNDAY

How important is it that you:

> - Have opportunities to work as a 'volunteer' for a charity or in a political campaign?
> - Spend time with your family and friends?
> - Are involved in caring for children or elderly parents?
> - Play sport or participate in your favourite hobby?

Perhaps it does not matter if your work takes over the whole of your life, because what you plan to do is going to be so important to you.

It is not for ever
We all change, and our circumstances change. You are not committing yourself irreversibly to a course of action when you make career plans.

If you no longer want to continue with the sort of work you have been doing, it does not mean you were wrong to start doing this sort of work in the first place.

What matters most to someone at the age of 20 is not necessarily going to be what matters most to the same person at the age of 30 or 40. On the other hand, there may be things that you have always wanted to do or to try out but, for some reason, in the past have never had the opportunity to do or never thought it would be possible for them to be the basis of paid employment.

It is not too late
It may not be easy to change career direction, especially if it means leaving a well-paid secure job to start again at the bottom rung of a career ladder, or becoming a student again; but lots of people have done it.

Over the next six days we will work through the remaining six steps in planning your career. We continue on Monday by looking at job interests.

Summary

We have spent Sunday examining the crucial issue of what we want from work. In doing that we have looked at:

- the barriers to career planning
- why you need to plan your career
- your own reasons for reviewing your career
- a framework for career planning
- understanding your work values
- where work fits with the rest of your life

Week One

MONDAY

What kind of job would you enjoy?

Jobs differ in a wide variety of ways. Today we focus on trying to identify the sort of work that you would find interesting. Forget whether you have the skills, the knowledge, or even the experience; concentrate on finding out what kinds of work you would *enjoy*.

In doing this you are continuing with the process of learning about yourself. This is the essential first step to career planning. You may feel you already have a pretty good idea of what your interests are, but even if this is the case, there are several reasons why it is worth spending some time reviewing your interests. In particular, it is possible that those interests may have changed since you last thought about them. It is also helpful to be able to articulate your interests, especially when you start getting interviews for jobs. One of the favourite questions of job interviewers is, 'Why are you interested in this job?'

The map of work interests

Having got some idea about what is important to you, you need to start thinking about the direction in which you want to go. However, when embarking on any journey a map is required to show us what is out there. It is just the same when planning a career, although in this case several maps are required. Today, we are going to be looking at the first of these maps. This map is called *work interests*.

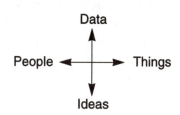

23

MONDAY

The first thing to do with any map is to orient it, and to do this we need a compass. The four points of the compass on the map of work interests are data, ideas, people and things.

The contents of jobs vary in many ways but some of the most fundamental differences concern whether they involve dealing with people, things, data or ideas. Of course, many types of work combine these four elements in varying proportions.

How to use the map

This map of work interests has several uses. First of all, if you are currently working, you can try to locate yourself, that is, to find out in what area of the map you are now. On the other hand, if you are not working, you need to find out where you were on the map when you last worked or studied. You also need to decide whether this is where you want to be or whether you really want to be somewhere else. Where would you like to be in an ideal world?

Once you have some firm ideas about where you want to be, you need to find out what sort of work opportunities exist there.

The problem is that there are so many jobs, and even the same job can seem quite different in one setting from how it feels in another. At this stage you are only trying to identify the territory in which you would like to be. Tomorrow you will have to determine whether you have, or can develop, the skills to survive there.

Establishing preferences: types of work activity

To help you determine what your work interests are, carry out the two exercises that follow. These look at interests in relation to six different types of work activity which combine a focus on people, things, data and ideas in various ways. The activities are:

- *Entrepreneurial* – activities found in business and management work.
- *Administrative* – activities found in administrative and organisational work.
- *Practical* – activities found in technical and practical work.
- *Intellectual* – activities found in scientific and research work.
- *Creative* – activities found in artistic and creative work.
- *Social* – activities found in social and personal services work.

MONDAY

The diagram shows how these six sorts of work activities relate to the two dimensions of our map: people – things and data – ideas.

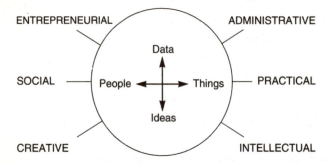

Exercise 2: your work interests

For the six sets of statements set out below, ask yourself:

'How interested am I in work that involves . . .'

Circle one number alongside each activity using the scale from 1 = no interest to 5 = strong interest

Entrepreneurial (data/people)
1 2 3 4 5 Persuading and influencing other people
1 2 3 4 5 Making business decisions
1 2 3 4 5 Managing/leading people
1 2 3 4 5 Taking business and financial risks
1 2 3 4 5 Getting people interested/involved in a project

Administrative (data/things)
1 2 3 4 5 Using a computer
1 2 3 4 5 Organising a filing system
1 2 3 4 5 Working with figures
1 2 3 4 5 Getting all the details right
1 2 3 4 5 Clear structure and routine

Week One

MONDAY

Practical (things)
1 2 3 4 5 Working with tools/machinery
1 2 3 4 5 Fixing and repairing things
1 2 3 4 5 Good hand-eye coordination
1 2 3 4 5 Working outside
1 2 3 4 5 Developing practical skills

Intellectual (ideas/things)
1 2 3 4 5 Understanding/being curious
1 2 3 4 5 Researching/analysing information
1 2 3 4 5 Asking questions
1 2 3 4 5 Solving problems in your own way
1 2 3 4 5 Learning about new things

Creative (people/ideas)
1 2 3 4 5 Using your imagination/expressing your ideas
1 2 3 4 5 Designing and making things
1 2 3 4 5 Performing/participating in artistic activities
1 2 3 4 5 Watching plays, films/listening to music
1 2 3 4 5 Working alongside creative people

Social (people)
1 2 3 4 5 Teaching people
1 2 3 4 5 Helping people with their problems
1 2 3 4 5 Meeting and talking to people
1 2 3 4 5 Building relationships with people
1 2 3 4 5 Looking after and caring for people

Add up the score for each set of items (maximum score for each area is 25). Then list in your notebook the six types of activity in rank order from rank 1 for the highest-scoring set of items to rank 6 for the lowest.

MONDAY

Patterns of scores may vary in lots of different ways. You may score much higher on one or two of the interest areas than on the others. Alternatively, you may find that you seem to score highly in nearly all areas, or not score very highly in any area.

Before we go on to explore the meaning of this interests' profile, let's complete another exercise. This is a different way of looking at the same six types of work activity.

Exercise 3: preference for work activities

The purpose of this exercise is to examine your preferences for the six types of work activity.

Circle the type of activity you prefer in each pair:

Practical	Creative	Social
or	*or*	*or*
Creative	Social	Administrative
Social	Entrepreneurial	Intellectual
or	*or*	*or*
Entrepreneurial	Intellectual	Social

Week One

MONDAY

Intellectual *or* Administrative	Administrative *or* Practical	Practical *or* Intellectual
Practical *or* Social	Creative *or* Intellectual	Entrepreneurial *or* Administrative
Creative *or* Entrepreneurial	Entrepreneurial *or* Practical	Administrative *or* Creative

Count up the number of times you have circled each type of activity and record the scores in your notebook. The maximum possible score for each type is 5. When you add all the scores together they should total 15.

Now compare the three highest-scoring activity areas in the two exercises:

	Exercise 2	Exercise 3
Highest		
Second		
Third		

What do the results of the two exercises show? Have you identified the same work interest areas in both exercises as being of most importance to you?

Do your results show that you have one or two particularly strong areas of interest, or are several of your scores from these exercises similar?

MONDAY

If you have clearly identified a preference for one or two interest areas you should find it easier to make career decisions because you have well-formed preferences about the sort of work that will interest you.

On the other hand, if your interests seem to be in several different areas, it may be that you will need to do some research about jobs and how they differ before you can tell where your specific interests lie.

It may be that you have been put off a certain area of work by a bad experience – for example, an unsympathetic boss – or from trying to do a job without the necessary training.

You also need to find out whether your interests seem to be pointing you towards one single part of the map or to several different parts. You can find this out by going back to the diagram which shows how the six interest areas relate to the two axes, people – things and data – ideas. Are the two interest areas for which you have the strongest preference alongside each other in this diagram?

If they are, this suggests that the sort of jobs that are available in this area will offer you opportunities for interesting work.

If you find that your interests are in areas which are not alongside each other in the diagram, this suggests that you may have to look more widely at jobs from the two or more areas that might interest you. However, many jobs can satisfy more than one area of interest. Frequently, you can identify a type of work that satisfies your strongest area of interest but choose to pursue it in an environment or work setting that will satisfy your other area of interest. In this way you could work alongside people doing different jobs but who have similar interests. For example, working as a secretary in an advertising agency or a social services department is likely to offer very different kinds of work colleagues.

Are you where you want to be?

By completing the two exercises you should have identified the sort of activities you would enjoy in your work. Now ask yourself whether your present job (or alternatively your last job) contained these sort of activities.

The easiest way to do this is to repeat Exercise 2, only this time ask yourself as you complete it: 'Does my current [last] job involve . . . ?'

How does your current or last job compare with your preferences? Does it offer you the sort of activities that you enjoy?

If it does, this does not necessarily mean that you should not be reviewing your career plans or even looking for a job

MONDAY

change, but it should reassure you that you are already in the right area of the map of work interests. This is likely to help in your planning, because you are more likely to know about jobs similar to your present one.

If your current or last job does not offer activities that are important to you or offers only some of them, this is one important reason for reviewing your career plans.

By identifying the sort of activities you enjoy, you have now identified where you want to be on the map of work interests in an ideal world. You should now be in a strong position to review your skills, knowledge and experience to see whether you are equipped for the sort of work opportunities that are available there.

Summary

We have spent today:

- learning about the key dimensions of work interests
- reviewing the work activities that you enjoy
- considering the extent to which your current or last job satisfies your work interests

TUESDAY

What are you good at?

Having thought about where your job interests lie, you now need to move on to think about your skills, knowledge and experience. This means both being aware of why you need to assess yourself as well as having some techniques for carrying out this assessment. This requires:

- understanding the need for self-assessment
- using exercises to review your skills and experience
- deciding whether you like what you are good at

In thinking about what you are good at, it is important not just to think about what you do in your present job but also to include what you have done in previous jobs and outside of paid work.

Understanding the need for self-assessment

If we were concerned with selecting someone for a job, we would want to assure ourselves that they were capable of

doing it. What sort of evidence of their ability to do the job – their 'competence' – would we consider relevant?

Almost certainly we would want evidence of the kind of work they had done previously. This would help us determine whether they were likely to have the skills, knowledge and experience required for the job. We might also want to know about their educational qualifications. Educational qualifications give both a broad indication of overall level of ability and show whether someone has the specific skills and knowledge required for certain types of work. We would also want to check whether they have certain key skills e.g. basic IT skills, communication skills.

The weight given to each of these components will vary considerably for different sorts of jobs. Qualifications are important for technical and professional jobs; they may be less important for non-technical and managerial jobs, where skills and experience are the main indicators of suitability. Selectors will also give more weight to recent work history than to qualifications that were gained many years ago.

It is just the same for you when trying to determine whether you are qualified to do certain sorts of job. You have to review your skills, knowledge and experience, as well as your educational qualifications, to work out what sort of jobs you may be capable of doing.

Assessing skills and experience

Of course, you are not yet at the stage of being selected for a job. Rather, you are trying to work out what jobs you might be able to do. *How are you going to do this?*

TUESDAY
Week One

Answer 1: using your expert knowledge

In some circumstances, selectors go out and measure the performance of people who are currently doing the same job elsewhere, to build up an objective picture of the skills required for the job. In this process they may use tests, measures of work output (e.g. production figures), ratings of performance from managers and so on. Frequently, however, it is not possible to collect this kind of objective information. Selectors therefore have to make their own judgements about the skills, knowledge and experience that are required for the job. It is generally assumed that selectors are able to do this because of their expert knowledge.

This is what you are going to do today. You will use your expert knowledge of yourself to review the skills, knowledge and experience you have acquired throughout your life.

TUESDAY
Week One

The strength of this approach is that no one should know you better than you know yourself. However, for this approach to be successful requires strict honesty in assessment. After all, someone who is not honest in self-assessment fools no one but themselves.

Answer 2: using exercises

The remainder of today is going to be spent in completing and interpreting two exercises. These exercises are designed to help you review your skills, knowledge and experience. The first exercise aims to give you an opportunity to make an overall assessment of your skill level, while the second one aims to generate a more detailed list of the skills, knowledge and experience you have acquired.

Of course, two short self-completion exercises do not constitute a thorough assessment of your skills; the aim here is to get started on the self-assessment process and to enable you to see in what broad areas you feel you have skills.

Exercise 4: identifying your areas of strength

This exercise asks you to judge how your skills compare with those of other people. Think about your skills in relation to the four compass points of our work map:

People: work skills involved in working with people might include managing and organising people, persuading and negotiating with people, supporting and giving help to people, teaching, entertaining or understanding other people.

Week One

TUESDAY

Things: work skills involved in making or constructing things might include the manual skills in using tools and working with machinery, the ability to understand how things work, having good hand-eye coordination.

Data: work skills involved in handling information might include interpreting a graph, working with figures on a computer, deciding how best to present and communicate information.

Ideas: work skills associated with being creative might include designing or adapting things, improvising, being innovative, having an interest in ideas and how to develop them, experimenting and investigating.

First of all, rate yourself in comparison to people in general. Compared to other people, how good are you at working with people, things, data and ideas? Circle the appropriate phrase in each case:

People Excellent	Very good	Quite good	Not very good	No good at all
Things Excellent	Very good	Quite good	Not very good	No good at all
Data Excellent	Very good	Quite good	Not very good	No good at all
Ideas Excellent	Very good	Quite good	Not very good	No good at all

How do you rate yourself? Have you given yourself a similar rating for each of the four skill areas, or do you think that you have a higher level of skills in some areas than in others?

Next, try rating yourself again, only this time making your comparisons in terms of people doing the sort of jobs in which you are interested.

These are your self-ratings of your skills. They are a measure of how you see your skills in relation to those of other people.

How accurate are these judgements? One way of testing this is to get someone else who knows you well to rate you in these four skill areas. Some of us are modest and tend to underestimate our skills, while others of us are more generous in the way we rate ourselves. Getting a second opinion is one way of finding out whether our perceptions match those of others (friends, work colleagues, or family).

The next exercise aims to review in more detail your skills, knowledge and experience.

> **Exercise 5: reviewing your skills, knowledge and experience**

The only way to do this is to review things you have already done and to think hard about what they involved. This exercise uses the same four headings as in Exercise 4; this makes it easy to look at the results of both exercises together. This exercise needs to be done in several stages.

The first step is to think of things you have done: for example, your current job (if you have one), a previous job that you liked, a previous job that you disliked, something you have carried out (a serious hobby or outside interest), a role you have experienced (parent, student). There is no limit to the number that can be listed. Try to list two or three to start with.

TUESDAY
Week One

Next, you need to identify the activities that were involved in the jobs or roles that you have listed. Write some of the activities that make up each job or role on a new page of your notebook. Looking at these activities will help you identify the skills, knowledge and experience you have used.

Now, using a fresh page, write at the top the name of the job or role you are reviewing then write down the left-hand side the three headings, *Skills, Knowledge, Experience,* equally spaced down the sheet. You will need a new page like this for each job/role you examine.

Now try to list the *skills* that are associated with each of the activities that you have listed. Include both general skills and more specific ones. You will need to ask yourself these kinds of questions for each job or role:

Did you work with people? If so, in what way? Persuading them or selling something to them? Teaching or training them? Communicating with them? Was leadership involved?

Did you work with things? What sort of things? Machines or tools? Working out how to make something? Were physical skills, like hand-eye coordination, important?

Did you work with data? How? Did you have to organise or administer it? Were you collating information or figures? Were financial skills involved? Was attention to detail important? Were IT skills used?

Did you work with ideas? Were you creating something? Did this include designing something? Researching or finding out about it? How did you plan this work?

Week One
TUESDAY

Next list the *knowledge* that you used when carrying out the activities in each job or role.

Did you have relevant educational, academic or professional qualifications? What knowledge did you acquire from doing this job/role?

Third, list the *experience* you gained from doing this job/role. Did you work as part of a team or on your own? What special experience do you associate with this job/role? Was there anything you really disliked about it?

Before the final part of the exercise, make several copies of the form opposite. One copy can then be completed for each of your roles.

Having written your entries under the three headings *Skills, Knowledge, Experience*, you can then go on to classify them under the four headings *People, Things, Data, Ideas*, and write them onto one of your forms.

Once you have completed one job or role, repeat the process for the second one, and so on.

TUESDAY
Week One

Exercise 5

	IDEAS	DATA	THINGS	PEOPLE

SKILLS KNOWLEDGE EXPERIENCE

TUESDAY

Putting it all together

The final stage of the exercise is to go through all your completed forms and look at what you have listed. For each entry, whether it is under skills, knowledge or experience, you must decide whether you were good at it.

Now make another copy of the master form and summarise, in the appropriate box, the things that you are good at.

Making sense of all this

You should now be in a position to review what you have learned about yourself.

First of all, can you see any pattern in skills, knowledge and experience you have acquired? Have some things come up several times? Are they in the same categories?

Are you good at them? Is there a pattern in the things you are good at? What are you *really* good at?

Looking at this list of things you are good at, it is now appropriate to ask yourself: Do you like doing these things? Of these, which ones are really important to you? Which ones would you like to do more?

Linking skills to jobs

As well as the very detailed profile you have now built up about yourself, you also need to be able to summarise where you think you should be located on the map of work types.

Look at the 'wheel' diagram opposite. Colour, tick or mark in some other way the sectors of the wheel where you now

Week One

TUESDAY

know you have skills, knowledge or experience. The areas can be related to the results from Monday's exercises on work interests.

Check back with Exercise 4. Do the results of the two exercises agree? Having completed Exercise 5, do you want to change the way you have rated yourself on Exercise 4?

Are your skills in:

- Adjacent sectors?
- Opposite sectors?
- More than half the sectors?

Are your areas of strength the same as your areas of interest?

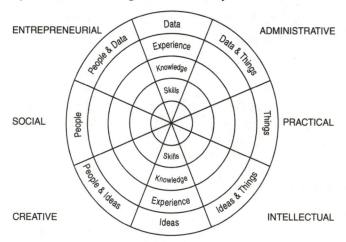

Learning for the future

As work will continue to change, one key skill for everyone is being prepared to learn new skills. Nowadays, nearly every job requires some IT skills, for example. Employers are increasingly interested in our willingness to learn and try out new things. Our attitude to learning can be just as important as our existing skills, knowledge and experience.

Summary

We have spent Tuesday reviewing what you are good at. We have set out to:

- understand why you need to do this
- review your skills, knowledge and experience
- see how they relate to the four areas of data, ideas, people and things
- map out these areas
- show why learning new skills is important

WEDNESDAY

Identifying your career options

You have started the career planning process by learning about yourself: examining your own values, interests, skills, knowledge and experience. Now it is time to turn to the second major building block of the career planning framework: learning about jobs. We will spread this task over the next two days. Today, we start by thinking as widely as possible about career options.

You may find that some career options which look exciting turn out to be less attractive or less achievable when you know more about them. You may need to go through the process of generating options and researching them several times before you move on to make a career action plan.

Today we will examine:

- what is happening to jobs and careers
- what kinds of jobs there are
- your own career options

What is happening to jobs and careers?

In thinking about our own career options, it is important to bear in mind general trends in the world of work. The job market is always in a state of change and this turbulence has been increasing over the last 20 years.

The economy
The state of the economy clearly affects our job options. In a recession, opportunities are likely to be in short supply. In a period of rapid economic growth, there are more job

vacancies. These are not caused just by new jobs, but also by people moving more freely from job to job. It will be easier at such times to re-enter the labour market or make radical career moves.

Also, the job market varies between sectors of the economy and parts of the country. Some types of employer can be recruiting while others are reducing numbers.

The media report such economic information, often mentioning aspects of the job market. We should use this knowledge to decide the tactics of our job moves. Given the turbulence of economic conditions, however, we should not let short-term economic changes dominate our longer-term career strategy.

Longer-term changes in jobs and careers
More important to longer-term career options are underlying shifts in the employment structure. These vary in detail by country, region and sector, but some broad shifts are apparent in most Western nations:

- A reduction of employment in so-called primary sectors: agriculture, fishing, mining, etc.
- Relatively fewer jobs in manufacturing industry.
- Relatively more jobs in the service sectors, e.g. retailing, financial services, health and personal services.
- An increase in the relative importance of employment in smaller organisations and of self-employment.
- The 'contracting out' of some work from larger organisations (e.g. in security, catering, cleaning) to smaller organisations or the self-employed.

WEDNESDAY
Week One

- A growth in temporary and part-time employment.
- A decline in less skilled jobs and a growth in high-skill, professional and 'knowledge' jobs.

These changes have resulted in significant levels of general unemployment, coexisting with shortages of people with particular skills.

These shifts in employment, plus alterations to the way large organisations operate, have also changed careers:

- A 'job for life' is not a realistic expectation. We should expect several major changes in occupation during our working lives, and many more in job or employer.
- We may do several types of paid or unpaid work activities at the same time – the so-called 'portfolio career'.

Week One
WEDNESDAY

> - Flatter organisation structures mean more of us will have to make sideways rather than vertical career moves.
> - Large organisations expect their employees to manage their own career moves and skill development.

Managing our own career

To manage our own careers, we need to develop new skills:

> - flexibility and adaptability
> - ability to learn new skills, especially higher-level, interpersonal and technological skills
> - willingness and ability to manage our own careers
> - ability to develop and use personal networks to get work
> - ability to see and understand trends in the labour market

Kinds of jobs

Most of us are restricted in our career planning by our very limited knowledge of the jobs that exist. We know about the jobs that our parents, friends and teachers do or tell us about. There are many jobs we never consider because we do not know about them. So how do we start thinking about jobs?

A useful starting point is to take the same concepts we used on Monday to map work interests. We can look at jobs in terms of whether they predominantly involve working with people, things, data or ideas.

WEDNESDAY

We used six headings to think about activities and interests, and the same categories can be used again to think about broad 'families' of jobs, as follows:

- 'entrepreneurial': business and management jobs
- 'administrative' or organisational jobs
- 'practical' or technical jobs
- 'intellectual': scientific and research jobs
- 'creative' and artistic jobs
- 'social' and personal services jobs

Within each family there are jobs at various levels, in various sectors and with a range of specific content. A few illustrations might help your imagination to get going. While reading this section, keep a note of any jobs which seem worth exploring.

Entrepreneurial jobs include: jobs in business and management, marketing and selling such as telephone sales, marketing manager, retail manager, shop assistant, buyer, personnel manager, estate agent.

Administrative and organisational jobs include: clerical, secretarial and administrative jobs, jobs in finance, actuaries, tax consultants, management accountants.

Practical and technical jobs include: a vast number of jobs working with different materials and technologies and at a wide range of levels, from labourers to nuclear engineers, such as jobs in construction (building trades, surveyor, etc.), in manufacturing (operators, technicians etc.), in transport, engineering, leisure (domestic staff, chef), agriculture and horticulture (gardener, tree surgeon, vet).

WEDNESDAY

Intellectual jobs include: jobs in research, science, medicine and social sciences, such as laboratory technician, geologist, statistician, radiographer, nutritionist, surgeon, economist, maths teacher.

Creative and artistic jobs include: music, dance, theatre and the visual arts, director, producer, journalist, professional sport, advertising, fashion work, architecture and design, photography.

Social and personal service jobs include: playleader, teacher, lecturer, social worker, counsellor, hotel receptionist, air steward/stewardess, beauty therapist, prison officer.

Of course, there are jobs which combine elements of more than one family. For example, technical jobs in the arts – theatrical electrician, sound technician – combine creative with technical skills. Many jobs in health and the law – nurse, barrister – combine personal and scientific or research skills.

WEDNESDAY

Week One

Identifying career options

Now it is time to generate your own list of career options. It is important that at this stage you think as widely – even wildly – as possible. Even if you eventually decide to stick with the same job, or a very similar one, such exploration will reassure you that you *are* in the right line of work, at least for now.

Types of career options
You can think about your career options in terms of how far away they are from what you are doing now, or did most recently when you were last at work.

Types of options might include:

- changing the content of your current job
- moving to a job for which you have the skills
- moving to a job requiring some further training or job experiences
- making a major career change into a new area of work, often requiring new qualifications
- other changes, e.g. taking a break from work, voluntary work, going back into full-time education, becoming self-employed, etc.

Generating a list of options
There is no single best way to approach this task. You may already have several options in mind; or you may be starting with a blank sheet of paper.

Here are some of the starting points you could use in listing your own career options. Jot down any ideas that come to mind as you think.

Week One
WEDNESDAY

- Do some of the 'families' of jobs described above excite you or contain jobs you have always wanted to do? Look back at the work you have done on your values (Exercise 1), interests (Exercises 2 and 3) and skills (Exercises 4 and 5) to identify at least some job families which are likely to suit you.
- If job families seem too general, some more detailed careers material contains lists of jobs within each of these families.
- Think about the different types of career option listed above.
- Fantasise about the perfect job. What would a perfect working day consist of? What would you be doing, and in what surroundings?
- Talk to family, friends and colleagues.
- Look at job advertisements in newspapers and journals.

WEDNESDAY

- If you are in employment, look afresh at your current job and consider whether it would meet your needs if you could change it in some way.
- Think too about jobs elsewhere in your current organisation – not just promotions but also jobs in other locations, in other departments or units and in other functions or occupations.

For each of your options, try to think about where your desired activities or jobs might exist. Identify:

- Possible sectors, types of employer or particular organisations.
- Whether any options involve things other than conventional paid employment, e.g. voluntary work, self-employment, full-time study, etc.

It is important to think too about some of the implications of each option, such as money, working time, geographical location or the need to study.

Listing and summarising your career options

This part of our process should have helped you to generate several career options. You should summarise these before moving on.

Exercise 6: summarising career options

First write a simple list of each of the career options so far identified. Remember you can always come back to this list and add more options later if you choose.

Week One
WEDNESDAY

For example, someone re-entering paid employment after several years caring for their young children might be considering:

- going back to teaching
- educational psychology
- some form of self-employment – perhaps writing

A young graduate accountant might include:

- gaining faster promotion to partner
- moving to a larger company
- finance work in another sector, perhaps retail
- doing something quite different once qualified: taking a management course, travelling

Now you need to complete a summary sheet for each of your options, recording the most important things about it. A sample format for this summary is shown opposite.

In looking at each career option, it is important to be honest with yourself about its likely pros and cons. Think about how they might affect your partner or family as well as yourself. Are there trade-offs between the contract of employment (money, location etc.) and how attracted you are by the work itself? What about the kinds of people you might be working with and the likely workplace culture?

Pay attention to how you *feel* about each option as well as your more objective assessment of it, before you go on to research it further.

WEDNESDAY

Career option summary

Name/title for this option:

Type of option (*circle one or add your own*):
- changing content of your current job
- moving to a job for which you have the skills
- moving to a job requiring training/experience
- a major career change
- other

Job family, job activities or occupations involved (*including possible jobs if known*):

Possible employer or job context (*particular employers or types of employer, voluntary work, self-employed, full-time education, etc.*):

Implications of this option (*finance, patterns of work, location, requirements for education or training*):

Pros and cons of this option:

Week One
WEDNESDAY

Summary

We have spent Wednesday considering:

- what is happening to jobs and careers
- what types of jobs there are
- your own career options

T H U R S D A Y

Collecting information

Now you have drawn up a list of career options, how do you move towards an action plan? It is tempting to move straight to choosing an option or applying for jobs. It is also unwise. We usually need to know a good deal more about each of our options before we are in a position to make judgements about them. This phase of 'active job research' makes all the difference between good career decisions and poor ones.

Today you need to turn from a dreamer into a detective. Your elusive quarry will be the real job. Only when you have a good understanding of what each of your options really involves can you make a wise choice.

We will be examining:

- your information needs
- career paths
- sources of information on careers and jobs
- using information interviews

Week One

THURSDAY

Your information needs

There are three main sets of questions you need to answer when you are researching jobs:

What would this option really be like?

> - In what environment would you be working?
> - What would you be doing?
> - Likely conditions of employment.

What would you need?

> - What skills are required?
> - What knowledge or qualifications are required?
> - What previous experience is required?

Will there be opportunities available?
Once you have the answers to these questions, then you can compare them with your own values, interests, skills, knowledge and experience to decide which options will suit you best.

The same questions can be applied to career options which are not just job moves. For example, if you are considering self-employment you can ask yourself what that change will really mean for you, what skills you will need, and whether you can create a realistic opportunity for yourself.

| Exercise 7: career option research |

This exercise goes a step further from the brief description of each option you generated yesterday. The blank form shows some headings you might use for each option to structure the

THURSDAY
Week One

information you collect. The notes on the headings suggest some of the specific things you should be finding out.

Career Option Research
Name/title of career option

What would this option really be like?
Work environment (*employers, values, environment*):

Job content (*role, level, responsibilities, activities*):

Conditions of employment (*pay, hours, etc.*):

Requirements for this option
Skills/knowledge:

Qualifications:

Previous job/career experience:

Likely levels of opportunity

Work environment matters as well as the content of a job, and choosing an environment which is compatible with your work values can be crucial. From a practical point of view, you need

Week One

THURSDAY

to find out who your likely employers might be. You also need to know with what sorts of people you will be working, the physical environment you can expect, and the culture of the organisation. Later on, these items will tell you to what extent each option is compatible with your personal values.

Job content is of paramount importance, including:

- What is this job there to do (job role) and how does it fit into the organisation?
- If the job exists at more than one level, into which job levels might you fit, perhaps in both the short and the longer term?
- What are job holders' responsibilities?
- What would a typical working day involve?
- How predictable is the work? Is it stressful? How much freedom and autonomy do job holders have?

Conditions of employment need to cover the financial and domestic implications of each option e.g. pay, benefits, pensions, costs of education courses, working hours and patterns (real not just contractual), travelling or working away, possible relocation.

Work environment, job content and conditions of employment tell you what each career option would really feel like. They apply just as much to full-time education or self-employment as to conventional jobs.

Skills and knowledge requirements tell us:

- what we have to be able to do
- what we have to know about

THURSDAY

You will be using this information later to assess your suitability for each option, and to present your curriculum vitae (CV) in the best way.

It is often possible to extrapolate from job activities to the skills and knowledge required. For example, the school-teacher thinking of writing educational materials would have to get ideas accepted by publishers, research, design and write. Skills required would include imagination, persuasion, negotiation, research, writing at the right level, IT skills, project and time management. Knowledge of the market would also be critical and the ability to learn how to run a small business.

Formal *qualifications* are used by employers as another 'filter' for applicants. For some jobs, including many professions, they are a statutory requirement. Many career paths require qualifications to get beyond a certain level so you need to find out which qualifications are necessary or preferred for your chosen option.

There is a rough association between job level and level of qualifications required:

- *No formal qualifications*: mainly unskilled and semi-skilled jobs.
- *General qualifications from school*: many clerical and craft jobs, often followed by specific vocational training.
- *Higher-level qualifications*: many jobs require good school-leaving qualifications plus specific training, but not a degree.
- *Degree or professional qualifications*: most specialist jobs and, increasingly, management.

THURSDAY

Skills and knowledge are what we need to do a job, but employers often use what we have done before – our *previous job/career experience* – as an indicator of these. In many walks of life there are jobs which are difficult to enter without having done some of the activities before, often at a more junior level. Sometimes you may be able to convince an employer to take a chance on you, even if you do not have the usual background experience. However, you still should arm yourself with the knowledge of what previous experience is normally expected. You need to know:

- the types of jobs and job levels at which you can enter your desired organisation or occupation
- the subsequent sequences of job experience – career paths – which are most often followed
- the range of experience expected for your desired job

Mapping career paths

If you find the career paths hard to think about for any of your particular options, it can help to try and map them. This is especially helpful for options which involve quite a few job or training steps between where you are now and where you want to be. Career path maps can be drawn for an occupation (e.g. entering educational psychology as a new career) or for more specific options within a given employer (e.g. the young accountant wanting to make his/her way to a partnership).

Exercise 8: drawing a career path map

Try drawing a map for some of your options which involve several job steps. Show boxes for relevant types of job

THURSDAY

experience. Put more junior jobs lower down on the page and more senior jobs higher up, with job levels in different work areas roughly lined up across the page. Arrows show career moves between boxes, which may involve a change in:

- level or job role
- department, unit or location
- function (e.g. production, personnel, sales etc.)
- employer

If you are trying to enter an organisation, you should mark the jobs where external recruitment occurs.

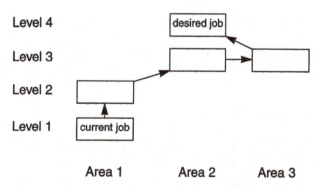

The typical career map shown here illustrates a career option involving a desired job type three levels above the current job (these may be from trainee, to qualified, to supervisor, to manager). It also shows moving to an area of work (Area 2) different from the current one (Area 1). To achieve this, it may be necessary to gain experience in a third area (Area 3).

These areas of work may be functions (production, finance, sales, etc.), different parts of the same function, different units (factory, head office) or different locations (a small-town bank, a large city branch, an overseas operation, etc.). They might also represent different employers. Often the map will show more than one possible route to where you want to get.

You can use these maps to identify more clearly short- and longer-term job goals.

Likely levels of opportunity

We have already discussed changing employment patterns and the labour shortages and surpluses they bring. It is important to be aware which career options will offer plenty of opportunity and which will be very competitive.

High levels of opportunity are found in:

- New or rapidly growing areas of activity or new technologies.
- Occupations for which few people have been training, and where shortages may develop.
- Occupations from which many people are about to retire, and where replacements will be needed.

Your job research should ask:

- Is the number of jobs growing or shrinking?
- How many vacancies exist at present?
- Are there large numbers of applicants?
- Do opportunities vary geographically or from one employer to another?
- Are you likely to face particular barriers in pursuing this option because of age, gender, race, disability, etc.?

Week One

THURSDAY

Information sources

Your information needs will be quite wide ranging, but there are many sources of job information. The process itself can be fun and interesting. Your main access to job information will be through:

- people you know – your personal network
- external information sources
- information within your own organisation
- people doing the job – through information interviews

People you know (colleagues, friends and family) may know about the job you have in mind, or have a friend who does. They may know about the organisation you are considering, or the college course you might take. It is always better to talk to someone who has had real contact with a job, rather than just listen to general opinions. If you know 100 people, and they each know 100 people, that gives you 10 000 people to ask – assuming you all have different friends!

THURSDAY

External information sources include:

- Brochures and reports from potential employers.
- Press and journals: job advertisements and articles on job and career trends.
- Reference books, career directories and reference material, available in public libraries.
- Careers services and educational institutions.
- Recruitment agencies.
- Industry and professional bodies: these often produce the most comprehensive information both on careers and on qualifications required.
- Trade unions and employee organisations.

Much of this information is now also on the internet.

Information within your own organisation can be very useful if you are currently employed and considering career options within the same organisation. However, make careful judgements about whom you talk to and when. Choose people who will keep a confidence if asked to.

There are many other internal information sources:

- Business information, e.g. annual reports, newsletters, business plans or objectives, is usually freely available.
- Job vacancies are often put on notice-boards.
- The personnel function usually holds information on jobs, e.g. recruitment literature, training schemes, organisation charts, job descriptions, skill and qualifications requirements.

Week One

THURSDAY

- Some employers have special libraries containing information on careers and training.
- Successful people in the job area you have in mind provide useful clues as to what career paths are valued, and what skills are required.
- Senior people, including your own boss, are often happy to advise or take a 'mentoring' role. Try and approach people who you think will support you. Use your own friends and informal networks to find out who might be best to speak to.

Once you have done some preparatory research it can be extremely valuable to talk to someone who actually does the job you have in mind. We call this an *information interview*.

Information interviews do not just help your research. They also give you a chance to meet people who might be willing to help you later on, or to recommend other useful contacts.

UH-HUH — THAT'S FROM MY PERSONAL EXPERIENCE

Week One
THURSDAY

When conducting an information interview:

- explain that the purpose of the interview is to help you find out more about a type of job in which you are interested
- prepare in advance what you are going to say and ask
- take good notes
- keep it short
- be pleasant and not too pushy, but take a CV with you just in case
- send a thank-you letter
- treat other contacts you may be given with discretion

Exercise 9: the information interview

Try out an information interview. Practise the technique on a friend or colleague first if you wish. Some questions to ask include:

- What does the job involve on a day-to-day basis?
- Where does it fit in with the rest of the organisation?
- Are there significant changes going on in the job or the organisation?
- What skills are most important in the job? (Remember to ask about general skills, like IT, as well as job specific skills.)
- Are any qualifications required/preferred?
- What training or development is available in this job?
- What are the career backgrounds of job holders?
- When people leave or move on, where do they go?
- Are there likely to be vacancies in future?

THURSDAY

Using people you already know to help you find your way to people with the information and advice you need is an important part of career planning. Such 'networking' has always been important in types of work where jobs are fluid and often not formally advertised. As the whole labour market becomes more fluid and fast-moving, networking is increasingly important to us all.

Summary

Today you have researched your career options by:

- defining your information needs
- mapping possible career paths
- identifying information sources
- using information interviews

Now we have completed the second building block of career planning – understanding jobs. We are now ready to go on to the third and final stage of career planning – making a choice and taking action.

Remember if you are not happy with any of the career options you have generated so far, you can go back to the options thinking stage and try again.

FRIDAY

Making a choice

The main task for today is to pull together what you have learnt so far this week. You need to examine how the career options you have researched measure up with your values and interests and whether they meet your personal requirements. You also need to consider how well your skills, knowledge and experience match up with those demanded by your options, and whether opportunities are likely to be available.

By the end of today you should have a firm sense of direction, so that you can move on to taking action. This means that there are a number of important questions that you must try to answer today. Most importantly, you must try to decide whether you have identified a career option that is both *attractive* and *achievable*.

FRIDAY

Many career plans will involve skill development, and in the final part of this chapter, we will review how to go about accessing development opportunities at work or through education.

Pulling together what you have found out

By now you should have identified several possible career options and researched them in some depth. The stages in deciding between your various options involve:

- Deciding how attractive they are by comparing them with your work values and work interests.
- Reviewing the impact of any factors that may constrain your choice of options.
- Deciding how achievable each option is for you by comparing your options with your skills, knowledge and experience, and levels of opportunity.
- Weighing the pros and cons of each option.
- Determining your overall preference between options.

Start by trying to decide which option is most attractive to you. First, gauge the extent to which each option matches up with your work values.

Comparing options with your work values
One way to do this is to review each of your options against your self-rating of work values (Exercise 1). Consider the three work values that you identified as most important and ask for each of your possible career options:

FRIDAY

Will the work involve this value? (Answer YES or NO)

How does each option score? It is worth rating your current job as well (if you have one).

How do the options compare? Will they satisfy the values that are most important to you?

If your options satisfy values that are not important to you, it may not matter. For example, the fact that an option is likely to provide a high salary or a friendly work environment is not going to put most of us off. However, you may be trying to avoid work that involves certain work values – risk, for example.

Comparing options with your work interests
You have already identified your profile of work interests. Now you need to see whether your options are likely to

FRIDAY

involve activities that interest you. If you have researched your options thoroughly you will now know something about what they involve.

One way to do this is to construct a profile for each of your options in just the same way that you constructed a profile for yourself. You can do this by going back to Exercise 2, where you rated yourself, and using the same framework to rate each option in turn.

For each option, ask the question:

Does this option provide opportunities for . . .?

Use the 1 to 5 scale giving scores from 1 for an option that will provide no opportunity for this activity to 5 for an option that will provide plenty of opportunity for this activity.

Now you can compare your own score profile with that of each of your options. Some key questions are:

> - Are the two highest activity areas for each of your options the same as or different from those that you found you preferred?
> - Are all your possible options scoring highly in the same interest areas?
> - How do your options compare with your current job?

What do you learn from this? How attractive are your options to you? Are they the sorts of jobs that you would enjoy? How do they match up with your real priorities?

Week One

F R I D A Y

At this stage you may be in one of three different situations.

1 Options match interests and values.
You are ready to go on and see how you measure up against your options in terms of skills, knowledge and experience.

2 Options match interests and values to some extent.
Should you go back and review your options? Can you think of any other options that you ought to consider? Or have you changed your mind about your interests and values?

3 Options do not seem to match up with interests and values.
More work is required. Review your values and interests. You may also want to review your options. It may be helpful to ask someone else for a second opinion (friends, work colleagues, family). You should not expect to make your career plan on your own, so this may be a good time to involve someone else.

It is possible that you are not yet ready to make a career plan. You may need to do more work on the first two building blocks of the career planning process – *learning about self* or *learning about jobs*.

Practical constraints
In assessing the overall attractiveness of different options, remember the practical constraints on your work choices, which we looked at on Thursday. How do you want work to fit in with the rest of your life?

> - *Working patterns* – How much time do you wish to give to your work? Are you constrained by domestic and caring responsibilities, or other activities and interests? For example, do you wish to work part time or term time only?

FRIDAY

Week One

> - *Work location* – How far are you prepared to travel to work? Are you willing to move house? Would you like to work from home?
> - *Pay and benefits* – Will your requirements for pay and other benefits be met?

Comparing options with your skills, knowledge and experience
A key purpose of our research into possible options has been to find out their demands in terms of skills, knowledge and experience. You should now be able to use the information generated about your skills, knowledge and experience to determine how well you match with each of your possible options.

You may need to go back and look at the results of Exercises 5 and 7 to check whether the skills and knowledge you currently possess match up with those of your job options.

FRIDAY

Skills and knowledge are often acquired through education. Are there qualifications that people doing these jobs are expected to have? *Do you, or are you about to, have them?*

Are there other skills or knowledge that are necessary to do this job? Can you provide evidence that you have acquired these skills and/or the relevant knowledge?

Do you have the necessary experience to convince someone that you can do the job? Do you feel you have the experience, but would find it difficult to convince someone that it is really relevant? Alternatively, should you be thinking about how you are going to get the experience?

For most types of career option, you will find yourself in one of three situations.

1 You already have the skills, knowledge and experience required.

Next step: choosing options prior to action planning.

2 You have most of the skills, knowledge and experience required.

Next step: think how you might acquire the few additional skills, knowledge and experience needed. Key steps are:

- More research to find out how people acquire the sort of experience you need. What jobs do they do? Can you get one of those jobs?
- Consider going ahead with your action planning, *on the assumption that you believe you can access the development you need.* The issue of access to development is considered in the later sections of this chapter.

3 You currently lack the skills, knowledge and experience required.

Next step: review the possibilities for acquiring the skills, knowledge and experience needed before you can pursue your desired career option.

Comparing options with likely levels of opportunity
Using the labour market information you have collected, you need to make a judgement about the likely level of opportunity, both now and in the future, for each option. Are they in fields that are expanding or contracting?

Choosing a preferred option
At this stage, try to make an overall judgement between the different options you have been considering. Before doing that there are a few points to consider.

- Do you have a plan B as well as a plan A? If your preferred choice was impossible, what would you do?
- Are your options extending your future work possibilities or closing them down? Remember that work is changing continuously and we must plan for future change.
- Do your possible options feel right to you? Are you looking forward to them? If not, rethink your choices.

The next exercise aims to help you make a final choice between your different options. Ideally, there should be a perfect match between your preferred option and yourself. In practice, you may have to compromise.

Week One

FRIDAY

Your decision should be based on the extent to which options:

- cater for your interests, values and constraints
- are within reach of your skills, knowledge and experience
- have sufficient levels of opportunity

Exercise 10: preferences between career options

You may find it helpful to rate each of your career options on the following scales:

Attractiveness		Ideal
Values	0	10
Interests	0	10
Constraints	0	10

FRIDAY

Achievability

Skills	0	10
Knowledge	0	10
Experience	0	10
Opportunities	0	10

Overall rating   0   10

- How do your options compare?
- Do you have a preference for one option?
- Which option presents the best combination in terms of attractiveness and your ability to achieve it?

Accessing development

Your preferred career option may be in itself a return to full-time education or training; in this case you will have already started thinking about possible courses. However, the need for further skill development is common to many career plans. Development may involve:

- an educational course (full time or part time)
- training at work (through on-the-job coaching or training courses)
- a job move or project which gives you the experience you require to get closer to your career goal

FRIDAY

In this section we look at how to access development, in the form of both educational courses and development at work.

Educational courses
In many ways going back to education is getting easier. The range of colleges and courses is expanding, and prospectuses are easily available. The internet gives access to a huge amount of detailed information on education. There are many part-time courses and we can also study from home (through so-called 'distance-learning'). However, we also have to realise that competition for places on some courses is stiff and the costs of education can be high. Educational qualifications cannot guarantee you the job you want, although the right qualification will improve your chances of success.

Before choosing a course, you will need to identify what *level of qualification* might be appropriate. On Thursday we related levels of qualifications to levels of jobs. We can think of levels in terms of academic qualifications (GCSE, A level, degree, professional qualification) but there are also many vocational qualifications. The UK has a unified system of classifying vocational qualifications (NVQs and GNVQs) by broad level. Colleges and employers can advise you on the appropriate level of course to aim for, or the educational path to take through several courses.

FRIDAY

Week One

Other aspects of courses to clarify are:

- subject or subject mix, curriculum and options
- key skills taught as part of the course (e.g. IT)
- location of colleges/distance learning options
- full-time or part-time options
- entry qualifications required
- precise qualification awarded
- recognition of course, if relevant, by professional body or employers
- length of course
- opportunities to gain work experience, e.g. placements, block releases
- facility to change course if desired
- fees and availability of grants/sponsorship
- special government or industry schemes
- pattern of terms and hours of attendance
- teaching methods and staff/student ratios
- methods of assessment (exam, coursework, etc.)

FRIDAY

Career development processes at work

Most of the development we gain in our working lives happens on the job or near to it. Your job research may have already given you clear ideas about job moves you need to make for development reasons. However, development at work will not just fall into your lap. You will need to understand the processes used by employers to develop their staff, and learn to use those processes to gain access to the training and job moves you need.

Personnel management has its own jargon and the diagram opposite shows some of the processes we should try and find out about. We need to know:

- What each process is used for: how it affects the jobs people get and the training they receive.
- Whether we can use the process to obtain career information, send signals to the organisation about what we want to do or have a better dialogue about possible options.

Four important types of use shown in the diagram are: *assessment, job-filling, development* and *career planning*. Processes can have more than one use. For example, an appraisal interview can be used to assess (openly or secretly), to discuss career plans, and to identify training and development needs. The output of this appraisal may influence whether the person being appraised is eligible to apply for jobs and whether he or she is selected.

FRIDAY

Some processes are used primarily for *assessment*: identifying our strengths and weaknesses. Appraisal of performance and/or potential by a manager is the commonest, but larger organisations may also use assessment centres. These consist of a series of tests, exercises and interviews applied to a group of people often over two or three days. These may act as the gateway to a particular job level (e.g. senior management) or special development programmes.

The processes for *filling jobs* are crucial but often elusive. You will need to understand how vacancies are notified, what the selection criteria are for the jobs you want, and how the selection process really takes place. Company Intranets are now often used to advertise and apply for internal vacancies. If skill criteria (e.g. communications, teamworking) are specified for jobs they can give you clues to the skills you need to show you have.

FRIDAY

Informal influence and networking are often important in making internal job moves. You need to establish who takes short-listing and selection decisions, and who they are likely to consult about candidates, so you can gently raise your profile in the right quarters.

A range of processes combine planned job replacement and *development*. These include development schemes or programmes, and fast tracks for 'high potential' employees. Succession plans, still usually secret, plan possible job moves for some individuals. Project assignments and secondments give valuable development. Other *training and development* processes include formal or informal coaching, off-the-job training and facilities for sponsorship.

As the trend to self-development has taken root, newer processes, such as career workshops, are aimed at helping *career planning*. Development centres combine assessment with development planning. *Learning resource centres* contain career and training information, as do Intranet sites. Mentoring puts employees in touch with someone more senior who can help them develop their career.

Learning to understand and play the system using these processes can be vital to us achieving our own career goals. Understanding career processes comes from a mix of reading formal descriptions (increasingly on company Intranets) and informal discussions with colleagues.

Week One

FRIDAY

Summary

Today you have:

- examined your career options against your values, interests and skills
- chosen one or more career options to form the basis of your action plan
- identified educational courses you may need
- looked at how you might use development processes at work

S A T U R D A Y

Taking the first steps

Now that you have settled on your preferred career option, you need to set about producing an action plan to make your vision of the future a reality. This may involve quite small changes in your current job or in your life outside work; or it may be a major upheaval including a change of job, employer and location or re-entry into education. Some action plans will therefore be quite simple while others may involve a commitment to several years of retraining and change to get to where you want to be. In either case you need to clarify and schedule your actions. Today we will be examining how these first steps are taken:

- clarifying types of action required
- preparing to present yourself through CVs and application forms
- applying for jobs and courses
- getting support
- setting goals and a timetable
- monitoring progress

SATURDAY

Clarifying types of action required

Earlier we identified some of the main kinds of career options as:

- Changing the content of your current job.
- Moving to a job for which you already have the skills (this could be with your current employer or elsewhere).
- Moving to a job requiring further training or job experiences (again, with your current employer or elsewhere).
- Making a major career change into a new area of work, often requiring new qualifications.
- Other changes, e.g. return to full-time education, self-employment, voluntary work, etc.

This way of looking at options can be helpful when you come to consider the main focus of your career action plan. Typical actions may include:

- renegotiating the content of your current job
- applying for jobs inside your own organisation
- external job search
- accessing training or development at work
- applying for educational courses
- exploring other options and changes outside work

Some career options are more likely to require each of these types of action than others, as suggested by the ticks in the boxes on the action planning grid shown above. You can use this grid to think through the main focus of your action plans. Remember that changes to your life outside work can also be identified and recorded in your action plan.

Marketing yourself

One of the major hurdles in getting the sort of job you want is the selection process. This requires you to convince a potential employer that you are the right person for the job. Even if you are planning to be self-employed, you will have to convince potential customers or financiers of the viability of your venture. Essentially, you have to look at marketing yourself as though you were a product.

SATURDAY
Week One

How do you market yourself
The first thing you must know if you are going to be successful in the job hunt is why you want the job. Primarily, this is about understanding your own motivation for applying. If you really understand your work interests and values, you will be in a good position to do this.

Second, you must be able to convince your customer, in this case your potential employer, that you have the skills that they require. Once again, the work you have already done on reviewing your skills, knowledge and experience should be of help here.

In what ways will you have to market yourself?
Almost always you will have to write about yourself. Either you will have to fill in an application form, or you will have to prepare a curriculum vitae (CV) that summarises your work history. Some organisations now conduct the initial application stage in electronic form via the internet or e-mail.

Second, you will usually have an interview with your potential employer. Almost everybody wants to meet someone they will be working with. This also applies to job moves within your current employing organisation.

Frequently, there are other components to a selection process. For example, there may be tests and presentations that have to be completed, or an assessment centre to attend. You might be asked to bring along examples of your work, or be required to provide the names of people who can give you a reference.

SATURDAY

It is important to realise that many selection procedures involve a number of stages, and the employer is effectively weeding out applicants at every stage of the process. This means that you must give each aspect of the selection process your best shot. There will be no second chance. Education and training providers also use similar procedures.

You should also be aware that, in general, selection procedures, particularly those used by major employers, are becoming more rigorous. There are several reasons for this. They include a greater concern for fairness, that is, not to discriminate against applicants unfairly. There is also a desire at all costs not to select people who will be unable to do the job required. The cost in time and money of running selection procedures is also an important factor for many employers.

SATURDAY

Putting something down in writing
This is usually the first stage. Even in the most informal selection process, it will usually pay to have a curriculum vitae prepared that you can hand over.

The main difference between completing an application form and writing a CV is that with an application form it is the employer who has decided what questions to ask; with a CV you have to decide what information to present to an employer about yourself.

For more information on how to write your CV, turn to Week Three of this book.

Hints for application forms
Take a photocopy of the form before you begin and make detailed notes of what information you are going to put in each section, especially for open-ended questions. Fill in the photocopied version first as a draft. Ask someone else to have a look at it and only then complete the actual form.

Week One

SATURDAY

Make a photocopy of the completed form so that you have a record of what you wrote about yourself. Check over this before you go to an interview.

You may be able to fill in the form electronically or it may be designed to be filled in by hand. Pay attention to any special instructions about how to complete an application form. Does it say use black ink? (The form may well be photocopied, so black or dark blue are usually the best colours to use.) Have you written in capital letters (e.g. for surname), when requested to do so? Presentation counts for more than it used to; write neatly and check that your spelling is correct.

If you are applying for jobs where there will be hundreds of applicants, be mindful that getting any of these little details wrong might result in the rest of your application never being read. The first sift of a pile of application forms is frequently just to check that they have been completed correctly. Perhaps just 30 seconds is allocated to your form. Some applicants fail at this hurdle.

Don't lie! It may catch up with you and will almost certainly mean you lose the job. How is the employer to know that this is the only lie you have told them?

Answers to questions on application forms should always be written concisely. However, sometimes there will not be sufficient space to write in all that is relevant. In this case it is normally appropriate to use a continuation sheet. Such sheets should always have your name on, and should specify to which section of the form they apply.

SATURDAY

Don't leave questions unanswered; write 'None' or 'Not applicable'. Think carefully about doing this, as too many answers like this could create a negative impression.

Some employers now concentrate on looking for evidence of key skills, and the ability – or 'competence' – to cope with particular aspects of the job. So, for example, an application form might ask how you would deal with a difficult customer. Or it might ask you about your own experience of handling difficult people. Answer such questions as fully and clearly as you can. They are likely to be a critical part of your application.

Getting support

Once we are committed to making some changes in our working lives – however modest – we need to discuss our plans with other people. In some cases, for example with friends, this has the function of helping us check out whether our plans seem sensible to other people who know us. We may also get help from our friends in tackling the job market through their knowledge and networks of contacts.

When it comes to families, some career plans may simply require their emotional support, for example in seeking a change in the content of a current job. Other options, for example a radical job move, a relocation or a return to education, have profound implications for other family members. These are clearly family decisions and need very careful discussion.

Week One

SATURDAY

Broaching the subject of career change at work can be quite difficult. How you deal with your manager and colleagues will depend on whether you think they are likely to be supportive and whether you need their help in moving job or accessing development.

Think too about how you can give yourself support. A major career change can be a very upsetting event to contemplate. You may feel frightened and uncertain. If you are job seeking after redundancy, or trying to return to work after a long period at home, you may face many setbacks before you achieve your goal. You need to think how to keep your spirits up and give yourself a reward for successful steps along the way.

If you are finding it very difficult to identify a satisfactory option, or to find the job you are looking for, there are other sources of support or professional help you can turn to, including:

- careers advisory services
- job clubs set up for job hunters to get together
- career counsellors

Setting goals and a timetable

Now it is time to try to list some of the specific goals or actions you need to take to pursue your preferred career option. This is, in essence, your career plan.

SATURDAY

Your plan will often be a mixture of short-term and longer-term actions. For example, if the teacher we thought about earlier decides to write books from home, the list (with timetable) might include:

> - sort out a small working space (this week)
> - find another parent who will 'swap' childcare occasionally to cover travel in set-up phase (this month)
> - map out three or four good ideas for books. Work one up in some detail (next two months)
> - identify three most likely publishers and write to them (next two months)

In this case she/he is likely to know within a few months how feasible this plan is, and will either persist with it or adopt a different short-term goal (e.g. supply teaching) while thinking again.

The young accountant we thought about might decide to:

> - give current company at most one more year to signal promotion intentions
> - meanwhile make contacts in two or three larger companies expanding in Europe (six months)
> - get CV up to date (this month)
> - start working on improving rusty French (next month)

If your plan includes looking for other jobs, then it is better to focus on making a small number of very thoughtful approaches to employers rather than sending off hundreds of standard letters. Make sure you know how these employers notify vacancies and fill jobs. Only go for jobs which really are an improvement on your current situation or take you in the direction you want to go.

If you have not changed job for a long time, you will need to allow more time for research and preparation than if you have been applying for jobs recently. In setting a timetable you should also bear in mind the amount of effort involved in each action, and when you will fit these activities in. Goals should be challenging but achievable. Discussing your goals and timescale with someone else can help you to ensure they are realistic.

Exercise 11: your career plan

> Make a list of some practical goals and approximate timescales for achieving them. A simple list is more likely to help than a very complex or elaborate one.

Monitoring and adapting your plans

As with any planning process, career plans should be frequently monitored and reviewed. Are you doing the things you planned to do? If not, is the problem lack of motivation or shortage of time, or do you now think that the goal was inappropriate? Even more than other kinds of plans, career plans must not be seen as rigid and unchanging:

SATURDAY

- They have no absolute timescales and direction may matter more than speed of progress.
- They will be affected by external events and must be modified accordingly.
- They depend wholly on your own desire for change and your determination not to let them fizzle out.

The key is to see career planning as a learning activity. We are learning more about the world of work and ourselves all the time. Sometimes a setback means that a goal will be achieved more slowly. Sometimes we learn that part of our plan will not work out, and we need to think again and modify our plan. Very often, our plans are conditional on labour market opportunities, and what we continue to learn about ourselves. For example, we often discover we have skills we did not identify at first.

You should not, therefore, feel that you have failed if you need to adapt your plans. What matters is that you use career planning to give yourself a direction, and the best chance of moving in this desired direction. As long as you are learning in this way and acquiring skills as you go, you are ensuring your future employability.

Career planning can be a challenging, sometimes uncomfortable, process. It can also be very hard work. However, if you don't do it, you are likely to end up at best dissatisfied and at worst unemployable. The choice is yours.

Week One
SATURDAY

Summary

Today you have built on your earlier work of learning about jobs and about yourself. You have moved forward from your preferred career option to building a plan for action. This has included:

- types of action required
- marketing yourself through CVs and application forms
- setting goals and timescales
- monitoring and adapting plans

Job Hunting

HILTON CATT
PATRICIA SCUDAMORE

WEEK TWO

CONTENTS

Week Two

Introduction		101
Sunday	Understanding the modern job market	102
Monday	Availability, accessibility and application	112
Tuesday	Targeting	122
Wednesday	Attacking the visible market	132
Thursday	Attacking the invisible market	148
Friday	How to get headhunted	164
Saturday	Applying selectivity to your job search	178
Conclusion	Job hunting as part of a career strategy	187

Week Two

INTRODUCTION

There's a much bigger market out there for your talents than you think and this book is going to show you how to access that market and profit in the process – all in the space of a week.

The benefits for you? Cast your eye down the following list:

- Give your job hunting a sense of direction. See better results for your effort.
- Cut down on the number of 'no thank you' letters you get. Avoid the discouragement that goes with unsuccessful job applications (the kind of discouragement that can lead to you giving up).
- Get a true picture of what the job market has to offer you.
- Understand the modern job market and how it works. Learn to play it to your advantage. Learn also where the dangers lurk.
- Learn how to access the elusive invisible market (the jobs that aren't advertised). As a result give your job hunting an extra dimension.
- Boost your chances of being headhunted. Put yourself in line for the *crème de la crème* of appointments.
- Get in tune with the twenty first century. Bring your job hunting up-to-date.

Week Two

SUNDAY

Understanding the modern job market

Here is your list of jobs for today:

- Develop your understanding of the modern job market and the way it works.
- Learn about the elusive invisible market (the jobs that are never advertised – the jobs that are rumoured to be the best jobs).
- Get a basic appreciation of proactive and reactive sourcing and what these terms mean.

The job jungle

Imagine you're setting off on a journey through the jungle all on your own. The first few steps you take will be bold ones until you find out the jungle is a strange place where there are no paths to follow and no signposts to show you the way. You press on regardless, hoping everything will be ok, but after a while you're thrashing around in the undergrowth hopelessly lost. Sooner or later despair takes over and all you want is the quickest way out.

Going out on to the modern job market can be a bit like this. At times it seems impenetrable and hostile. At times it feels like all you're doing is going round in circles and achieving nothing. At times all you will want to do is sit down on the ground and put your head in your hands.

> *WARNING!*
>
> **Discouragement**
> Discouragement is what happens to people who thrash round in the job jungle with no clear sense of direction. In job hunting, discouragement is what you need to avoid at all costs.

Job hunter's concerns

A few years ago we asked a random sample of candidates for junior to middle management posts in the engineering industry to list what concerned them most about modern job market conditions. This is what they came up with:

> - The sheer volume of competition for good jobs – the difficulty in even getting interviews.
> - Bad manners (employers not replying to applications or letting candidates know how they got on at interviews).
> - The so-called invisible market – the rumoured 90%

> of jobs that aren't advertised; how to find out about such jobs.
> - The risk attached to changing jobs; the fear of making bad moves and what could follow.

Understanding the modern job market

So what's going on here and why do so many people see the modern job market as such a 'difficult' place? Let's take a closer look and see what we can find out.

Few of us need any reminding that the world in which we live and work has changed very substantially in the last 20 years. Big smokestack industries have for the large part gone. Dozens and dozens of small start-up businesses have taken their place – to the extent that the small firm sector is now an important provider of quality employment (a fact no-one should ignore).

Even with big firms, the need to cut costs has driven many of them to downsize and streamline. What's more, this downsizing and streamlining has been accompanied in many cases by breaking up once large structures into smaller, more manageable units (fragmentation).

How do these changes affect the way recruitment is handled? Let's see first of all what used to happen in the good old days.

Classic recruitment
We have coined this term to describe most people's conception of what the recruitment process involves. An example will help.

SUNDAY

Week Two

> *Example – Company X*
> Company X has a vacancy for an IT Manager. Company X is a major player in the automotive components industry and it employs approximately 5,000 people spread across three locations. The instruction to proceed with recruitment is given to Company X's Human Resources Department. Advertisements are placed in various newspapers and journals and the vacancy is also given to two firms of recruitment consultants specialising in IT staff. As a result, 30 applications are received from which the Human Resources Department picks out 15 for preliminary interview. From these preliminary interviews, a short list of five candidates is put forward to the Chief Executive for final selection purposes. At each stage unsuccessful candidates are informed in writing.

Recruitment today
Big companies Classic recruitment still goes on of course, but in many big companies where classic recruitment used to be practised, very different circumstances now prevail.

For a start, Human Resources Departments suffered more than most in the various phases of headcount slashing we have seen in recent years. Viewed as peripheral to the core activity of businesses they have, in some cases, been disposed of altogether while in others they have been reduced to mere shadows of their former selves. The result? We see recruitment today pushed more and more on to the shoulders of line managers meaning the standard to which it is done depends on:

- how much time and resources they can give it (bearing in mind they have other functions to discharge as well)
- how experienced they are

Time and resources are, of course, major areas of concern for all practising managers but, to add to the problems, the delayerings, restructurings and downsizings of recent years have left many of them with little or nothing in the way of administrative support. Witness the fact that the armies of secretaries and assistants who once used to surround senior managers in big companies have to all intents and purposes gone. Today the same senior managers are more likely to have to do their own fetching and carrying, take their own phone calls and, in some cases, type their own letters as well.

Small companies
Small companies have never carried human resources departments (at least not as a rule). Recruitment has always been dealt with by busy managers with other responsibilities. What's different about small companies is that there are a lot more of them about.

Bad manners?
Why are employers so remiss about responding to applications these days? Has there been an outbreak of bad manners as some job hunters seem to think?

Not that we wish to excuse employers who don't reply to candidates' letters but the explanation, very often, is not rudeness but some hard-pressed manager faced with the problem of finding a replacement for a key member of staff who has decided to leave. What happens is this: An ad is put in the paper and maybe a few firms of recruitment consultants are contacted. Where the job is a good job, the result is a glut of applications. Bearing in mind our manager is probably not too used to such situations, he responds by picking out a couple of letters which catch his eye then puts the rest to one side with the intention of dealing with them later. Another crisis crops up followed by another and, like any good manager, he responds by prioritising. As a result, jobs like replying to a bunch of unsuccessful applicants get pushed to the bottom of the pile from where they may never surface.

Quick fixes
Another facet of the down-sized delayered world we live in is the way gaps in the ranks of key people quickly cause companies problems.

Week Two
SUNDAY

> *Example – Company Y*
> Company Y is a manufacturing plant employing 600 people. Previously company Y had a three tier management structure:
>
> Manufacturing Director
> ▼
> Section Managers (5)
> ▼
> Cell Managers (30)
>
> Five years ago, faced with intense global competition and the urgent need to cut operating costs, Company Y decided to take out the section management tier from its structure leaving Cell Managers reporting directly to the Manufacturing Director. As a consequence of this, wherever a cell manager's position is vacant, shop floor personnel have a direct line to the Manufacturing Director – a situation the Manufacturing Director finds difficult to deal with. A further consequence? The Manufacturing Director does his level best to get any vacant cell manager slot filled as quickly as he can.

The invisible job market

Classic recruitment is time consuming and hard work. It has little appeal therefore to hard-pressed managers with vacancies that need filling fast and a thousand and one other concerns clamouring for their attention. So what happens in these situations? The answer is they do what all resourceful managers do. They look for short cuts.

SUNDAY

Here is an example of a short cut:

> 'If we advertise positions in the press we find ourselves inundated with response – 90% of which is totally unsuitable. Rather than give ourselves this kind of hassle we prefer first of all to see if there is anyone we know in the trade. If there isn't, we usually go to a few firms of recruitment consultants and ask them to put up a short-list of candidates from their files.'

A vast and largely untapped invisible job market has emerged in recent years – jobs that are never advertised and are filled by one of three methods:

- **Approach** Companies sourcing people through their networks of contacts within given industries or trades or using headhunters to do this task for them.
- **Recruitment consultants** Accessing candidates by asking firms of recruitment consultants to search their files for suitable candidates.
- **Previous applicants** Revisiting previous applicants including unsolicited CVs.

There are other reasons other than the ones we have touched on already for the growth in the invisible market. Let three senior executives from the new breed of small knowledge-based businesses explain:

> 'The people we're interested in won't necessarily be looking for another job. This is why advertising doesn't work for us.'

Week Two

SUNDAY

> 'We're seeking people with scarce and very defined skills. We find the only way of getting such people is by going to specialist firms of recruitment consultants.'
>
> 'Picking up a square peg in a senior management job is a major area of concern for us because of the damage it could do to a team-based business like this. When we recruit, therefore, we always enlist the help of headhunters. We feel happier about people who come to us with a headhunter's recommendation.'

The key points to pick out here are:

- The increased awareness today of the downsides of making poor selection decisions particularly where the vacant slot is a position of responsibility; not only is there the damage to the business to be considered but also the prospect of litigation if the bad choice has to be exited quickly.
- The impact of skills shortages on businesses: the widely held view that recruiting people with scarce skills calls for something 'special'.
- The growth of headhunting as a preferred method of recruiting particularly where senior executive appointments are concerned; the 'comfort' factor that headhunting offers.

> *There are just three things you need to appreciate about the invisible market:*
>
> - it's big
> - it's getting bigger
> - you need to get in on it

S U N D A Y

Proactive and reactive sourcing

The last job for today is to introduce you to some useful terminology.

Reactive sourcing
This is where the stimulus is provided by the employer – usually in the form of advertising. Here you are responding to an invitation to put yourself forward and the quality of your response is what counts. Reactive sourcing is used to attack the visible market.

Proactive sourcing
This is job hunting aimed at the invisible market – where, to penetrate the walls and get your face in the frame, the stimulus needs to come from you.

> Successful job hunting today means having the capacity to attack both the visible and the invisible markets which in turn means using a 'mix 'n' match' of proactive and reactive sourcing. Too many candidates put all their effort into the latter (replying to advertisements), meaning they miss out on some of the better opportunities the market offers.

Summary

Make sure your job hunting is tailored to today and that you are not using methods designed for market conditions that disappeared years ago. Adapt. Learn new strategies. Don't get left behind by the times.

Week Two

MONDAY

Availability, accessibility and application

Today we are going to learn about three principles that are the underpinnings to successful job hunting in modern conditions. These three principles are known collectively as the 'Three As'. They are as follows:

- **Availability** The importance of 'being there', being easy to contact, being able to attend interviews as and when employers require.
- **Accessibility** Making sure it's clear to everyone exactly (a) who you are, (b) where you're coming from, and (c) what you're seeking to achieve.
- **Application** Being ready for the hard slog. Being ready too for the harsh treatment that the job market can dish out occasionally.

Availability

Being in the right place at the right time helps with most things in life and job hunting is no exception Being there, being easy for employers to contact, having the capacity to attend interviews as and when required, all go a long way to ensuring successful outcomes in modern market conditions. This is why you need to audit your availability before you set foot into the job market, i.e. *before* lack of availability becomes the reason for you not having much joy.

How do you do this? Go through the following checklist and answer the questions as truthfully as you can:

Week Two

MONDAY

> *Availability checklist*
>
> - How would prospective employers get on if they needed to get hold of you in a hurry? Would they have phone numbers where they could contact you?
> - Similarly, if the same employers needed to speak to you out of hours, would they have phone numbers where you could be reached?
> - Could contacting you involve hassle in the shape of 'phones that aren't answered or lines that are engaged for long periods of time?
> - What would you answer be if an employer needed to get you in for an interview in office hours some time within the next seven days? Would you be able to get the time off work or would it be difficult for you?

Going through this checklist will help you to expose flaws in your availability. Hopefully, it will also throw up some points for action like:

- Re-doing your CV so that telephone points of contact are included. By this we mean your home, work and mobile telephone numbers. In the case of your home number, you also need to give an indication of the time when you normally get in (e.g. 'after 6.30 p.m.').
- If you're away from your desk a lot, investigating the possibility of installing a voice mail facility on your office phone extension.
- Introducing a few disciplines at home like telling members of the family to keep their phone conversations brief especially early in the evening (when people like

employers, headhunters and recruitment consultants could be trying to get through). Alternatively you could install a second line or ask the phone company to supply you with a call waiting bleep.
- Always keeping back a few days' holiday in case you need to go for interviews.

Clean up your answer tape

With the prospect of employers, recruitment consultants and headhunters ringing you up, now's the time to take those silly messages off your answer tape!

WARNING!

Lack of availability sometimes has unusual causes. Often you are the last to find out about them.

Week Two

MONDAY

> *Did you know?*
>
> Today the phone is used more and more for contacting job applicants. In part this is a reflection of the instantaneous, paper-free world we live in, in part the pressure on management time, and in part the increasing involvement of people like headhunters who do most of their business on the 'phone. As a consequence, interview lists are frequently decided on the basis of who can be contacted and who can't. Candidates who are difficult to get hold of are candidates who get given the miss.

Accessibility

A prospective employer needs to be able to see who you are, where you are coming from and what you are capable of doing in a very compressed period of time. Needless to say, accessibility has got a lot to do with the design of your CV. It has particular relevance to two situations:

- **Visible market** Where you are applying for a good job which has been widely advertised. Here the problem is going to be competition. You will be one of many applicants and somehow your CV has got to stand out from the rest.
- **Invisible market** Where you're mailshotting your CV to employers on the off chance there may be something suitable for you. Unsolicited CVs tend to get the 'quick read' treatment automatically arriving, as they do, with the rest of the morning mail. Again, they need to catch the reader's eye to prevent them from being binned instantly.

MONDAY

Writing your CV

It goes almost without saying that you won't get very far on your trip into the job jungle without a CV. If you don't have a CV, for any reason, then take steps to get one prepared. Turn to Week Three for a more in-depth look at writing your CV.

A useful image to have in mind as you go through your CV is that of some stressed-out overworked senior executive given the task of wading through a hundred job applications with a view to picking out a few for interview. Just to add a bit of flavour, let's say our senior executive decides to leave this task till the end of the day when the telephone traffic has died down but when he won't be at his best for giving his full and undivided attention. Typically, he'll cast his eye over each application searching out key points that look ok (e.g. a certain type of experience). From this quick flick through he'll put the applications into three piles: the ones that interest him, the don't knows, and the no-hopers. When he's finished doing this, he'll probably look at the 'yes' pile again just to make double sure he's picked out the right people. If the 'yes' pile thus reduced happens to coincide with what our senior executive views as a reasonable number of people to call in for interview, that will be that as far as the preliminary sifting process is concerned, i.e. the don't knows will be joining the unsuitables in the turndown pile. If the 'yes' pile is a bit thin on numbers, however, the don't knows might just get a second airing. The point to grasp? That even though all recruitment may not be dealt with in this way, your CV has still got to be capable of surviving this kind of treatment. It has got to hit our weary senior executive in the eye first time because, if it doesn't, it stands a good chance of ending up in places where it is unlikely to ever see the light of day again.

Before leaving our senior executive to his after hours' reading, it is worth pondering on the fact that, once he's finished putting his interview list together, he could round off the evening by ringing the candidates he's picked out. Here is where your availability comes in. The ones he manages to contact will be invited for interview. The ones he doesn't may not get another chance.

Application

One of the big challenges you face on your journey through the job jungle is having the tenacity to keep going and not be put off by any of the difficulties that you encounter. Partly this is to do with avoiding discouragement and partly to do with keeping your expectations in line. With the latter:

Week Two

MONDAY

> - don't expect to be invited for an interview every time you apply for a job (it won't happen)
> - don't expect everyone to be nice to you

Picking up on the second of these points, employers' standards vary enormously and not all the treatment you receive will be to your liking. The mistake, however, is to let bad experiences get to you so they become a source of discouragement and a reason for you throwing in the towel prematurely.

Employers who don't reply
Going back to yesterday, we saw the concerns about employers who don't reply to applications or don't let candidates know how they got on at interviews. We saw at the same time, however, that these omissions are not always manifestations of bad manners – as some job hunters seem to think – but evidence of organisations in turmoil or managers under pressure – in short, nothing very unusual in the modern day business world.

The message? Don't get wound up about employers whose communication skills are lacking and, to some extent, condition yourself to accepting this kind of treatment as the norm. Certainly don't let the general standards of employers' behaviour become the reason for you giving up because you feel you can't take any more.

> *Unsolicited CVs*
>
> Don't expect anyone to reply to an unsolicited CV – even if you enclose a stamped addressed envelope.

MONDAY

Week Two

As we shall be seeing on Thursday, mailshotting prospective employers is an excellent way of accessing the elusive invisible market. The aim, however, is to sow seeds rather than chalk up streams of polite acknowledgements. Judge the performance of your unsolicited CVs on what matters, i.e. on the number of interesting interviews you get invited to attend.

Prepare for the hard knocks
Even if you can learn to live with employers who don't reply to your applications, because of its diversity the modern job market can still be a hostile and unpredictable place. Expect, therefore, your path to success to be littered with bad interview experiences and brushes with employers who don't seem to know what they're doing. Try to find ways of hardening yourself against the knocks.

Week Two

MONDAY

Anything else?

What other preparations do you need to make before you set out on your job hunting expedition?

Time off work
Having the capacity to take time off work to attend interviews is, as we have seen, an important part of your availability and, for this reason, you must always keep back a few days of your holiday entitlement.

The point stretches a little further, however. As part of your preparations for going out on to the job market, you must condition yourself into viewing your time off work time as precious and something not to be squandered. An example of squandering time off work is using it to attend interviews for jobs that wouldn't interest you even if they were offered to you. We will be exploring this use of time off work time in more detail tomorrow when we will be looking at targeting (making sure the jobs you're applying for are the right jobs).

> For most of us, the time we can get off work is limited and even stock excuses like 'going to see the dentist' can start to wear thin after they've been used a few times. Not all employers will be happy to do interviews out of hours and this is certainly something you shouldn't be banking on.

Giving up smoking
This is territory we enter with some trepidation yet enter it we must because anti-smoker discrimination is rife in employment – meaning, if you're addicted to the weed, there

are great benefits for you career-wise if you can succeed in giving it up.

'Do you smoke?' is increasingly a question that gets asked at interviews and on application forms. So much the better for you, therefore, if you can answer truthfully 'no.'

> *Tip to non-smokers*
>
> If you don't smoke, advertise the fact somewhere on your CV – for example, in the section giving details of your medical history. Who knows, it might just tip the balance when it comes to deciding whether to include you on the interview list or not.

Summary

Appreciate just three things about the modern job market:

- it's highly competitive – the better the job, the stiffer the competition
- it won't always be nice to you
- it won't spend much time on you

Successful job hunting is based on the acceptance of these realities.

Week Two

TUESDAY

Targeting

Today we are going to look at targeting. Targeting is about having it clear in your mind exactly what kind of job you are looking for. Your programme for today is as follows:

- The importance of being realistic – targeting jobs you can do and jobs that the market has a reasonable chance of providing.
- Targeting benchmarks – getting the specification right.
- The problem of pay: knowing when you could be asking for too little or too much.
- Targeting and accessibility.

Targeting is important. Targeting is what gives your job hunting its sense of direction. It is an exercise you need to do, therefore, before you set out on your expedition into the job jungle because, if you don't, you run the risk of ending

TUESDAY

up thrashing around aimlessly – and, for most people, this is the prelude to giving up.

Aims of targeting

Targeting has two aims:

- **Reducing failure** Not getting chosen for interview or going for an interview and finding you don't get put on the shortlist has a discouraging and demoralising effect. The less of this you have to deal with, the better.
- **Reducing time-wasting** Job hunting is time consuming. The time you give it has to be put to most effective use.

> Targeting is about being **selective** with your job applications. Applying for hundreds and hundreds of jobs just because they happen to be there has no virtue to it at all. You succeed in doing nothing except:
>
> - Chalking up large numbers of 'sorry but no thank you' letters (inviting discouragement).
> - Frittering away your time off work time on utterly pointless interviews (loss of an important part of your availability).

Realism

Targeting needs to be done in the context of what the job market can reasonably be expected to deliver. If you set off in pursuit of unattainable targets then, practically speaking, it is almost as bad as setting off with no targets at all.

Week Two

TUESDAY

Jobs you can't do

Although we're all entitled to have our dreams, there are some jobs that quite clearly we can't do because we don't have the necessary experience or qualifications. These jobs that are out of our range are usually self-evident to us, but occasionally we need reminding that we may be trying to take a step too far.

The signs of over-reaching? Inevitability, the number of applications where you find you don't even get as far as the interview list. The big danger in over-reaching, however, is that if you carry on doing it, you finish up feeling dejected and discouraged. The answer is, therefore, to take stock from time to time. If your job hunting has been largely fruitless, ask yourself if you could be falling into the trap of applying for jobs you can't do. This is a case of acting on the feedback that the market is providing you with – feedback that's telling you you're trying to achieve something that's unattainable, practically speaking.

Week Two

TUESDAY

> *WARNING!*
>
> In a world where selection standards are not always consistent, there is the chance you could be offered a job that's beyond your capabilities. If you accept, needless to say, your celebrations are likely to be short-lived. Your lack of capability will be found out pretty quickly and it won't be too surprising if you find yourself on the receiving end of the short sharp exit treatment.

Jobs that don't exist

Incredible though it sounds, there are a lot of people out there pursuing jobs that don't exist or jobs that are in very short supply. Here are a few examples:

- Doug – who wants a job where he doesn't have to do shifts but where, at the same time, he won't have to take a drop in the high level of earnings he gets for working unsociable hours.
- Gaenor – who works in customer support and who wants a job where she can have every Wednesday off to go to college.
- John – who makes good money doing work he finds boring. John wants to make a complete change in career without having to take a drop in his earnings.
- Steve – who wants a senior management job where he won't have to put up with the hassle he gets now.
- Ruth – who wants a high powered career in marketing without having to travel any further than ten miles from where she lives.

Week Two

TUESDAY

The conditions that Doug, Gaenor and the others are imposing on the jobs they're looking for effectively wipe out most if not all of the available market. What they are attempting to do really is dictate to the market and, not surprisingly, it doesn't work.

The lesson? Again to listen carefully to the feedback. What is it telling you? Could it be telling you, for example, that what employers have to offer and what you are looking for simply don't match up? If it does, stop what you're doing immediately and take stock. The mistake – and plenty make it – is to flog on in pursuit of these near impossible aims year after year till discouragement sets in.

> *Feedback*
>
> Feedback or experience is an important part of job hunting because, at the outset, few of us have any meaningful idea of what the market for our particular talents really has to offer. What all successful job hunters do is learn from their experience and, in this way, accumulate quite formidable stores of knowledge on the demand for people in their niche occupational area. Listening to feedback is therefore important. Ignoring it is something you do at your peril.

Targeting benchmarks

Having dealt with the problems of targeting jobs you can't do and jobs that don't exist (or only exist in very small numbers), we want to turn our attention to looking at how to set about targeting jobs properly. To do this we need you

TUESDAY
Week Two

to get some fixed points of reference or *benchmarks* in your mind. Targeting benchmarks will be there to help you when it comes to deciding which jobs to apply for and which to leave alone. They will help you to deal with people like recruitment consultants (people who will be using their contacts and know-how to search for jobs on your behalf). They also act as a fail-safe – making sure you take the right jobs and leave the wrong ones alone.

Targeting benchmarks can be broken down as follows:

The job
This should be the easy part. What are you seeking to gain from your job hunting? Is it promotion, for example? If so, what's the next job up the ladder?

The pay
More pay is often the reason why people look for another job. Pay is tricky and this is why we will deal with it separately (keep reading).

The area
How mobile you are clearly has a bearing on the kind of jobs you will be applying for. For example, are you a truly global person who is happy to work anywhere in the world or, at the other end of the scale, do partners' jobs and/or family commitments tie you to looking for work within commuting distance of where you live now?

The risk
Would you only be interested in a secure job with a big name employer or would you be happy to entertain something with a little more risk attached to it, e.g. a start-up business?

Again, a lot here will depend on your domestic situation. Are you the sole breadwinner for your family, for example? Or does your partner have a secure, well-paid job meaning perhaps you can afford to take a few risks?

The hours
Some jobs involve working strange or anti-social hours. How would you feel about this? Alternatively are you just looking for something part-time or hours that fit round your other commitments?

The prospects
Is this important to you? If so, it will rule out any employers where the prospects are limited, e.g. very small firms in static or low-growth situations.

Anything else?
What we're fishing for here is anything peculiar to you that will have a bearing on the kind of job you can go for. For example, do you have a medical problem that could preclude working in certain industries or environments? Alternatively, would your family circumstances make it difficult for you to have nights away from home?

> Simple though it seems, this exercise in setting out your targeting benchmarks is what will give your job hunting the structure and direction it needs. Targeting, remember, is about being selective. This means that, any job that falls short of your targeting benchmarks is a job you won't be applying for. Another way of looking at this is, the more focused you are on the target, the more chances you have of hitting it.

TUESDAY

> **WARNING!**
>
> Don't fall into the trap of scanning the ads and applying for jobs simply because they're there. If weeks go by without seeing a job that comes up to scratch, view it as evidence that your targeting is working.

The problem of pay

Pay, as we noted a few moments ago, is an awkward area mainly because a conflict can and does arise between:

- your estimation of your own worth
- what the market is capable of offering at any one given point in time

One of the bigger problems here is that, at the outset of job hunting, you will have little or no idea of what the market can provide – in short, whether the kind of figures you have in mind are going over the top, not enough or somewhere in between.

Sources of information on going rates of pay
When setting your pay targeting benchmark, try tapping into three sources:

- The visible market – the jobs you see advertised in newspapers, journals or on websites (jobs which call for people with similar skills and experience to yours).
- Your networks – contacts in your profession who may be able to give you some valuable inside information on what other employers pay.
- Recruitment professionals – somewhere along the line

Week Two

TUESDAY

you will be talking to people like recruitment consultants, people whose job it is to know about going rates.

From these sources you will be able to form a quick overview of whether the figure you have in mind is realisable or not. Incidentally, don't rule out the possibility of finding out that you're not so badly paid after all – meaning:

- If your only reason for changing jobs is more money, you may want to think again.
- If your problem is something other than money (e.g. security, lack of prospects), you may have to contemplate stepping sideways pay wise – or even backwards.

Fine tuning your pay targeting benchmark
Fine tuning your pay targeting benchmark is something you do in the light of experience. For example, if the feedback you get from your job hunting suggests you may be asking for too much then be ready either:

- To tweak your benchmark down a few notches,
- To stick with your original benchmark but realise that you're targeting just a narrow segment of well-paid jobs (top-end targeting), or
- To call off your job hunting altogether.

Targeting and accessibility

If you go back to yesterday's lesson, you will remember the point we made about making employers aware exactly where you're coming from and what you're seeking to achieve. You will remember also that the main vehicle for this transparency and accessibility is your CV.

TUESDAY

Help employers to spot the mismatches

A common misunderstanding of the purpose of a CV is to see it only as the means of getting you interviews. Whilst this is important, it is equally important that your CV conveys enough about you and your ambitions to enable employers to spot any mismatches between what you want and what they've got to offer. Don't therefore, be tempted to use your CV to pull the wool over people's eyes. Present yourself exactly as you are and help employers to make the judgement as to whether the job is right for you or not. Getting interviews is no good if the jobs are time wasters.

Summary

Today's lesson has been about giving your excursion into the job jungle the right compass bearings to strike off on – notably:

- not to set out in pursuit of difficult or unobtainable objectives
- to define your targets properly and in the form of benchmarks
- to listen to the feedback you get from the market and to use this to give your targeting fine tuning

Week Two

WEDNESDAY

Attacking the visible market

The subject for today is attacking the visible market – the jobs that are advertised. Your programme is as follows:

- sources of visible market jobs
- deciding which jobs to go for and which to leave alone
- dealing with competition

Take it as read that any good job that surfaces on the visible market is going to attract large numbers of applicants. The biggest problem you face, therefore, is one of competition. Somehow you've got to make yourself stand out from the crowd.

WEDNESDAY

Sources of visible market jobs

> *Reactive sourcing*
>
> Reactive sourcing is the term that describes the way in which you engage the visible market. Reactive sourcing, remember, is where the stimulus is provided by the employer – usually in the form of advertising. How you respond to this stimulus determines how effective you are in engaging the visible market.

For convenience we've broken down sources of visible market jobs into the following:

- ads in newspapers and journals
- the internet
- other sources

Ads in newspapers and journals
Advertising in newspapers and journals is still one of the most popular ways of recruiting people. 'Scanning the ads' is, therefore, an important part of job hunting. It is where most of us start out on our search for a new job.

The choice of newspapers can be baffling and, with job hunting in mind, it is sometimes difficult to know which ones to take.

Local papers These vary quite a lot in the quality of the recruitment advertising they carry but, on the whole, they are essential reading from the job hunters' point of view. Local papers frequently have 'jobs nights' or nights on which they feature jobs in certain fields (e.g. engineering and technical appointments).

Week Two
WEDNESDAY

> *Did you know?*
>
> If you are looking for a job out of your area, you can arrange for a copy of the local evening newspaper to be sent to you on subscription. Simply phone the subscriptions department and at the same time ask them if the newspaper has a special night for jobs (so you know which edition to order).

National papers Some national papers have strong toe-holds in certain sectors of the market, e.g. the Daily Telegraph has a long standing association with jobs in sales. Other than this, 'pick 'n' mix' your choice of national papers and ring the changes from time to time. The same goes for Sunday papers.

> *WARNING!*
>
> Don't try and scan the ads in every newspaper. You haven't got the time.

Journals Journals and periodicals that carry recruitment advertising divide into two types:

- journals published by professional associations
- trade journals of the kind that circulate in certain industries

> *Verdict on journals?*
>
> **Good points:** well targeted job wise (some journals put out by professional associations are regarded as top sources of jobs in their particular fields).

WEDNESDAY

> **Bad points:** tend to be national or international publications meaning the jobs will be 'anywhere and everywhere' (a less attractive feature for those who are targeting jobs in specific areas).

The internet. More and more employers are using the internet for sourcing staff – indeed the day may come when all recruitment is done online.

> Recruitment web sites divide into two types:
>
> - Dedicated sites – these, if you like, are the internet equivalents of employment agencies where employers pay to have their vacancies posted on job boards.
> - Employers' sites – organisations using their own web sites to advertise vacancies (in the main these are large employers with well-known names).

Using the internet to source jobs
Although an established method of recruitment in some sectors (e.g. graduates, jobs in IT) the internet is still a novelty as far as most mainstream employment is concerned. Don't therefore rely on it exclusively – as some job hunters in their enthusiasm to embrace new technology have been tempted to do. See the internet instead as yet another way of accessing the visible market. In other words see it as complementing your methods of reactive sourcing.

Other sources

Advertising on the radio, advertising on electronic billboards sited in public places, advertising in newsletters put out by the local branches of professional associations – the methods employers use to attract applicants are almost endless. The message is keep your eyes and ears open.

Deciding which jobs to go for

With any job you source, the first decision you have to make is whether to apply for it or not. Here is where you go back to your targeting benchmarks. Does the job match up to your specification or doesn't it? If it does, then the green light is flashing at you to get moving. If not, an equally strong signal should be beaming out to you to go no further.

WEDNESDAY

> **WARNING!**
>
> **Applying for the wrong jobs**
> Never view it as a foregone conclusion that you will be applying for every job you source – indeed applying for the wrong jobs is fraught with all kinds of dangers:
>
> - You can find yourself squandering precious time off work time on pointless interviews.
> - Employers can usually spot square pegs so wrong jobs tend to be jobs you don't get – chalking up turndowns like this leads to discouragement.
> - The experience will be misleading, for example if you apply for a lot of poorly paid jobs you will form the impression (wrongly) that the poor level of pay is the norm.
> - Worst of all, you could find yourself in the wrong job.

Advertisements without salaries

Being selective about the jobs you apply for by running them across your targeting benchmarks is all well and good, but a problem you frequently have to face up to is the ad that makes no mention of salary other than the meaningless jumble of words such as 'negotiable' or 'commensurate with the responsibilities'. The job looks ok but, without any insight into the pay, how do you know whether it's worth applying for or not?

As we all know, pay is a difficult area shrouded in mists of secrecy. Why don't employers put salaries in ads? In most cases, the reason will be one of the following:

Week Two
WEDNESDAY

> - Confidentiality (not wanting the world at large to know what salaries they pay).
> - Their salaries are poor and they don't like to say.
> - They're fishing (they want to see what you're earning first so they can decide whether they can afford you or not).

How do you deal with ads with no salaries?

On the face of it, the sensible approach to the problem seems to be to ring up and ask. You don't want to waste anyone's time so, before you put an application in, could they give you a rough idea of the kind of figure they have in mind please? Sensible though it sounds, anecdotal evidence of this approach actually working is rather thin on the ground. Often all you get is a lot of cagey answers that don't move you forward very far.

Make your pay expectations accessible
Going back to Monday's lesson, we stressed the importance of always making it crystal clear to employers exactly where you are coming from and what you are seeking to achieve. In the case of pay, this means two things:

- your current earnings
- the level of earnings you're aspiring to

This information is what needs to figure prominently in your CV and mentioned again in my letters of application you send in. Because of the secretiveness and sensitivity that surrounds pay and because of the special problems arising from ads without salaries, this kind of accessibility acts as a fail-safe to ensure that your application goes no

WEDNESDAY

further if the employer's ideas on pay don't fall into line with your own. In short, deal with ads with no pay as follows:

- Check first of all to make sure all your other targeting benchmarks are met.
- Revisit your CV and satisfy yourself that no-one reading it will get any wrong ideas about your pay aspirations.
- Put together an equally accessible accompanying letter.
- Send off your application and see what happens.

> *WARNING!*
>
> There is a snag with the above approach and it is this. Not many employers will own up to not being able to afford you so the likely response if the pay available falls way below your targeting benchmark is a standard 'sorry but no thank you' letter. Since 'sorry and no thank you' letters are a source of discouragement, when replying to ads with no salaries you need to condition your expectations accordingly. If you get turned down, tell yourself it's an even chance that the job's to blame – not you. This is all part of getting your expectations into line that we talked about yesterday under the subject of application.

Read advertisements properly
Ensuring that jobs match up to your targeting benchmarks sounds easy enough so why is it so many people get it wrong? The reason in a lot of cases is not reading the ad properly or rather, reading it selectively so that, consciously or not, we ignore:

- Any stipulations that render us unsuitable, e.g. 'candidates must be able to converse fluently in Mandarin Chinese'.
- Job conditions that come into conflict with our targeting benchmarks, e.g. 'the work can involve anti-social hours including weekends'.

This blanking out of things we don't want to see usually happens when the job is a good job – typically one where a good salary is on offer. In the excitement to get an application off, we omit to go through the small print in too much detail or we see the bit that jars in our minds but decide to give it a whirl anyway.

Read job ads carefully. Employers usually go to a lot of trouble to draft the copy so that unsuitable candidates aren't drawn into applying. They are as concerned as you are that no-one's time is wasted.

Dealing with competition

Engaging the visible market means facing up to competition. The amount of competition you have to deal with depends on two things:

WEDNESDAY

- how good the job is
- how widely it has been advertised

Where there is a lot of competition, being suitable for a job is no guarantee that you will get an interview. What you also need to ensure is that:

- Your suitability comes across in one quick read of your CV (your accessibility).
- You can be contacted without any fuss and bother, plus the fact you can come in for interviews quickly (your availability).
- Any strong points you have are brought into prominence (your super accessibility).

We dealt with the first two of these bullet points on Monday. Now let's look at the third.

Bringing out your strong points
Strong points mean your strong points *vis-à-vis* a particular job application. What it doesn't mean is what you see as your strong points generally. For example, you may have had a lot of very interesting experience with a certain brand of computer-aided design software but this won't cut much ice at all with an employer who uses a completely different package. The point here is to get you to see each job application as a fresh challenge. There will be more on this as we move on.

WEDNESDAY

Week Two

> Strong points are the matches between what the employer is looking for and what you have to offer. A strong point could be the fact that you hold a particular qualification. Alternatively, it could be your experience with a certain technique or that living out of a suitcase for months on end is something you're completely used to. The clues to these matches can be found in the ad itself – in what employers have to say about themselves and in what they see as desirable attributes in candidates (another good reason for making sure you read ads properly).

Bringing your strong points into prominence
At the application stage you normally have three ways of bringing your strong points to the attention of an employer:

- in your CV
- in any supporting letters you submit
- in any application forms you fill in

WEDNESDAY

Use their words This is one of the golden rules to getting across you strong points. In a world where there is an ever increasing use of buzz words and jargon, a very real danger exists of the strong point you're trying to bring out falling on stony ground because it isn't understood or fully appreciated. The way to avoid this difficulty is by putting your own preferences to one side and always using the same buzz words and jargon as the employer (the same words as those used in the ad).

> **Did you know?**
>
> Preliminary scanning of CVs is sometimes done by computer, meaning your application could end up in the turn down pile without it ever having been seen by human eyes. What CV scanning software is programmed to do is search for key matches between what appears in your CV and the specification for the job. It does this by identifying certain key words and phrases – all of which lends a new importance to the choice of terminology you use.

Customising your CV This should present no problems if you keep a copy of your CV stored on disk. Simply get it up on screen and edit it. What you are seeking to achieve here is to bring your strong points into prominence without breaking the rule about keeping your CV short and concise. Be warned, however, this may mean taking out some cherished piece of information to make the necessary space. Console yourself with the fact that the strong point will have more bearing on whether you get picked for an interview or not.

Week Two
WEDNESDAY

Accompanying letters The letter you send in accompanying your CV is another place to get across your strong points. Don't worry about repeating what's already in your CV.

Application forms Most larger firms have standard application forms and there's a fair chance you could be asked to complete one at the early stages of an application, i.e. before you know whether you've been granted an interview or not.

> Application forms usually have a section headed 'Any other information you wish to add in support of your application.' Use sections like these to list your strong points.

> *WARNING*
>
> As a general rule people give insufficient attention to filling in application forms. They dash them off quickly and this is a mistake. Remember next time you fill in an application form that it will probably get a better reading than the CV you spent hours preparing.

Follow the instructions
In the tailpiece to every ad you will find instructions on how to apply. These instructions usually include:

- The name and/or job title of the person to whom your application should be sent.
- The form in which the application should be submitted, e.g. a current CV together with an accompanying letter.
- Any references you should quote.
- Any closing date for applications.

WEDNESDAY

- How your application should be submitted – by post, fax, or e-mail, or you may have to ring and ask for an application form to be sent to you.

What is important about these instructions is that you follow them to the letter and that you don't substitute your own ideas on 'what's best'. With large numbers of applicants and employers recruiting for more than one position at the same time, there is always the danger of individual applications getting mislaid or put on the wrong pile. Needless to say, you won't make a very good job of engaging the competition if you're not there to do it.

Don't procrastinate
Even though there may be no mention of a closing date for applications, don't let the grass grow under your feet when you're attacking the visible market. Remember, the world won't wait while you're finding the time to put the finishing touches to your CV or other distractions seem more pressing. Application, the third of our three As, is the watchword here.

Week Two

WEDNESDAY

Get moving.

Selection consultants

Finally, today, a passing acknowledgement to the fact that a lot of visible market jobs are advertised by firms of selection consultants. This reflects either:

- the need for the employer's identity to remain confidential (not necessarily evidence that someone is about to get the sack), or
- the need for expertise of the kind the employer doesn't have (expertise the selection consultants can offer).

> ### Look after the job you've got
>
> With advertisements placed by selection consultants, is there a danger you could find yourself applying for your own job?
>
> Whilst this may be an extremely remote prospect, what is more worrying perhaps is that the application you sent off to Boggis & Associates, Selection Consultants, could somehow find its way into the wrong hands – namely the hands of your boss. Not knowing the identity of the employer behind the ad is a real area of concern for a lot of people. Could it be, for example, a company that is in the same group as your own?
>
> Firms of selection consultants sometimes offer a confidential reply service meaning you can list out the names of any employers you don't want your details sending to. Failing this, ring the consultants up and ask them how else they can address your concerns. If

Week Two
WEDNESDAY

> you're still left feeling uneasy then it may be best to give the job a miss. When job hunting, your first priority always is to look after the job you've got and never to put it at risk.

Summary

Successful job hunting on the visible market is about facing up to and seeing off competition. Focus on this fact and attack the visible market with your most powerful weapons – your strong points.

Week Two
THURSDAY

Attacking the invisible market

Is it true the best jobs are never advertised? Today we will be looking at the so-called invisible market. Your programme is as follows:

- why the invisible market exists
- accessing the invisible market
- cold calling
- mailshots
- professional networking
- registering with recruitment consultants

Whereas successful job hunting on the visible market is about taking on and overcoming competition, the invisible market is entirely different. Here the challenge lies in accessing the market. Where do you go to find out about these jobs that aren't advertised? How do you start the search?

T H U R S D A Y

Why the invisible market exists

Going back to Sunday's lesson, we picked out a number of reasons for the growth of the invisible market. Let's now extend this list to give you a complete appreciation of why the invisible market exists:

- The cost of advertising – laying out large sums of money with no guarantee that the outcome will be successful.
- The resources and expertise needed to deal with response to advertisements – resources and expertise employers may not have.
- The fear of making bad selection decisions coupled with the increased prospect of employers have to face litigation from people they have sacked.
- The impact of skills shortages on recruitment. The commonly held view that 'advertising doesn't work'.
- Bad experiences with advertising – a double whammy when the cost is also taken into account.
- Employers in a hurry. In a technology driven age, the tendency for anything slow and ponderous to be viewed as intrinsically bad.

Invisible market methods

Against this background, more and more employers are turning to alternative methods of recruitment, notably:

- Recruitment consultants (agencies) – people who are usually prepared to work on a 'no placement, no fee' basis and can put up shortlists of candidates at 24 to 48 hours' notice.
- Contacts – putting the word round in the trade or to selected individuals (eg people who work for competitors).
- Revisiting CVs that are held on file.
- Using headhunters.

Week Two

T H U R S D A Y

Accessing the invisible market

Let's now look at what you need to do to access this vibrant and expanding invisible market.

> *Proactive sourcing*
>
> Remember, proactive sourcing? Proactive sourcing is the key to getting to know about jobs that aren't advertised. Proactive sourcing is where you provide the stimulus.

Cold calling
This is one very obvious way of finding out if employers have got any vacancies that they're not telling the world about – simply by ringing up and asking them.

There is a right and a wrong way to go about cold calling. The wrong way is to ring an employer once, leave your name, phone number and a few personal details then leave it to chance they'll remember you the next time a suitable vacancy comes up.

Snapshots At best, a cold call reveals a snapshot of what's available in an organisation at a particular point in time. Expect no more from it and you won't be disappointed. For instance, the chances of the person you spoke to remembering you in three months time when a vacancy comes up are extremely remote. The scrap of paper where he/she wrote down your name will have disappeared a long time ago.

A model approach to cold calling Done systematically, cold calling can be a very effective way of accessing the invisible market. Here is what to do:

Week Two
THURSDAY

- Start by picking the right employers – organisations who are likely to have the kind of job opportunities you are targeting. To an extent, this is inspired guesswork but clues to suitable employers can sometimes be picked up from reading the job ads, e.g. companies who are doing a lot of recruiting.
- Get the name of the right person to speak to, e.g. if you're an accountant, ask for the name of the financial manager. Don't be fobbed off here with the name of the personnel or human resources manager – even though they may be the normal channel that applicants go through.
- Keep it brief. Remember, cold calls can be irritating especially to someone who is busy. State simply who you are, what you're looking for and whether there's anything suitable for you at the moment.
- If you strike lucky, keep the momentum going. Suggest an interview and get in quickly, i.e. use your Availability to maximum effect.
- Alternatively if you find there's nothing doing, then, consistent with not outstaying your welcome, find out if the organisation ever has the kind of job opportunities you are targeting. This, if you like, is your market research.
- End the call by saying thank you. Leave the door open for calling again another time.
- Keep a record of your calls including the name of the person to whom you spoke and any useful information you picked up.
- Give each call a score from 0 to 5. Your 5s will be calls where the feedback has been encouraging (employers who are worth keeping in touch with regularly). Your 2s and 3s will be those who only have an occasional demand for talents such as yours. Zero mismatches along with

Week Two
THURSDAY

any employers who give you a hard time. Don't waste any more effort on them.
- Work out a call cycle. For example, put your 5s down for a call every two months or so, whereas your 2s and 3s won't need to be contacted quite so frequently.
- Stand by to revise your ratings (upwards or downwards). Each call reveals a little bit more of the picture.

> **WARNING!**
>
> Cold calling companies too frequently achieves little – the snapshot is still the same and you run the risk of getting yourself viewed as a pest.

Systematic and targeted cold calling eventually pays off. The number of companies on your call list diminishes whereas the target gets more accurate and defined. Sooner or later statistical probability takes over from pure chance and you start to connect with good jobs. Patience and persistence are the watchwords here (all part of Application).

> Cold calling is a good way of getting to know about vacancies before they're advertised or put out to recruitment consultants – a case of getting in before the competition arrives.

Mailshots
Sending your CV off to prospective employers is another way of accessing the invisible market. Again, there's a right and a wrong way of going about it.

T H U R S D A Y

Don't expect a reply: Whether employers should acknowledge every unsolicited CV they receive is a matter of opinion. The fact that many of them don't is, however, something you are going to have to learn to live with – a point we have touched on already.

Focus on the aim: Rather than getting wound up about matters of no importance, such as how many standard letters of acknowledgement you do or don't notch up, concentrate instead on what really matters, which is:

- That your mailshots may strike lucky and land on the right desk at the right time.
- Failing this, that your mailshots have enough impact to ensure that they get put on the right file (the file that gets revisited whenever vacancies for people like you come up).

Redesigning your CV: Yesterday when we looked at attacking the visible market we placed great emphasis on customising your CV and in particular, on setting out your strong points *vis-à-vis* each application. With the invisible market, this isn't quite so easy because there isn't an advertisement to look at for clues on what to put in and what to leave out. The answer? Use your imagination and try to customise each unsolicited CV you send out to what you think the employer will be looking for.

> ### Example
>
> If you're seeking a position in general management and you're mailshotting a small firm, perhaps you need to bring out your experience in managing small teams or

Week Two

THURSDAY

> your hands-on approach or your good all round business skills. Conversely, the experience you've had running multi-site operations won't have too much relevance and should therefore be relegated to a less prominent place.

Two important points about customising CVs:

- Print off a second copy (one you can keep on file so you will have a record of what you've said if you're invited for an interview).
- Don't neglect to do it because employers receive hundreds of unsolicited CVs and they automatically bin those that don't strike immediate chords with them.

A model approach to mailshots If you want mailshots to work for you, this is what you need to do:

- Again, identify the right employers – employers who are likely to have the kind of opportunities that match your targeting.

THURSDAY

- Ring before putting anything in the post. The object of this exercise is to get the name of the person in the organisation who would be responsible for employing people like you, i.e. the decision maker. Again, don't be fobbed off with the name of the Human Resources Manager. Human Resources Managers aren't decision makers (unless you happen to be looking for a job in Human Resources, of course).
- Put an accompanying letter with your CV. Keep this short and simple: who you are, where you're coming from and what you're seeking to achieve. Let it serve as an appetiser for the main meal (your CV).
- Mark your envelope 'Confidential'. This is the best insurance you can give your CV that it will be read by the right pair of eyes.

Fax shots and e-mails

An alternative to putting your CV in the post is to fax it or send it by e-mail. What's best?

Go back to your aims. Once your CV has passed through the preliminary read test and given there are no suitable vacancies at the moment, what you want to ensure is that:

- Your CV is put on file.
- When it is retrieved from file, it will still be in more or less pristine condition.

On the second count, fax paper doesn't acquit itself too well whilst, with e-mails, there is always the risk they don't get printed off – meaning they fail on the first count. At risk of sounding prehistoric, therefore – and unless there are any over-riding reasons for doing otherwise – put your unsolicited CV in the post.

Week Two

THURSDAY

Electronic storage of CVs A CV submitted by e-mail would seem to win hands down where it is the practice to store details of interesting looking candidates on an electronic data-base. One of the problems facing you, however, is knowing which employers do this and which don't. Since you will be sending your CV to individual named managers rather than to the Human Resources or Personnel Department (where these computer based systems tend to be located) the advice to 'put it in the post' still holds good.

> *Keeping control*
>
> Putting your speculative CVs in the post as opposed to faxing them or sending them by e-mail is a good example of **keeping control** – playing an active rather than a passive role in ensuring your job hunting moves to successful conclusions; facilitating the process as far as you can rather than leaving it to chance or how some hard-pressed manager happens to feel inclined on the day. Keeping control has particular importance when accessing the invisible market. We shall see more of it as we move on.

Professional networking
Professional networking is another way of accessing the invisible market – using your circle of contacts in business as a source of suitable job opportunities – something most people only think to do when they're out of work or their jobs come under threat.

Week Two

THURSDAY

> *Did you know?*
>
> More people find jobs by professional networking than by any other method.

Networking is for everyone A common misconception of networking is that it is the preserve of social climbers or extrovert personality types. Nothing could be further from the truth. Anyone in a career has his or her own professional network. Typically it consists of:

- Work colleagues past and present – bosses, peers and subordinates.
- Other people you come into contact with in the course of your work – for example, customers, suppliers, outside service providers.
- People you know through your professional body, e.g. the local branch of the Institute of Management.
- People you meet through going on courses or whilst getting qualifications – people in similar lines of work to yourself.

> *WARNING!*
>
> **The wrong ears**
> With the relatively small worlds that most of us operate in, sourcing jobs by professional networking carries the risk of our job hunting ambitions reaching the wrong ears. Take the case of Leonard. Leonard is a Sales Manager in the telecommunications industry. Leonard tried tapping into his contacts in the

Week Two
THURSDAY

competition to see what jobs might be available but unfortunately his boss got to hear about it. The result? Leonard was in very deep trouble indeed.

The lesson here is only network with people you can trust – people you can rely on to look after your best interests and who won't compromise your position by indulging in tittle-tattle. Conversely, give a wide berth to those who don't meet these criteria.

Neworking for jobs – a model approach The key to networking for jobs successfully is *keeping control*.

- Don't use your network contacts as sounding boards for your grouses and groans. It will feed out entirely the wrong messages – i.e. that you're only looking for an escape route from your present difficulties and any job will do.
- Instead make sure that the messages you feed out to your network contacts are *complete messages*. Give precise

THURSDAY

Week Two

guidelines on the kind of job you're looking for – including the salary.
- Set the perimeters by telling your contacts how far you want them to go for you. This would normally be to effect an introduction. In other words you should make it clear that you want any detailed negotiations left to you (always better done first hand).
- Stress the confidentiality. Lay down precise rules – like you want no discussions with any third parties without your prior knowledge and consent.

Registering with recruitment consultants

A large slice of the invisible market is handled by firms of recruitment consultants (employment agencies). Recruitment consultants keep details of candidates on file and interested employers can access these details at short notice. Here are examples of two employers who chose to use recruitment consultants for different reasons:

Example – Company D

Company D's IT Manager unexpectedly handed in her notice half way through a major project. With no suitable internal candidates to promote, Company D was faced with having to recruit someone from outside. The rigmarole of placing advertisements didn't appeal to Company D mainly because of the time it would take. Company D decided, therefore, to run their vacancy through a couple of firms of recruitment consultants specialising in IT staff to see if they had anybody on their books who would fit the bill.

Week Two
THURSDAY

> *Example – Company E*
> Company E's recently promoted Chief Accountant proved to be a total failure and they decided that he would have to go back to his old job at some stage in the near future. Before they broached this subject with him, however, they felt they needed to know if anyone more suitable was available on the market. A quick and confidential way of checking this out was to ask a leading firm of financial recruitment consultants to send in details of candidates they had registered with them.

No placement, no fee

Other than quickness, most firms of recruitment consultants offer their services on a no placement, no fee basis. This means employers like Company D and Company E can have a look at who's available without it costing them anything.

Week Two

T H U R S D A Y

Choose the right consultants In picking firms of recruitment consultants to register with, you will normally find you are faced with a bewildering choice. You need to apply the following criteria:

- The consultants must deal with the kind of appointments you are targeting. For example, if you're looking for a management position in the construction industry, it is pointless registering with a firm of consultants who deal mainly in general office staff.
- They need to be effective which is, in part, a reflection of their client base and, in part, a reflection of their general efficiency. (With firms of recruitment consultants, effectiveness should never be taken for granted!)

Conduct your search for the right firm of recruitment consultants in the following way:

- *Seek personal recommendations* – for example, does anyone on your professional network have any recent experience of dealing with a firm of recruitment consultants? If so, what information can they pass on?
- *Check the business telephone directories* – recruitment consultants often have display entries telling you what they do.
- *Scan the job ads* – recruitment consultants frequently run advertisements for vacancies that have been notified to them. From reading these advertisements over a period of time it is possible to tell which consultants are active in the areas of the job market you are targeting.
- *Ask* – if in any doubt, ring up firms of consultants, give them a brief run down of the kind of job you're looking for and ask if they can help.

THURSDAY

> **WARNING!**
>
> Don't register with too many consultants because it can give you two problems:
>
> - Too many requests to go to interviews (more than your availability will stand).
> - Two or more firms of consultants, putting you forward for the same job (this can queer the pitch before you even start).

Registering with consultants Registering usually involves filling in a registration form, attending an interview and possibly doing some kind of test. Some firms of consultants offer the facility to register online. This includes the new breed of internet-based recruitment consultants. Once you have registered with a firm of consultants they will be able to use their contacts and know how to find you the kind of job you are seeking.

Keeping control Those magic words again! Keeping control is the secret to success in dealing with recruitment consultants. Keeping control means:

- Make sure at the outset that they understand where you're coming from, i.e. go to great pains to explain your targeting, benchmarks and leave no room for doubt.
- Make sure that they know how to get hold of you. Recruitment consultants live in a fast moving world where they have to get results both for their clients and for themselves (a lot of them are paid on commission). Needless to say, candidates they find hard to contact don't appeal to recruitment consultants one bit.

- Phone up consultants from time to time to find out how they are getting on. Not only will it remind them that you're still there but you might also pick up some interesting feedback (like the salary you're asking for is too high). Prick up your ears for feedback. Feedback, remember, is what you use to give your targeting benchmarks their fine tuning.
- Very important – advise consultants whenever any information they are holding on you changes, e.g. you get a new telephone number or you decide to tweak your pay targeting benchmark down a notch or two.
- Ditch any consultants who don't perform satisfactorily – especially consultants who waste your time by putting you forward for jobs that are completely wrong for you.

Summary

Successful job hunting means sourcing both markets – the visible and the invisible. Too many candidates miss out on the latter because of its seeming inaccessibility. As a result they undersource – meaning they never discover the full extent of the market for their talents.

Today we have been looking at ways of penetrating the invisible market and its huge potential by using proactive sourcing techniques. The reward is accessing jobs for which there is frequently little or no competition (you got in first). In turn this means:

- much more chance of getting the job
- more flexibility when it comes to negotiating items like pay and perks

Week Two

FRIDAY

How to get headhunted

How about being headhunted? Today we're going to take a look at the glitzy world of executive search to see what's in it for you. Your programme reads as follows:

- the market for executive search
- projecting the person perfect and work perfect image: mastering your lifelong interview skills
- marketing yourself to headhunters
- dealing with headhunters
- keeping the approaches coming

On the face of it, being headhunted is an event over which you have no control. An approach comes straight out of the blue – as a rule when you're least expecting it.

Week Two

F R I D A Y

The market for executive search

Executive search consultants don't come cheap so the first point to grasp about headhunting is that employers don't go down this route unless there is a good reason. In most cases the reason is that the job is a very senior job (e.g. a board level appointment) where the person being sought is someone with exceptional qualities. Note: employers also use headhunting to recruit people with scarce and/or specialist skills.

What's in it for you?
Being headhunted is definitely something you can't afford to miss out on. There are two reasons for saying this:

- many of the best jobs are filled by headhunting
- the money's flexible (it's up to employers to come up with an offer that's going to interest you)

Projecting the person perfect and work perfect image

Is there anything you can do to enhance your chances of being headhunted?

How headhunters work
First let's look at how headhunters work. Professional headhunters – or executive search consultants, as they are more properly known – thrive on their connections in the business world.

> *Example – Company Q*
> Company Q, a brand leader in the widget industry, is looking for a new Chief Executive to replace the

Week Two
FRIDAY

> present job holder who retires in 12 months' time. Company Q contacts RST & Associates, a well known firm of executive search consultants, and briefs them on the kind of person they are seeking – ideally someone with several years' top management experience with a major widget maker. RST & Associates set about the assignment by tapping into their numerous contacts in the widget making world. Soon they have a list of names – people their contacts have recommended to them. From here they proceed to ring up each name on the list to find out who's interested in making a move and who isn't.

What the example of Company Q shows is that, to get yourself on to the receiving end of a headhunter's approach:

- someone has got to know you
- more importantly, what they know about you has got to be good

Projecting the right image

For the most part, by 'people who know you' we mean people who have come into contact with you in the course of your work. This includes:

- Colleagues, past and present (bosses, peers and subordinates).
- External contacts such as customers, suppliers and professional advisors.
- People who know you through your work on outside bodies such as professional institutions and trade associations.

FRIDAY

Week Two

> With being headhunted hot on the agenda, it is people like these who can influence the outcomes for you by:
>
> - mentioning your name at the right moment
> - saying the right things about you

This is where we ask you to focus your mind sharply on the image you project as you go about your day-to-day work.

The lifelong interview
An interesting contrast to draw here is between:

- The image you cultivate for going to interviews.
- The rather less well-managed image you project to those who have dealings with you every day of the week.

With the first, you are extremely mindful of being on your best behaviour whilst, at the same time, taking great pains over your personal appearance. You will be guarded in anything you say. You will certainly be going to great lengths to keep any grey areas in your track record under wraps.

Not so, however, with the second. You will be more inclined to let your hair down and a few of the less endearing aspects of your character may even creep out.

Part of the problem here of course is that we're talking about projecting an image all of the time rather than over the 45–90 minutes that's par for the course for most interviews. Harder? Of course, it is – and this is what we mean by the lifelong interview. The consistency and application called for are not easy to achieve.

Week Two

FRIDAY

The lifelong interview in practice

- You don't have off days.
- You have to be 100% reliable – you get back to people when you say you will and you complete your work to targets.
- Your appearance is always up to scratch (don't be the first to dress down).
- You refrain from running down your colleagues and your bosses behind their backs – you keep your opinions on people to yourself.
- You don't whinge and whine – you don't use your colleagues as a sounding board for your grievances whenever you feel you're being given a hard time.
- You learn to keep your flaws to yourself.
- You give some of the gloss you save for interviews to every day.

Week Two

FRIDAY

Person perfect and work perfect

Headhunters get their business by reputation, hence they play safe when it comes to putting forward the names of candidates to their clients. Don't expect headhunters to be very interested in you, therefore, if:

- they know of any defects in your character
- your work record is not up to standard

Rather, you must be seen as someone who is person prefect and work perfect and this is especially the case with top drawer jobs.

> *It's who you know and what they know about you*
>
> 'It's who you know' used to be the catch phrase to describe the way to success. Today it's truer to say 'It's who you know and what they know about you.'

Marketing yourself to headhunters

Headhunters have the reputation of being an aloof breed who move in elitist social circles – inaccessible to the Joe and Jane Ordinaries of this world. But is this true? Indeed, are there ways of bringing your credentials to the attention of headhunters so that you can enhance your chances of being the target of an approach?

Don't pepper headhunters with CVs

First, the wrong way to go about it. Don't pepper headhunters with copies of your CV – at least not until you've done some ground work first. Headhunters (proper ones) receive thousands of unsolicited CVs. Most of them end up in the shredding machine.

Week Two
FRIDAY

Where headhunters are coming from
Ask yourself why a headhunter should be interested in you. What do they stand to gain from having your name on their lists?

Headhunters are in business to make money – just like everyone else. What plays the biggest part in how they view you is whether they think they can make money out of you or not – in other words, whether they could place you with one of their clients.

Identify unusual areas of skill and experience
Headhunting assignments frequently involve finding people with unusual or special areas of skill and experience – people who:

- aren't in abundant supply
- advertising won't necessarily reach

> *Example*
> Ask yourself if you've got any interesting areas of skill and experience. Take Garth as an example. Garth is the Financial Manager of a company that has recently gone through a major expansion programme. Garth, therefore, has a lot of knowledge of takeovers, mergers and acquisitions – a lot more than the average financial manager would have.

Use your connections
Play headhunters at their own game – by which we mean use your connections to access them. This is easy if you've been headhunted before. Speak to the consultant you dealt

FRIDAY

with previously and say you're ready to make another move. Explain what it is you're looking for this time.

If you're not fortunate enough to have been the target for an approach before, find someone among your circle who has. With search becoming an increasingly preferred method of sourcing executive talent, there is almost bound to be someone you know who has been the focus of a headhunter's attention at some point in the past. Find out from them the headhunter's name then follow the plan of action set out below.

- Use the phone for making contact.
- Quickly establish the connection: 'I got your name from Ruth Sykes. You placed her in a position with Wired Up Electronics six months ago.'
- Equally quickly, move on to where you're coming from and what you're seeking to achieve (your target). Do this in three sentences maximum.
- Mention any interesting areas of skill/experience (another sentence).
- Ask the headhunter if he/she can help you.
- Stop talking and listen to the answer.

There are a number of possible outcomes here:

- *The headhunter may not deal with the kind of jobs you're targeting.* If this is the case, ask if he/she knows a headhunter who does. Start again.
- *The headhunter may ask you further questions.* This is usually a good sign. Answer as concisely as you can.
- *The headhunter may ask you to send in a copy of your CV.* Again a good sign.

FRIDAY

Key points to pick out here as follows:

- Headhunters do most of their business on the 'phone. You will do better communicating with them in this way than, for example, by writing to them or sending them e-mails.
- Connections are important to headhunters. The name-dropping you do at the start of your conversation will help to focus their attention on what you are saying.
- Long-windedness is no way to a headhunter's heart. By coming to the point quickly you will avoid losing the headhunter's interest.

The aim to your approach to the headhunter is twofold:

- To see whether any of the headhunter's current assignments match up with what you're looking for (an off chance).
- Failing this, to ensure that when your CV arrives it is put in the interesting candidates' file rather than consigned to the batch to be shredded.

Visibility

Headhunters often source candidates from media reports on companies or from other sources that are in the public domain. Here are two examples:

> **Sean** specialises in corporate law and became the target for an approach following an article he wrote for a leading business magazine.

FRIDAY

Week Two

> **Gemma** received three phone calls from headhunters after her name featured prominently in trade press coverage of the launch of her company's latest range of products.

Dealing with headhunters

Once you've got an approach from a headhunter, how should you deal with it? What's the best way of moving the approach forward?

Keep it to yourself
This is the first and most important rule for dealing with approaches. Don't succumb to the temptation to tell everyone. We say this for two good reasons:

- Approaches sometimes fizzle out. This can happen, for example when the company behind the approach changes its mind about recruiting.
- The fact that you've received an approach could send out a message to your principals that you're potentially a short-term stayer, meaning they're going to think twice before spending any more money on your training and development.

Don't let it go to your head
After an approach there is a tendency to feel flattered. Someone out there has at last recognised your talents.

Whilst a certain amount of self-satisfaction is only natural, letting an approach go to your head is fraught with danger.

FRIDAY

For example:

- If the approach falls through – or you don't get the job for any reason – it could deal a crushing blow to your ego.
- You could start to view the job with rose-tinted spectacles, meaning you fail to pick up on quite glaring mismatches with your targeting benchmarks.
- Feeling flattered tends to go with feeling grateful – not a good position to start from when it comes to negotiating the best possible deal for yourself.

Don't put up the shutters
Even if you're not looking to make a job move at the moment, always receive headhunters courteously and hear out what they've got to say. There are two reasons for this particular piece of advice:

- Because of the cost factor alone, jobs filled by headhunting tend to be very good jobs – in short, without knowing it, you could be turning your back on the opportunity of a lifetime. As we all know, opportunity seldom knocks twice.

FRIDAY

Week Two

- In today's uncertain world, you never know when you're going to need a headhunter. Keeping on the right side of them is therefore in your best interests.

State your position
Aware of the potential for time wasting, a headhunter will seek to establish at an early stage whether you are in the market for making a move or not. Your response here should be on the lines of, whilst you're perfectly happy with what you're doing at the moment (true or not), you would always be interested to hear about any opportunities that would move your career forward. Then this cues you up nicely to trot out your targeting benchmarks – including the kind of package it would take to tempt you out of your tree (irrespective of whether a figure has already been mentioned or not).

> *WARNING!*
>
> **Don't ask for too little**
> Employers normally enter into approaches with flexible ideas on the kind of pay and benefits package they would have to put forward to attract the right calibre of candidate. In short, there is usually plenty of latitude for negotiation. Don't, therefore, make the mistake of selling yourself short by naming a figure at the start that's too low.
>
> Remember:
>
> - It is easier to come down than it is to talk your way back up.
> - With a top job, you could create the unfortunate

Week Two

FRIDAY

> impression that you're lacking in personal ambition (a bad point).
>
> Headhunters are used to talking salaries in truly astronomical figures without the bat of an eyelid. Sentiments like 'being too greedy' or 'going over the top' have little meaning to them.

Move the approach forward
It's usually in your best interests to move the approach forward as quickly as you can and, whilst the headhunter will probably want to engage you in formal selection procedures such as interviews and psychometric tests, you should endeavour to **keep control** over the pace at which events move. For example, if the headhunter says 'I'll get back to you' ask for some idea of time scale. If you hear nothing by the date you've been given then get on the 'phone and chase them up.

Keeping the approaches coming

The first approach you receive may turn out to be a mismatch but there is a bigger picture here – one where you need the approaches to keep coming at you until eventually the right one turns up. What this means is cultivating headhunters and keeping them sweet. How do you do this? By incorporating some of the lessons we have touched on already, namely:

- *Be courteous*. Never shut the door in a headhunter's face and always hear out what they've got to say.
- *Be available*. Don't make headhunters' lives difficult by being impossible to reach.

FRIDAY

- *Be reliable.* Go back to headhunters when you say you will. Don't leave them to have to chase you.
- *Be straight.* If a job's not suitable for you, say so. Don't string headhunters along. Wasting their time won't endear them to you.
- *Be positive.* Tell the headhunter the kind of job you are looking for and what kind of offer would tempt you out of the tree.
- *Be engaging.* Encourage headhunters to keep 'phoning you.
- *Be pro-active.* Keep up the contact by 'phoning them from time to time.

Summary

Approach is the doorway to some of the best opportunities the job market has to offer. Make sure you don't miss out by:

- Concentrating on your lifelong interview and seeking to project a person perfect and work perfect image at all times.
- Using your connections to establish links with headhunters.
- Extending your visibility beyond your company.
- Marketing any areas of interesting skills and experience that you may have.
- Engaging headhunters in an ongoing dialogue (keeping the approaches coming).

Week Two

━━ S A T U R D A Y ━━

Applying selectivity to your job search

The crowning piece to successful job hunting should be when the offer of employment is put into your hands. But for a lot of people this is when the worrying starts. Should they take the job or should they turn it down?

Today we are going to look at applying selectivity to the jobs you source – in other words, which jobs to go for and which to leave alone. Following this we are going to look back over the week to see what you have learned and pull a few of the threads together. Your programme looks like this:

- assessing the risks in changing jobs
- avoiding rogue employers
- weighing up job offers – looking at the small print; getting all the information you need

- enticement: the dangers that lurk behind the offer you can't refuse
- job hunting as part of a broader career strategy

The risk factor

Irrespective of how much research you do into prospective employers, a job move is still largely a step into the unknown. You don't know how you will fit in. You don't know how you will feel about the job in six months' time.

Fears like these serve to deter a lot of people. They turn down perfectly good offers of employment for the simple reason that they develop cold feet. This is clearly no good and a waste of all the time and effort they have put in.

Upsides and downsides
Accepting that there is a risk attached to any change of job, you need to view the risk in its proper context – by which we mean view both the upsides and the downsides together then stand back and see how they balance up.

Upsides These are usually the advances in salary you make, the greater challenges and responsibilities the new job has to offer and so on.

Downsides This is what happens when the job doesn't work out. You find yourself back on the job market. You could end up making a sideways or even a backwards move to escape from the pain. It could be several years before you get your career back on track.

SATURDAY

Downsides are, admittedly, pretty frightening, but what most people neglect to do with their risk assessment is consider another set of upsides and downsides: those associated with turning the job down and staying where they are:

> **Upsides** The security of working for an employer you know.
>
> **Downsides** Continuing to underachieve, stagnate, be underpaid – whatever it was that drove you out on to the job market in the first place.

Make your job moves for the right reason
The bottom line to taking a balanced view of the risks is two golden rules:

- Don't make job moves for trivial or inconsequential gains, e.g. a small improvement in salary.
- Don't be driven out on to the job market by minor gripes, e.g. your company car is overdue for a change.

Week Two

SATURDAY

Rogue employers

> Not all the creatures you meet in the job jungle will have your best interests at heart. Indeed, the increasing diversity of the modern market means there is a far greater chance of you coming across a few slippery characters on your travels.

We all know of the odd hire and fire outfit (employers who are in a constant cycle of taking people on and laying them off) but there are some equally dangerous species about – people who will conceal important facts from you usually to get you to take the job.

How to spot a rogue employer

- Be on your guard the moment you feel you are being 'sold' a job. Good employers always point out the snags as well as the benefits. Rogues confine themselves to painting rosy pictures.
- Beware of employers who make big promises, e.g. on future pay increases – especially when they're not prepared to put their promises into writing.
- Sense danger if the answers to your questions are vague or evasive.
- Watch out for employers who give themselves let-outs, e.g. the offer is made conditional on the retention of a commercial contract.
- Be aware of employers who make you the offer you can't refuse (more on this in a moment).
- Trust your instincts. If you feel there's something fishy about an employer, let that be sufficient reason for you

giving them a wide berth. Listen to your inner voices. They rarely let you down.

> *WARNING!*
>
> A lot of jobs today (including management jobs) are short term or temporary – meaning you have to be very careful that what you are being offered is indeed a permanent position. Be warned that some unscrupulous employers try to disguise the fact that a job is temporary just to attract suitable applicants.

Weighing up job offers

Though it seems scarcely in need of saying, don't act on any job offer until you've got it in writing. Don't, for example, spread it round the office that you'll be leaving soon. Don't, whatever you do, hand in your notice.

Read the small print
Job offers are frequently quite detailed and/or they come with supporting documentation such as job descriptions, standard terms of employment and information on items such as pension schemes and company cars. Read all of these documents carefully making notes as you go along.

Pick out:

- any items that you feel need clarification
- anything at variance with information given to you at the interviews
- any items that appear to have been omitted

Week Two

SATURDAY

> What you are safeguarding yourself against here is not so much rogue employers but poor or inexperienced interviewers – people who don't get their facts right or leave out something important (important to you, that is).

Get all the information you need
Again, it scarcely needs saying, but don't accept any job until you've got all the information you need.

> *WARNING!*
> Whereas in most cases this will simply mean a quick phone call to the person who made you the offer, with really important issues such as the date on which a salary increment becomes payable or the details of a relocation package, it is advisable always to get the additional information put into writing. Any employer who is reluctant to do this should automatically be viewed with suspicion.

Revisit your targeting benchmarks
This, if you like, is your final fail-safe device. Does what you're being offered match up with what you set out to achieve by going out on the job market or does it fall short in any significant way? Asking yourself this question exposes three potential dangers:

- You could have allowed your career aims to drift (this tends to happen to people who have been on the job market for a long time). You could have lowered your sights without realising it.

Week Two

SATURDAY

- You could be allowing disenchantment with your present job to colour your opinion of what's being offered to you. You could be seeing the new job in a better light than it deserves.
- You could be succumbing to enticement (read on).

> *WARNING*
>
> There's no such thing as the perfect job. This is said to warn you against:
>
> - Being over-pedantic when it comes to viewing job offers.
> - Turning down good jobs because relatively unimportant aspects of the package are not in line with your expectations.
>
> Learn to consider your job offers 'in the round'. For example, see where a major improvement in salary (higher than the figure you targeted) far outweighs a slight reduction in holiday entitlement or a more restricted choice of company car.

Enticement

With some employers quite desperate to acquire people with scarce or sought-after skills, the field is wide open for enticement or making an offer in the knowledge that the person on the receiving end will find it hard to refuse. Enticement often goes hand in hand with headhunting.

SATURDAY

Week Two

> Enticement is perhaps the commonest reason why people make bad moves. 'I knew it was a mistake' you hear them saying. 'But with what was put on the table how could I say no?'

Enticement can come in many forms: pay, perks and, these days, big up front lump sum payments or golden hellos.

All offers are refusable

Needless to say, a job with a fat cat salary and a big flash car won't do you any good at all if it only lasts six months. You should beware of situations therefore where you feel you are being made an offer you can't refuse. Ok, it could mean you've hit the jackpot but it could also mean the employer you're in negotiation with is in dire straits and knows of no other way of getting you to take the job. The message? If the warning bells are ringing out at you, take notice of them. With job hunting, all that glitters is not gold.

Week Two

SATURDAY

Summary

Bringing job hunting to successful outcomes means being able to pick out winners and losers from the jobs you source and avoiding bad moves at all costs. The way to do this is by:

- putting the feel good and flattery that goes with being offered a job to one side
- picking up on any warning signs that are flashing out at you
- not allowing enticement to get in the way of your better judgement
- taking a long hard look at what's on the table before you say yes
- going back to employers if the information they've given you seems contradictory or incomplete

At the same time, don't be put off by the modern job market with all its difficulties and imperfections. See it rather as a place full of opportunities for those who can learn to master it.

CONCLUSION

Week Two

Job hunting as a part of a career strategy

Job-hunting for many people is something they turn to in moments of desperation. They do it, for example, when their jobs are put at risk or when the pressure starts to get too much for them. They do it when the pay rise they banked on doesn't materialise or when they get passed by for promotion. Desperation puts pressure on people to go for quick solutions. They end up taking the first decent offer that comes along, meaning:

- they're not on the job market for very long
- they only ever see a fragment of the complete range of opportunities available to them
- they build up little or no experience

Bearing in mind these short spells of frantic job hunting are usually interspersed by long periods of inactivity, the result is a view of the outside world that is rather like a series of snapshots – one where you only see:

- what's in the frame
- what's happening at one particular point in time

CONCLUSION

> *Example*
>
> These snapshots views can yield completely false readings of the true nature of the market. Take Tom as an example. Tom works in the construction industry. Tom has been on the job market three times in his life – each time when the construction industry was going through hard times and when he thought his job was under threat. Tom's job hunting experience is therefore confined to periods when:
>
> - jobs in construction were thin on the ground
> - there were plenty of other people like him (people shopping round for something more secure)
>
> As a result, Tom's view of the market for people with his talents is a distorted one. What Tom clearly hasn't experienced is the market in more buoyant times.

The bottom line for people like Tom is that they underachieve.

Keep the job opportunities coming

The two main messages in this week are:

- there's a much bigger market out there for your talents than you think
- source the bigger market properly and you could profit from it handsomely

There is one final piece to the infrastructure we need to put into place, however, and it is this. You need to have an ongoing view of what the market has to offer, not one that

Week Two

CONCLUSION

starts and stops depending on how life happens to be treating you at the time. In other words, this is where you ditch the series of snapshots and go into moving pictures.

How do you do this? The answer is by employing some of the lessons we have touched on during the course of this week:

- Don't be driven out on the job market by desperation.
- Keep in contact with the visible market by scanning the ads regularly. As a matter of course apply for any good jobs that catch your eye.
- Keep up the proactive sourcing. Keep up your presence on the invisible market by staying on the books of selected recruitment consultants. Mailshot selected employers occasionally.
- Keep your networks open. Let it be known to your contacts that you are always interested in hearing about good opportunities.
- Keep working on your lifelong interview. Make yourself a more attractive target to headhunters by continuing to project a person-perfect and work-perfect image.
- Encourage headhunters to keep calling you. Don't put them off by being negative with them.

> Because of the uncertainties of the world in which we live, good career management is about keeping options open and having irons in the fire all of the time. Keep on-line with the job market. Turn job hunting into an everyday part of your life.

Week Two

CONCLUSION

What have you learned this week

- Job hunting benefits from having your ideas thought out clearly first.
- Source the whole market and not just part of it.
- Don't miss out on the invisible market and what it's got to offer.
- Do everything you can to make yourself a target for headhunters.
- Be selective with the jobs you go for.
- Learn to leave some jobs alone.
- Make job hunting part of every day.

A final word

When everything seems to be going against you, shooting off a few job applications immediately makes you feel better. You are doing something positive. Avenues are opening up. The world is suddenly a bigger and more exciting place.

Writing your CV

WEEK THREE

STEVE MORRIS

GRAHAM WILLCOCKS

Edited by

Chris Baker

CONTENTS

Week Three

Introduction		193
Sunday	Thinking about you	195
Monday	Getting the basics right	206
Tuesday	Knowing you	216
Wednesday	Knowing me	230
Thursday	Getting down to the writing	243
Friday	Almost there	254
Saturday	Getting your CV across to the employer	268

Acknowledgement

The authors would like to thank Sue McKoen for her help in researching this section and Chris Baker for recent revises.

Week Three

INTRODUCTION

Everyone should write a curriculum vitae, a potted history of their life, a CV. However, for many people, writing a CV is a little like reading *War and Peace* – it's something they intend to do one day but not quite yet. For many other people the request for a CV is greeted with a cheery:

I've got one somewhere but it's a bit out of date I'm afraid.

This week will help you take the plunge and write a CV that gets results for you – an interview for a job. You will work step by step throughout the week and at the end you will have a first-rate CV and a covering letter to go with it. All you'll need then is a first class stamp, an envelope, and a dash of good fortune.

Week Three
INTRODUCTION

The steps you will work through as you write your CV are:

- researching yourself
- researching the company you will send your CV to and deciding whether to apply
- deciding on what CV format to choose depending on your circumstances
- avoiding the basic errors that would spell Do Not Pass Go
- writing the CV itself
- editing and checking it
- writing a professional, sharp and interesting covering letter
- popping everything in the post

Week Three

SUNDAY

Thinking about you

We will start the week by thinking about why we write CVs and trying to establish what you want to say in your own.

From our experience, very few people relish the prospect of writing their CV. Some see it as a boring chore, while others approach it with a real sense of dread. However, writing your CV gives you the chance to take stock and put down in black and white all your achievements. It should be seen as an opportunity rather than a tiresome necessity.

After all, the first impression that a prospective employer will get of you will come from your CV. Before the interview, before the aptitude tests, he or she will read your CV and make an instant judgement – 'Do I want this person working for me or not?'

If they open a dog-eared photocopy, littered with spelling mistakes and basic errors, they are unlikely to hurry to pick up the nearest phone. If, however, the CV is nicely presented and clearly written in a logical order, then they just might.

> *Rules, rules, rules*
>
> This is an ideal time to pause and say something about the approach this book takes.
>
> We are not going to lay down a set of arbitrary rules that must be obeyed at all times when writing CVs. Too many people try and turn CV-writing into some kind of pseudo-science. They want to create formulas and laws, where simple common sense is all that is needed.

SUNDAY

> Pick up three books on CVs and as likely as not each will advise you differently on tiny details – like whether to write a date as 3.4.98 or 3 April 1998. No wonder people sitting down to write CVs often don't know where to start!
>
> This book is not going to insult your, or your employer's intelligence by getting pedantic about these minor details. Rather we are going to help you make the most of the important information that you are going to include – information about yourself.

Some early thoughts

We have already said that CVs are the way to make that all-important 'good first impression'. They are the proverbial foot in the door that will help determine whether you actually get inside. You may not think that two sides of paper can affect your whole career – but they can!

SUNDAY

So we know why we are writing our CV, but it is worth asking ourselves why the recipient will want to read it.

Although many companies now rely on assessment centres and psychometric testing, the vast majority still require you to send in the humble CV.

> *Companies ask for CVs because:*
> - Writing a CV gives you a chance to present yourself in your own way.
> - It is a good indicator of how much pride you will take in your work.
> - It removes the need to draw up time-consuming application forms.
> - Employers can keep a CV on file and use it when further vacancies arise.

Now we have established why we are writing the CV, and why our prospective employer will want to receive it. It is now time to see how we can best make our CV work for us.

What are we really trying to achieve when we write our CV?

They allow you to tailor your message The important thing about a CV is to show that you are both **right** for the job and **different** enough to be worth interviewing. This is something that people often don't realise when they are writing their CV.

On the one hand you need to demonstrate in your CV that you understand what the company or organisation is looking for and that you match up closely with the criteria

Week Three

SUNDAY

they have set. If you are too wide of the mark you won't stand a chance. You also need to show where you are different or better than the competition – that you have the edge.

People often go wrong by going overboard on showing how different they are. This can lead to zany CVs that simply don't get past the door. So drawing up a CV is about balance and about making sure that you aim your arrows good and true.

CVs are universal You are never too old or too young to write a CV. Many people leaving school find writing a CV very difficult, because they find it hard to identify what it is about them that is marketable. Many older people who write a CV find it difficult to see the wood for the trees. They have done so many things in their working life that it can seem very difficult to get everything down in just a page or so. People who have had an unconventional life or career can find CVs difficult, because on the surface CVs seem only to cater for people who have walked a straight path.

Week Three

SUNDAY

You will see how to overcome all these anxieties as you work through the week. Put simply, a CV is for *everyone*.

CVs are infinitely adaptable You decide what to say and how. You don't just fill in the boxes on someone else's form. In fact CVs are as adaptable as you and your own circumstances need them to be.

One very important point is that the CV is not just your chance to talk about what you have done at work. It's also your chance to present other skills and experiences you have picked up during your life. Indeed in some circumstances you can show, through your CV, that your life experiences are more relevant and valuable than your work experiences. All areas of your life and work can be brought to bear – but sparingly and tightly focused on the job you are applying for. So a CV allows you to select the appropriate parts and leave out the interesting but irrelevant bits.

Where are you starting from?
Of course, where you are starting from and what you are aiming for will have an impact on your CV. So you may be any one of the following – and more than one at different times:

- You may be a school leaver with the problem that you have very similar qualifications and education to other people. The challenge in this case is to look at ways of adding value and showing how you are different, and how your experiences inside and outside of school actually mark you apart from your peers. So in your CV you might stress the clubs you have been involved in, for instance.

Week Three

SUNDAY

- You may be moving on from one job to another job in the field. In this case your CV is an opportunity for you to show that you have the capacity to move up a gear from where you are. So your CV may well be slanted towards presenting your experience and showing why you are capable of making the leap to the next level.

- You may be out of a job, having been made redundant. In this case your CV is your opportunity to get started again. This means you will be looking to show the ways in which your work experience is still valid in the workplace today and looking at any other attributes you have built up in your life that will help you get back into the job market. Take heart, there are routes back!

- You may have taken early retirement or be an older person. In this case you will probably have a whole host of life skills that you can draw on and experience that you will be able to present in your CV. It may also be an opportunity for you to show that you're still in touch with the job you are looking for, and to cash in on your most bankable asset – your experience.

- You may be a returner to the job market, having looked after or cared for relatives or brought up children. It's often tempting to think you are at a great disadvantage against all those people with a clear progression to show. However, your CV is an opportunity to stress all the valuable life skills that being a carer gives you, like budgeting, time management and negotiation with benefit agencies and schools. You may also have been involved in voluntary work, helping on the PTA or working in one of the care charities, for example.

Week Three
SUNDAY

- You may decide you want to make a career change. In this case your CV is your opportunity to identify transferable skills that will allow you to move between one career and another.

So, it's important to be aware of all these points before you start working on your CV. All too often people simply plunge in without any preparation or clear idea of the context a CV operates in. What you have done so far today will help you see how your CV is grounded within the general world of selection and recruitment.

Ask yourself:

- What do I want from a CV?
Be clear about the specific results you want it to achieve.

See the wood and the trees

The first step when drawing up your CV is to make sure you see both the wood and the trees, the detail and the big picture. This is probably the most difficult thing about putting a CV together. All of us have had experiences, all of us have lived lives. The hard part is to give an overall impression and at the same time to pick out the important bits that might get us that vital interview.

For many people the effort and discipline needed to pick out the key points makes them put their CV to the very bottom of their list of priorities. The best way to counter this is to have a more structured approach to take the pain out of it. The first step is to come up with the answers to some very simple questions. Try these for starters:

- What three things you have done are you most proud of?
- What three things are you good at?
- What three things are you not so good at?

SUNDAY

Week Three

> - What are three personal and professional landmarks in your life?
>
> *When you have written the answers to these big questions, think about other things that are important to you, like:*
>
> - What kind of job do you really want?
> - What kind of things wouldn't you do (for instance, relocate)?
> - What kind of work environment do you like best?
> - Are you the kind of person who likes responsibility?
> - Where and why were you most productive over the last five or ten years?
> - If you are meeting a total stranger, how would you describe yourself to them?

You can go on and make other questions up. The aim of this is to start unblocking your thinking and start seeing yourself in a positive way. It should also help you to start sifting through what is important to you and some of your achievements. Unfortunately, a lot of people find answering some of these questions extremely hard.

Be realistic
It's a characteristic of many people that they hate boasting. They're much happier telling other people what they are bad at than what they feel they are really good at.

> *Go away and boast*
>
> A consultant running a seminar on stress management told the twenty participants to go off in

SUNDAY

> pairs and to tell each other what they did better than most (or all) other people. They had to honestly believe their claims and be able to demonstrate their validity through some sort of evidence.
>
> After five minutes, six of the pairs came back. They said they simply couldn't do it. It was embarrassing and wrong to say good things about themselves. However, as the consultant pointed out, if the individuals didn't explain their strengths to other people, who else would? Who else knew more about them than they did themselves?

In other words, being honest about yourself is not the same as being boastful. If a succession of bosses and people reporting to you have told you you're a brilliant communicator, why not share this with the world?.. Suitably phrased, of course.

The best CVs have only the most crucial and relevant details selected. By asking yourself some straightforward questions like these, and giving honest answers, you can:

- Start the process of sifting out what is likely to be important.
- Clarify the kind of things you are likely to want on your CV.
- Get down on paper some ideas about yourself.

In many ways this should have helped you break the ice and start the process of more structurally putting a CV together.

And finally today

Finally, today is the day to start digging out all the bits and pieces you are likely to need as you go about drawing up your CV during the week. This will help you to feel fully prepared when you come to put pen to paper.

So, get together a pack or pile of all the documents you think might be relevant. These could include:

- Certificates from your formal education.
- Proof of training courses you have been on.
- Articles you have written.
- Addresses and phone numbers of your potential referees.
- Any testimonials written by people about you.

Basically you need to get together anything you think might help you, or jog your memory, or that you might refer to in your CV.

Summary

Today you have:

- Clarified what CVs do and why they matter to you.
- Thought about yourself and your main achievements.
- Got together the bits and pieces to help draw up your CV.

Week Three

MONDAY

Getting the basics right

Before you start putting detailed information together, it's worth looking at what makes a successful CV in most people's eyes. Then you can put your details into a framework you know is a good one.

There are a number of basic things to get right for your CV to pass the acid test. There's no point in beating about the bush with these. They really are as simple as they seem.

Anyone who has ever advertised a job will have come across CVs that include either all or some of the basic faults we talk about today. They crop up with depressing regularity – ask anyone who has read a lot of CVs.

Before we look at this guide it's important to remember that you are trying to make an impact with your CV. You are trying to show that you are worth interviewing. First impressions count, so you need to make your CV stand out, and not for the wrong reasons.

If you don't do the basics right then it is a case of Do Not Pass Go. Your CV will be filed in the bin.

So what should you do?

Be yourself

One of the things people often do wrong with CVs is try to invent a persona for themselves that doesn't really ring true.

MONDAY

Week Three

Obviously you want to stress the good things that you have done and stress your skills. But you want to ensure that you can talk about everything you write about. Don't use long words or phrases that, when you are questioned, show you can't really explain them. Try to use language you would normally use and feel comfortable with.

> *An example*
>
> A manager, talking about a CV he had received, said the person had written:
>
> *I enjoy working in a synergistic environment.*
>
> 'None of us knew what she was talking about and we suspected it was a case of using a word she felt would impress without understanding it herself. The phrase clashed with every other sentence in the CV and made me feel uncomfortable with the applicant. On almost that one sentence alone, I chose not to interview.'

Sometimes the CV agencies, who draw up a CV for individuals, write them in a language that doesn't feel comfortable for the person concerned. This sticks out a mile, and it's well worth taking the time to write your own CV. It may not be as standard as the kind of thing an agency churns out, but because of that you have all the more chance of getting an interview. And anyway, it's unlikely that the company will actually believe you are a part-time brain surgeon or heavyweight boxing champion.

Week Three

MONDAY

And one final thing, try never to copy or adapt someone else's CV, even one you see in a book on *How to write a CV*. Be yourself!

Read the ad

We'll look at this in detail on Wednesday. All too often people don't read the ad properly. They spend about one minute reading the ad and then two days putting the CV together. Their CV may be great, but because they haven't read the advert properly they miss the main points.

> I advertised a job for communications officer at the place where I work. You would be surprised how many people just didn't read the advert and what we were looking for. We actually got one CV in from someone who was a telecommunications worker. He

Week Three
MONDAY

> was an ex-BT person and had seen the word 'communications' in the title and thought the job was for a telephone engineer!
>
> Housing Association Manager

Another trap people fall into is sending a CV whenever they see a job they are interested in, even if the advert doesn't ask for one. This may make you feel better but it won't get you a job.

Often people just have a scatter-gun approach, sending CVs to any jobs they like the look of and not bothering to fill in application forms. If you do this, you will not get an interview, and it's just a waste of another first class stamp. It looks lazy and companies will not take any notice of you.

Be positive but don't lie

This goes back to being yourself, and being honest. On a CV it's important not to pretend or tell lies. If you lie it could give you serious legal problems later on and you may lose your job. What's more, you are unlikely to feel comfortable if you get an interview because you will be worried about being found out.

Length is important

It's important to get the right length for your CV. In general, the shorter the CV the better. Certainly you don't want to go over two pages in length, except for some very senior posts.

The received wisdom is that you should aim for a one page *resumé* type CV that gets all the basic points and leaves the person advertising the job wanting to ask you more.

The act of getting all the major points in about yourself briefly and succinctly is an important discipline. If you find your CV has crept up to more than two pages then get to work editing the sentences and cutting everything that is not relevant to the job. The best way of doing this is to check your CV carefully against the person specification for the job. We look at this later.

Broadly you may say that there are views on the right length of CV depending on the different types of job:

Week Three

MONDAY

- For analytical-type jobs – like banking or accountancy or anything to do with figures – try to get everything on to one page. For this kind of job you want to appear to be well organised, concise and clear thinking. If your CV for this kind of job goes on to two or three pages it may look as though you can't see the wood for the trees.
- More creative-type jobs. In this kind of job you may well go to two pages because you may want to give a fuller picture of yourself.
- If you are sending in a speculative CV to a company when they have not advertised a job, never write more than one page. Your task is to whet their appetite and encourage them to either contact you, remember you next time or keep your CV on file.

As well as these areas there are other areas to take into account. If you fail any of the following you will not pass go.

Week Three

MONDAY

Don't use gimmicks

In the past some people who have advised on CVs have stressed the need to be different. This has led to people sending in gimmicky and jokey CVs.

We have seen CVs that have come in on luminous paper, on transparencies, with elaborate shading, that include cartoons, that have been headed by family photographs and that are on paper sizes other than A4. One person sent in his CV for the job of swimming pool manager on the back of a pair of flippers!

These kind of CVs are very unlikely to impress. During the 1980s in a very small section of the market – advertising and so on – this kind of wacky approach to CVs was the norm. However, as recession has bitten, and organisations have started to take their business a little more seriously, it is almost bound to turn people off. Keep your CV personal, engaging and professional.

Another tip is, never try to be funny. Your idea of humour is likely to be peculiar to you. One man wrote in his CV under *Educational Qualifications*:

I was the original exam nightmare – I threw up before every exam!

What he meant was that he had no qualifications.

The nuts and bolts

The following is a checklist for getting the nuts and bolts right:

- The CV must be clean and tidy. It shouldn't be creased or have ink blots. Above all, avoid the dreaded white correction fluid. If you are still using a typewriter make sure you type absolutely perfectly. The mere sign of a

MONDAY

white patch covering a mistake will probably guarantee your CV a future in a rubbish bin. Organisations produce quality paperwork these days, so yours has to match their standard or they'll almost certainly reject it.

> *Join the 21st century, please!*
>
> The real advice here is to use a computer. With a PC (personal computer) you can store information and develop your CV over time.

- The layout must be clear and neat. There are varying opinions about how much margin to leave, but avoid cramped or crowded pages. It's important not to suddenly reinvent yourself as an ace designer and use 15 typefaces and various avant-garde type designs. Keep it simple, keep it professional. Remember that headings are important but don't go overboard. Above all, don't try to do anything too fancy, especially with typefaces.

- Spelling and grammar are crucial. We know of people who have won jobs on the basis that they knew how to spell, and could tell the difference between *principal* and *principle*. It's absolutely essential that you avoid spelling mistakes and grammatical errors. If necessary, get someone else to check it before you send it.

M O N D A Y

If you are not good at spelling, use the spell check on your PC, but don't rely on it. You may type a word wrongly but still not be alerted to it by the spell check – for instance you may type 'spell' as 'sell' and because both are correct the computer will let it go.

- Only handwrite the CV if the company insists on it, and then use black ink rather than blue. It photocopies better and makes their life easier. If you are going to use handwriting, be aware that some employers use handwriting analysts. If you send a handwritten covering letter or envelope, take time with your writing, and make sure it's neat.

- Politically correct terminology matters. If a specific terminology is important for the employer, you need to make sure that this is reflected in your CV.

- Keep something back. CVs often fail because of sheer overload. People become so exuberant and carried away with themselves that they put every possible fact and detail on their CV. It's very important to keep something back, so that you can talk about it at the interview and possibly surprise your interviewers. In the CV world less is definitely more.

Summary

Today you have looked at some of the basics of putting a CV together. If you get these right you will have at least jumped the first hurdle. And when you have jumped the first hurdle you can go on to tomorrow, which looks in more detail at researching what needs to go into the ideal CV.

Week Three

MONDAY

Avoiding the pitfalls of CVs means avoiding the obvious things like spelling mistakes and poor grammar. Make the CV look neat, tidy and professional. There are also some slightly less obvious things like the importance of being yourself and using language that suits you.

If you get these things right you should be able to build on today and put together a CV that really works.

TUESDAY

Knowing you...

One thing that many people forget to do when writing their CV is to find out about the people they are sending it to. What they end up with is a generic CV that they send off to a series of random companies, more often than not selected from a particular section of the phonebook.

By taking some time to research a company you give yourself the chance to decide whether it is somewhere you would like to work. (And so avoid the cost of a stamp if it isn't!) Sending a CV to a company you have no intention of joining wastes not only their time, but also your own.

> *Computers*
>
> There is no need to create a new CV each time you apply for a different job. You can compose individual paragraphs or key information for use when needed. Different aspects can be highlighted, or left out so that your CV is always relevant and addressed specifically to the concerns of the employer.

A cautionary tale...

Researching your prospective employers is a very useful habit to get into. It will not only help you gauge what to put in your CV, but is vital should you get to the interview

TUESDAY

stage. There is no excuse for going in blind, and hoping to bluff your way with natural charm. It might work occasionally – but it doesn't very often!

We know someone who made these mistakes when they were first applying for jobs. Having put together an impressive CV, he didn't bother to do any research and was left looking rather foolish in the interview.

Everything was going great. He had walked confidently through the door, given the all-important 'firm handshake' and scored well in the tests. Then, quite unexpectedly, he was asked why he thought he was the right person for the job. All of a sudden he was floundering. He had seen the advert in the Media section of the paper, so he tried his luck.

"Well I have always been interested in advertising, and I consider myself to be a pretty good writer."

By now, the expressions on the faces of the interviewers should have been enough to tell him that it was time to get his coat. And if he hadn't noticed them, then their next question was an even bigger clue…

"What exactly do you think we do here?"

Apparently he has blocked out the rest of the interview from his mind, but suffice to say that they were not an advertising company, and they did not want writers, but rather Media Accounts Managers. Unsurprisingly, he wasn't asked back for a second interview!

So what sort of research should you be doing to avoid the trapdoor that our poor friend fell into? There is the internet of course, and the company's web site. There might also be a booklet produced by the company. However, before all

TUESDAY

that there is the job advert itself. We will now take a look at ways to glean as much information as possible by just reading the advert.

Reading job adverts

It's important to realise that there is often a great deal more to a job than meets the eye. To be effective with CVs you must get to the real truth. The following rules should help you to start reading job adverts so you can decide whether or not to go for the job, and if you do, to tailor your CV to fit.

In a job advertisement, there are two levels to be aware of:

- The **surface level**. In other words there is a whole range of basic things you need to make sure you match up with, like the qualifications that are asked for and so on.

- **Below the surface**. The important thing with adverts is to do a kind of Sherlock Holmes exercise and do some detective work. When you read a job ad you need to ask questions like:

  – What does it really mean?
  – What kind of person are they really looking for?
  – What kind of work environment is it really likely to be?
  – Is this the job for me?

So, look at what the advert does say, and what it doesn't, and then make a judgement. A large part of tailoring a CV is to make sure your language and style matches up with the

TUESDAY — Week Three

employer's language and style. You can pick up lots and lots of clues from the job advert about the kind of culture in the organisation.

The following is a beginners' guide to reading job ads. We will then look at a couple of actual job ads and see what you could find out from them to help tailor your CV.

A guide to job ads

- What are the buzz words? Use a highlighter pen and pick out any particular buzz words that seem to relate to this company. Lots of companies use a kind of shorthand that means they are looking for a certain kind of person. If they mention self-starter or self-motivator for instance, the chances are they want people who don't need a lot of managing.
- Ask yourself whether this is the kind of place you

Week Three
TUESDAY

are looking to work at. What is the job ad hiding? Is there anything behind the wording that might point to something rather difficult or unpleasant? Have they left things out that you would expect to find? For instance, does the advert fail to mention salary, or that it is an equal opportunities employer, when all similar jobs mention this prominently?

- More to the point, if you know your job market well, is this job in character with it? If it isn't, beware! It may mean the company hasn't thought through the job properly and is confused about what kind of person they want.

- Ask yourself what can you learn from the style of the advert to help your CV? And, of course, will the culture of the job really suit me?

So, although it sounds obvious to say, 'read the advert', it really is important to study it carefully, both at the superficial level and below the surface.

Some job adverts

Look at the following job advertisements. The technique you'll use is one you can apply to all advertised vacancies, so it's worth trying it out a couple of times.

Week Three

TUESDAY

> **The Fabulous Group**
>
> Come and join one of Birmingham's fastest growing companies. We are dynamic and innovative, and based in brand-new, high-tech offices in the heart of Birmingham. We are currently wanting to recruit a part-time receptionist (hours 9.30 – 12.00).
>
> We want a well-presented, enthusiastic and experienced person to help in the busy atmosphere of our front-of-house reception. You need top-class communication skills and to be super confident in liaising with clients. You will need to show a flexible approach and be able to work without supervision.
>
> Please write in confidence, enclosing your current CV with a daytime telephone number to:
>
> **Mr Scottish Claymore, The Fabulous Group, Pinkerston House, 1 Victoria Square, Birmingham.**
>
> The Fabulous Group employs over 1,000 staff.

Search for clues

What does this job ad really tell us about the company? For a start, what kind of qualifications are they looking for? What kind of skills do they want?

When you have done this kind of exercise you can start to decide whether you actually have the skills and mapping them out in your CV. Apart from the obvious things like excellent communication skills which the advert asks for, what else is there behind the ad?

Week Three

T U E S D A Y

> *Something to do*
>
> Write down what you think the company will be like, and what you think the job will be like.
>
> What do you think they will be looking for from a CV?

There are lot of interesting things about this advert, including the words *dynamic* and *innovative* early on. It's probably a lively and rapidly changing company, unlikely to be particularly bureaucratic. You need to ask yourself if you would like to work in this kind of environment, where companies can grow rapidly and decline just as fast, or whether you would be happier in a settled place. The choice depends on you.

The advert also asks for a well-presented person, so you need to be smart, clean and tidy. It may also mean that the company is obsessed with image, and if you aren't this kind of person the job could be wrong for you.

TUESDAY
Week Three

The job is part-time, and you need to ask if you would be happy with this, especially as it seems they are looking for a high level of responsibility. Some people want part-time jobs because they aren't highly responsible, and you need to make a decision here.

The company is a large local employer – this is useful because you might start to do some research to find out more about the company.

The whole advert stresses the importance of confidence and enthusiasm. It's a front-line post dealing with lots of enquiries and people. It may well involve dealing with irate clients and problems. Again, you need to ask yourself whether this is the kind of place you want to work.

Finally, you need to work without supervision, so you might have to solve most problems yourself. You need to ask yourself whether you could cope with this kind of job, or whether you would thrive in this kind of atmosphere.

So, if you decided to go for it, your CV would need to stress your:

- self-reliance
- ability to manage yourself
- dynamic and independent nature
- ability to get things done and to deal with people

Week Three

TUESDAY

A different kind of job

> **Senior Youth Worker**
>
> **Coronation Youth Centre, The Borough of Swaffham**
>
> **£20,000 - £23,000**
>
> We need a person who will be at the forefront of developing a new style of youth work at our centre. We are located within the northern wards which are part of a council-wide development. You will need to be adept at following council policy and developing the Council Equal Opportunities Policy too. You must have a recognised JNC qualification plus two years' full-time experience, or four years' experience as a full-time youth worker.
>
> You must have the ability to plan and deliver a programme of youth work and work with council officers to make sure the council policies are delivered effectively.
>
> We offer a casual car allowance and car loan facilities.
>
> We are an Equal Opportunities employer and we welcome applicants from all sectors of the community. Disabled people meeting the job requirements are guaranteed an interview. Employees are not permitted to smoke at work. We have a work-based nursery.

TUESDAY

> *A question*
>
> What does this tell you about the job and the organisation?

This advert tells you masses about the job. For a start, you need a range of experiences and qualifications to get past the first hurdle, and qualifications and experience come pretty near the top, so the employer obviously thinks they are important. You would need to stress these areas early in your CV, to stand a good chance of getting an interview. However, there are lots more clues to pick up in this advert.

There are two references to council policy. The chances are it's a relatively bureaucratic organisation and it's likely you will be quite closely supervised by your political masters. There is more than one reference to equal opportunities, and you need to decide how much this reflects the ideology of this particular council. You need to be in sympathy with this approach, or at least accept it, to apply for this job. If you are very anti-equal opportunities or like getting on with the job on your own, this is not the job for you.

Finding out more

If you can, try to find out more about the company, to help you tailor your CV to fit. There are lots of avenues for doing this, and it's worth putting some time in.

The following check-list gives some ways of finding out more about the company you might be sending your CV to.

TUESDAY

- Companies will send you annual reports, prospectuses and customer information leaflets – but watch the delivery time if you're up against a deadline. Documents like these can give valuable insights into what the company thinks and the way it works. You may even find from the documents that you have done work in a similar kind of area, and this can only help your cause and strengthen your CV. Staff magazines are also good because they give you a better idea of the company culture and the way it operates. In fact, some staff magazines tell you more than almost anything else, certainly about the atmosphere and what the place is like to work in.

- The public library keeps directories on business and the public sector. These are often split into areas of interest, for instance media, retail, finance and so on. In these directories you will find details of what the business is, where it operates, and its size. Ask the librarian and check the reference section. You can also visit specialist libraries like the City Business Library in London, which has lots more in-depth detail about companies.

- The media is a good source. Check all local press coverage and you may well find stories about local employers that can help you again to tailor your CV. On the other hand you may well find references to problems which may make you think twice. You may also find stories about recruitment drives and community involvement which could help you shape your CV.

- Every trade or profession produces specialist magazines aimed at people working in that trade or profession already. Again, the library can help here. These can make quite interesting reading and they can certainly give you

T U E S D A Y

Week Three

a way of finding out more about a particular company, or at the very least about the sector.

- Don't forget the informal network: friends, relatives and contacts through your leisure activities and hobbies can give you a great insight into local employers. Someone who already works there can give you a lot of low-down on the kind of place it is to work. These people can also help you to tailor your CV to the way they think will help get you that all-important interview.

Red light or green?

So, what's it to be? Will you go on and do a CV for this company? Or will you decide the job and the company are not for you after all?

Summary

One thing that should have come through clearly today is that what you write needs to match what the person

TUESDAY

advertising is looking for. We haven't said, 'if they say they want someone with a driving licence, tell them you've got one', because you know that matters. What we have said is that you need to stand back, think and research before starting to put down the details. Once you have the big picture it is relatively simple to see the shape and fill in the details.

You have looked at the importance of reading job adverts in great detail and looking above and below the surface, to find out as much as you can about the job.

You have also looked at ways of doing research into organisations to find out more about them. Armed with these two crucial elements you can go about creating a CV that is tailor-made. It also shows that you have thought about the company. It's this kind of thing that can really help you get an interview.

TUESDAY
Week Three

Anyway, even if you don't get this particular job, if another job comes up in the sector, none of your research will have been wasted. In the CV game you get out what you put in. Tomorrow you are going to get down to the business of starting to write your CV.

Week Three
WEDNESDAY

Knowing me...

Today gets the ball really rolling for your CV. After all the CV is about you. It's your way of saying something about yourself that will get you that all-important interview. It is also a job that requires selection and judgement. You can't write everything about yourself – save that for your best-selling autobiography. On the other hand you can't write a CV in a two-line telegram.

Yesterday we gave you several clues for linking your work experience to the requirements of the company – matching your experience to what they see as important. Today you'll look at yourself more broadly, and choose a format for the CV that fits the company and you.

A useful technique for getting a clear picture about yourself is called retrieval mapping.

Retrieval mapping

The idea behind retrieval mapping is actually quite simple. Retrieval mapping is a technique for pulling out or retrieving key experiences you have had and skills you have built up, that you can then use to help develop your CV. Follow the simple, step-by-step guide below to your own retrieval mapping process.

Step 1: division
Divide your life up into significant blocks that you can concentrate on. This will allow you to focus on different parts of your life rather than see the whole thing as a jumble. It is an organising tool.

WEDNESDAY

The kind of divisions you might come up with are things like: school days, late teens, twenty to thirty, thirty to forty, forty to fifty, fifty plus; or school, university, early jobs, management jobs, senior management jobs; or school, and outside school. It's up to you to divide the cake in whatever way you think would be most helpful.

The key is to give yourself manageable chunks that you can actually focus on, and then think about what you did, what you learned, and what skills you developed during that period.

Step 2: blocks
Write on a large piece of paper one block that you have identified above. You may want to have different pieces of paper for each of the different blocks you have identified.

Step 3: arrows and bubbles and things
Now place the block in the middle of the page and draw lines or bubbles or arrows from it, linking everything you did that you thought was interesting or you learned something from.

Week Three
WEDNESDAY

Step 4: patterns and shapes
When you have done this for each of the blocks put them all on the table in front of you. You can now start looking for patterns and common areas between the blocks. As you look through you might want to use a highlighter pen and highlight every time when similar responsibilities came your way.

You may start seeing a pattern in things like:

- you've often worked with teams
- you've often led teams
- you have a consistent pattern of doing administrative jobs and enjoying them

The choice is yours, but what this activity will show you is where there has been a repeatable pattern of events throughout your working and other life.

So you should be able to highlight:

- your skills
- your experiences
- your achievements

You can use these in your CV. You may also start identifying highlights that you definitely want to talk about. Flag these up using a different coloured pen.

Drawing the picture
This is a simple example of what we mean, done by a woman who has a wide range of experience in each of the blocks she picked out. The one shown here is for the *school* block.

Week Three

WEDNESDAY

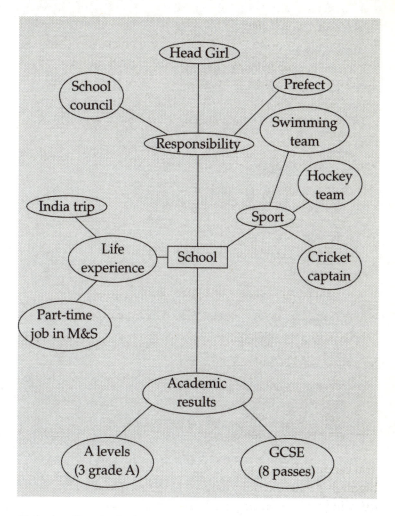

Drawing the conclusions
The following shows the results of this individual's retrieval mapping, putting the blocks together. She has condensed the information into what she feels are the key points to make it manageable.

Week Three
WEDNESDAY

> **School**
> Head Girl
> Cricket captain (not usual in girls' school, then)
> 3 A levels, grade A
> Travel to India
>
> **University**
> Degree
> Amateur dramatics
> Edited university newspaper
> Travel to Indonesia
>
> **Early 20s**
> Researched report on lawyers
> Cricket captain
> Worked as researcher and team leader
>
> **Conclusions**
> There is a pattern of:
>
> - leadership
> - an enjoyment of physical activity
> - thinking work
> - a broadness – reflected by the travelling

So, now you know what the company wants and what you have to offer, it's a question of sorting out the best format for the specific circumstances.

Choosing a format

One of the beauties of CVs is that you can construct them in a way that best suits your purposes. This means you are not stuck with a standard format that might not actually suit you.

WEDNESDAY

Week Three

The key today is to think about some of the different kinds of format, and then select one that will do the job you are looking for.

The basic formats

It is important not to feel that choosing your format is a complicated or technical affair. In fact the choices are quite simple and the advantages and disadvantages of each are straightforward too.

> There are two basic formats of any CV. These are:
> - chronological
> - functional

There are some other options as well, like going for a completely free-form approach, or tailoring your CV specifically for one job. We won't look at these in detail

WEDNESDAY

because these are on the extremes of CV writing. Instead we will concentrate on the two major areas, and look at the benefits and problems associated with each. By the end of the day you will be able to choose which suits you best, and helps you to get that job.

The chronological CV
As the title would suggest, the chronological CV starts with your most recent job, and then works backwards. This format gives your most recent job the most space and emphasis. Commonly in this kind of CV you will see that the title of the organisation is prominently displayed. A chronological CV may look something like this:

1990 – present

First Offer Housing Association

Development manager. Managing development projects and putting together funding bids. Preparing spreadsheets for management committee. Managing a team of three development officers. Handling a budget of £500,000.

1985 – 1990

Dyfed Community Housing Trust

Development officer. Project managed building projects on site. Carried out regular financial audits of the department. Set up tenants liaison group.

WEDNESDAY

The case for The advantages of this chronological format for a CV is that it emphasises the continuity and the way your career has grown gradually and progressively over time. It also allows you to bring out the names of employers which may in turn help you get an interview.

If I see a CV from a person who has worked for one particular company, I automatically give them consideration because I know the excellent training they offer. Everyone who's good has basically worked for that company at some time.

Personnel Manager

Another real advantage of this format is that it is very easy to follow – after all it follows a simple order.

So this kind of CV is best when you have had a pretty clear career direction, and you can paint a straight-line picture. It's also good if you have worked for some well-known employers.

The advantages also include:

- Showing you have worked in the same field for a number of years.
- Helping to establish continuity which may be important in more traditional employment areas.

And against The disadvantages of this kind of approach are obvious. If you have had a career history that is a little patchy, then it can be difficult to do this chronological type of CV. This is because the gaps tend to show up clearly.

This kind of CV is also difficult if you have had a career change and decided to retrain in a completely different direction at some point.

In today's market people often change jobs quickly, and this has meant that the chronological CV has become less and less useful. If you have to list six or seven recent employers it can make you look flighty.

Another problem with this kind of approach is that it can highlight if you have been in a job for a very long time – which might make you look like a stick-in-the-mud – and of course it also highlights when you have had a big career break.

Finally, this kind of CV is no good if you are fresh into the job market. It emphasises your lack of work experience – and may make you seem lightweight.

The functional CV
This is the alternative to the chronological CV and gives you the option of presenting a view of your main skills areas. The following is an example of a functional CV for a restaurant supervisor.

The benefits Looking at this CV you can see the real benefits of this approach. For a start it allows you to be clear about the skills you are able to offer and the areas in which you have worked. The actual titles of your jobs and your work history are in a more secondary position. This approach adds focus.

WEDNESDAY

Week Three

> Peter Flemming
> 56 Flightborn Road
> Persham
> Middlesex UB5 7QT
>
> **Staff Management**
>
> Supervising 12 staff during busy shifts. Carrying out appraisals. Organising rota system. Running the team rewards system.
>
> **Budgetary Control**
>
> Controlling and managing a budget for the restaurant of £180,000. Checking time sheets and authorising expenditures. Presenting financial report to management each month.
>
> **Customer Care**
>
> Dealing with any customer complaints. Setting up and running customer care training programme for team members.

The advantages of this are that it can give you great flexibility and allow you to avoid repeating yourself as often happens in a chronological CV with many similar jobs.

This kind of CV also overcomes the fact that you have not had a lot of experience at work. The emphasis on your functional skills and experience allows you to blur some boundaries and smooth over some of the gaps – after all in this kind of CV you are not emphasising progression.

Week Three
WEDNESDAY

You may also want to use this approach if you are looking to make a career change because it allows you to emphasise transferable skills that will help you make the transition. By the same token you can use the functional approach if you are returning to the job market after a gap. You just present what you learned during the gap.

The problems This kind of CV isn't useful if you want to emphasise continuity and growth, and it may not be right for more traditional jobs. Many jobs want to see a progression up the career ladder.

If you take this approach it might also mean you lose the impact of any prestigious companies you may have worked for.

Working on the words

The final thing you will do today is think through some of the words you will use when you come to look at your work history tomorrow.

Week Three

WEDNESDAY

All too often CVs are written in a rather limp, non-committal way, using phrases like 'my duties include', 'I have been involved in'.

What's more, the act of putting together a CV is sometimes seen as a glorified administration job – with you simply pulling together lots of existing material and slapping it down on a piece of paper. Not true.

Instead you should see putting your CV together as a writing job. It is a job where you need to work hard on the words and choose them carefully – after all, you only have limited space to get the message across. So every word counts!

Using active words

The main way to get away from a rather flat delivery is to use active words to describe your skills, experience and achievements.

Active words allow you to concentrate on the results you have achieved and present them in a focused and up-beat way.

The following is a prompt list that should help you. Each word in the list is the kind of positive action word you can use when drawing up your CV. They help impress a potential employer and really bring home to the full what you do.

Achieve	Create	Manage
Analyse	Develop	Organise
Capable	Economical	Process
Consistent	Expand	Sell
Control	Guide	Specialise
Coach	Improve	Train
Co-ordinate	Lead	Wide background in

WEDNESDAY

Something to do

- Add some positive words of your own.
- Now write some sentences describing your skills, experience and achievements using these words.

Summary

Today you have reflected on your strengths in some depth and some different options for CVs. You have looked at retrieval mapping and at two approaches, chronological and functional, to preparing your CV. In addition you looked at the use of positive words when describing your work history.

Put together, these should help you tomorrow when you come to putting together the first version of your CV.

Week Three
THURSDAY

Getting down to the writing

Today you are going to get down to the nitty gritty of writing your CV. You might think it odd that you have waited so long before you actually start the writing process, but being prepared is important.

With the preparation you have done, the writing should come easy and you should be able to get it right first time. Of course you will want to come back and edit your CV, checking it for spelling, grammar and punctuation, but the point is that all the preparation should help you see clearly, and it is this that makes a good CV. It's in the thinking and planning that a tip top CV is made.

So you have chosen your model, you've had a think about the style and some of the words you are going to use. You have also done a retrieval mapping exercise where you have dredged up the most important things in your life and career and then started to look for patterns. So now it's time to get to it. You can't put it off any longer.

Over the next two days you will write your CV.

Thinking through the sections

There are many different ways of doing this, but it's important to be clear about some of the sections which you might use in a CV. This means stopping and thinking before writing it down.

Week Three

THURSDAY

Put yourself in their place

The most powerful way of structuring the sections and the content of your CV is to pretend you are reading it for the first time. Put yourself in the position of the person you're sending it to and make a short list of the most important factors you'd be looking for. If you can step into their shoes you will be able to really choose information that is relevant to them. You don't want to bore them or turn them off.

It's hard work

The manager of a large furniture department in a chain store says that she sometimes gets over 100 CVs for fairly junior management posts. The first thing she does is scan the CV and within four or five seconds makes a decision whether it goes on the 'A' pile (the desk) or the 'B' pile (the bin). It's as tough as that and her advice is to make sure that what you write is going to seem immediately relevant to her.

In other words, think it through and put yourself in their shoes – write what they want to read, not what you want to write.

THURSDAY

Week Three

There are probably as many differing views on which sections and what information should come where, as there are managers reading the CV. We will look at these a little later. The important thing is to be aware of what the basic sections are likely to be in any CV. Then you can decide on the order and the emphasis to suit your situation.

A model you can use

1 Personal details

This section will include your name, address and other details personal to you.

2 Education

There is some debate about whether this should come early in a CV, or towards the end, although the more experience you have, the further towards the end of the CV it should come. Here you put the names of your schools and colleges and the qualifications and training you have received.

3 Employment

This is the crux of any CV. It is where you carefully match your working life against the demands of the job you are applying for. In fact, you have already done substantial preparation for this section through:

- the initial retrieval mapping exercise
- thinking through the right format for you
- choosing power words to describe what you have done

THURSDAY

Week Three

Packing it in or packing it together

If you had 17 jobs in selling during the early years of your career, don't list them all. It is too long and too boring, and it could give the false impression you don't stick at anything.

Think about grouping together early experiences that aren't individually exciting and making something more chunky out of them, like:

Between 1982 and 1990 I built up considerable experience in sales, marketing and management with national and local firms in the electronics and food processing sector.

4 Interests

All too often this goes horribly wrong for people, or at the very least you can miss an opportunity to impress. The interests section is your chance to show that you are a rounded human being and to show how interesting you are.

Cricket captain

The retrieval mapping you looked at earlier showed a woman who had been cricket captain. The interest in sport was demonstrated by the other activities as well, but having been cricket captain in a girls' school is something that will grab the attention of employers and make the CV stand out from many others.

Week Three

THURSDAY

5 Extra information

This is your chance to put in anything that doesn't fit well elsewhere and paint a picture of some of the skills you have. You can also use this section to say why you are interested in the type of work you are applying for.

> *Getting it wrong*
>
> The job of a Careers Officer can involve helping students compile CVs and identify their strengths and weaknesses. One CV from an applicant for a Careers Officer post said, under the heading 'Additional Information':
>
> *My father is a Principal Careers Officer.*
>
> That's all it said. As an example of terrible role modelling for the job it was classic. The individual was not interviewed.

Week Three

THURSDAY

6 References

This section speaks for itself. It is where you give the names and addresses and phone numbers of the people you have asked to give you a reference.

> *Would you mind...*
>
> Notice the words above – 'people you have asked to give you a reference'. NEVER put someone's name down and then try and contact them to tell them you've done it. For a start, it's simple bad manners and anyway, it could go radically wrong. If they feel annoyed at being taken for granted, or are now going to have to give a reference but they don't actually rate you as much as you thought, the results for you could be negative.

What to do today?

Because we are taking a step-by-step approach, today you are going to look at the first couple of parts of this broad model.

> *A thought*
>
> The important thing with a CV is to try and stress the unusual and present information about yourself that will impress the reader. People often include details of any travelling they have done on a CV for this reason. Your travels can often be an interesting way of presenting yourself as an individual.

THURSDAY
Week Three

> However, it is important not to go mad and stress too many zany things about yourself. If you are an expert in colonic irrigation, our recommendation is that you keep it to yourself.

Personal details

This section is straightforward, but it's important to start with some don'ts before we get on to the dos.

Where people often get this section wrong is to put too much detail in. So, don't give details of:

- your weight
- your age
- your place of birth
- your next of kin

Week Three
THURSDAY

- your National Insurance Number
- your health
- your marital status and whether you have any children (especially if you are a woman because this may be used to discriminate against you)

Sadly, in the ageist society we live in it is not advisable to put in your date of birth if you are over 40.

The layout in this section

All too often this personal details section also becomes stilted.

One of the problems here is that people run text down the left-hand side of the page in the following way:

Name: Peter Morris
Address: 54 Orchard Close
             London
             W6 3BR
Telephone: 020 8634 7252

This starts your CV on a highly formal and uncomfortable way. Much more effective is simply writing your name and details like this:

Peter Morris
54 Orchard Close
London
W6 3BR
020 8634 7252

If you want to add any more details about yourself, why not add them to the additional information section. Using this

THURSDAY

section also allows you to get quickly to a real hook – either your education or your work experience.

By presenting your name in this human and straightforward fashion you have made a statement about yourself. It also allows you to be slightly less formal with your CV whilst still being professional and getting all the important information in.

There are a few options in this section. If you think it would help you get the job, you could also mention whether you have a clean driving licence, for instance.

Remember though, you don't want to take up too much space with this section, and you want to make a crisp start with your CV and get onto the stuff that will get you that all-important interview.

Education
The debate is where to put your education. Maybe the simplest answer is to decide how important the person reading the CV will think it is. If you have been Managing Director of a multi-national company, maybe your seven GCE 'O' level passes aren't that crucial?

Traditional CV advisers have always stressed that education should come up front in a CV. However, the more experienced you are the more likely you are to relegate your education to almost the last item on your CV.

Of course, if you are just leaving school or college then your education is very important and it should be at the beginning of your CV. The judgement on this is really yours.

Week Three

T H U R S D A Y

The main problems people have with putting together their education sections are:

- how much detail to put in about the education
- how to set this section out

The detail
In this section don't be shy to put all your qualifications at school. You don't need to give the grades for GCSEs if you went on to do 'A' levels. Don't give details of exams you failed.

The key here is to put down all the qualifications you have, because it's likely to impress. You may then want to add a separate section where you list your training.

All too often people tend to downgrade the value of training, but to many employers the training you have received is every bit or even more important than your formal education. After all, the employers who trained you thought it was important enough to spend money on, so why shouldn't other employers?

So put down here every training course you have attended and any certificates you have. Today's modern organisation values training, so use this opportunity to tell them about what courses you have done.

Do try to leave out irrelevant certificates and awards like the fact you earned a fire-lighting badge in the scouts or passed your cycling proficiency test.

THURSDAY
Week Three

The layout
This section often looks messy because people are left with a large block of text with both their place of education and their qualifications. A way of counteracting this is to break the section up into easily definable chunks.

So, you might have a section headed *Places of education*, which lists the schools or colleges you went to, and where they are. Don't mention your primary school here.

You can then have a separate section headed *Qualifications*. Again, contrary to normal advice, we think a good idea is to start with the most recent qualifications you have. So if you have a degree, start with it and then work backwards.

Summary

Today has seen you start the CV proper. You have looked at the sequence and content of the early sections from the perspective of the person reading it.

Tomorrow you'll finish it off.

Week Three

F R I D A Y

Almost there

It's Friday, and you're almost there with your CV. You have put a lot of work into getting the first draft of some of the key parts of your CV, and now it's time to round it off. But remember, when you have rounded it off, you still need to go back and check it carefully. Make sure it does the job you want it to and that the spelling, punctuation and grammar are correct. Attention to detail is all-important.

You've done personal details and education, so on to the next part.

Work experience

This is vital and it is here that your CV will either succeed or fail. There are a number of key things to bear in mind when you write this section.

Keep it relevant
Many jobs these days will send out a person and job specification and you can use this to match your work experience section with what the job requires and the person to do it.

> So go through the job and person specification and pull out all the:
>
> - special skills – the things you really need to be able to show you can do

FRIDAY

and

- experience – the areas you need to have worked in over the years

that are needed.

Write these down on a sheet of paper or highlight them in the specs.

Then for each, write down your skills and experience to match. If you find you do not have a perfect match with your work experience you may be able to match using things you have done or learned outside work.

Working through the specs in this way will help you put only the relevant details into your CV. Don't put in things that seem interesting just for the sake of it.

Show what you have done…
… rather than simply tell. For instance rather than telling the reader:

I am computer literate,

show that you are computer literate:

I am an advanced user of Excel and have designed integrated spreadsheets. I have a good knowledge of Word and a basic knowledge of the database program Access.

Remember to use those power words we looked at earlier. But always keep it concise and to the point and keep on matching your CV with the person and job spec. If a company goes to the trouble of putting together a person spec, then they will use it. So don't ignore it.

Don't be put off
Be realistic but don't be too easily put off. If the specification asks for five years senior management experience for instance and you only have three, don't be too put off. Often companies are prepared to bend the rules.

However if it asks for five years experience and you only have five months worth, then it probably isn't worth making the application. You will need the skills of a professional magician to conjure up this job and present a convincing CV.

What's in a name?
It is important to think through what job titles you want to use on your CV. Very often, organisations give you job titles that in no way reflect what you actually do.

The following list shows some of the job titles you might want to consider:

FRIDAY

- Accounts Manager
- Customer Services Manager
- Clerical Manager
- Carpenter
- Managing Editor
- Development Officer
- Executive
- Press Officer
- Operations Manager
- Printer

and the list goes on.

If you have opted for a functional CV then you might also want to spend some time thinking about the functional headings you can use to group your ideas under.

The following are just some possibilities:

- Advertising
- Banking
- Budgeting
- Communications
- Entertainment
- Managing
- Problem-solving
- Team building
- Supervising

and so on.

FRIDAY

Expanding on your personal skills

You need to pick up on your personal skills. All too often people are shy or coy about their personal skills.

The following is a check-list of some of the personal skills you may be able to identify in yourself and then use.

> *Expanding your list of personal skills*
>
> The following are just a few of the personal skills you may identify. Have a look and see whether there are any on the list you could claim for yourself.
>
> advising people
> arranging events
> calculating numerical data
> checking for accuracy
> coaching people
> compiling figures
> co-ordinating events
> counselling people
> dealing with difficult people
> delegating responsibility
> drawing up plans
> editing documents
> selling products
> setting up demonstrations
> speaking in public
>
> handling projects
> inspecting quality
> interviewing people
> managing resources
> motivating people
> operating equipment
> persuading others
> planning agendas
> preparing charts
> raising funds
> reviewing
> running meetings
> supervising staff
> teaching
> writing reports

Now add any of your own to the list.

You should try to get as many of these personal skills as possible into this work history section. And remember, always link them with action words if you can.

Smoothing over the years
All the research shows that very few people list all their experience down to the last month. Often they gloss over a gap or two or the odd dreadful and short experience by adding a couple of months to the previous job and bringing forward the start date for the next one. We're not telling you to lie, obviously, just telling you what the research says.

If you have had career gaps, career changes, or are returning to work, you may choose the option of going for a functional CV to help smooth over the years. However, one other way of doing it is to list your jobs in terms of years not months. This will allow you to cover up any gaps you have. The other option here is to be up front and honest about any career breaks you have had. You may well do something like this:

Career break 1991 – 1993.

I took a career break to look after my mother. During this time I used my time management skills, and further developed my negotiating skills with the local authority and medical agencies.

Other tips for this section are not to put down why you left a job, and not to mention the salary you were receiving.

Are you interesting?

What you need to tackle in the next section is your interests.

All too often these are a lost opportunity for people.

Week Three

F R I D A Y

For instance, if you just put down that you like reading and walking the dog, you won't look like a very interesting person. You are likely to rank somewhere below Steve Davis in the 'interesting' stakes. So, make a list of all the different things you might list as interests. This could include being involved in sport, the arts, or running clubs. The trick is to give a balanced, portfolio approach to your interests. Putting down that you like playing cricket, rugby and football may make you look a bit light on the old grey matter.

One of the tricks with 'interests' is that you must be honest. Don't put down that you have a lifelong fascination with pop music if you wouldn't know your David Bowie from your George Michael.

As you write down your interests, think through what the employer is looking for as well. Try and work out why what you write could matter to them. If it's a job that involves

Week Three

F R I D A Y

lots of management you might decide to highlight an interest that reinforces this, for instance putting on a production at the local amateur dramatics society, rather than just acting in it.

The key is to make yourself look like a lively and well-balanced person. You need to show you have a life outside work, and how you believe your interests will actually help you do the job you are applying for.

The following prompt list might help:

> ### About your spare time activities
>
> The following prompts might help you construct an interesting Interests section. Leisure activities are given alongside ideas showing why they might be relevant. These are just ideas and aren't the only possibilities by any means.
>
> ### Possible leisure activities
>
> - Painting — creative, calm
> - Mountain climbing — achieving, fit
> - Playing a musical instrument — creative, achieving
> - Woodwork — creative, practical
> - Keeping fit — good health at work
> - Golf — competitive, active
> - Bird-watching — dedication, research
> - Watching live music — artistic, relaxed
> - Cycling — fitness, self-managing
> - Motor racing — enthusiasm, technical

FRIDAY

> *Possible social activities*
>
> The chances are a prospective employer will want you to have some kind of social life even if they work you too hard to have one for very long. Involvement in the following examples of social activities can demonstrate a range of personal qualities, including most of those listed above, as well as a willingness to work with others and put something into the system.
>
> - Parent-teacher association
> - Drama group
> - Choir
> - Sports team
> - Youth club leader
> - Voluntary work
> - Photography club

Extra information

This is the section where you can give a broader picture of some of the skills you have and maybe why you want the job as well. You can also tailor it to fit the job you are applying for.

For instance, if you were applying for a job in housing, then this is where you would mention that you do some voluntary work for *Crisis at Christmas*. This will allow you to add credibility to your application and show you care about the field you are applying for.

FRIDAY

This kind of section is particularly important if you have gaps to deal with in your CV and you feel you haven't dealt with them adequately in the rest of your CV. This is where you may be able to explain the gap, and show what you got from the experience.

You can also write here if you have travelled, or indeed anything that has taken you away from the normal steady progress of a career and adds relevant interest to your CV.

In this section you can also put other key skills and experiences you think might help you, like owning a car, having a clean driving licence, being a qualified first aider.

When you write this section you usually write it in full – in an informative and friendly style. For instance:

In my spare time I produce the community news letter. I write and edit it and design it on an Apple Mac computer using Microsoft Word 5.1. I then organise for it to be distributed around my local streets.

So it's here you can pick out something interesting that may just be the difference between getting an interview and not getting an interview. And it is the winning edge you are looking for.

Personal achievements

Even Rab C Nesbitt probably has some personal achievements – so don't be afraid to mention yours.

FRIDAY

Many people add a short section to their CV outlining their main achievements and responsibilities. This is another way of using power words and of focusing in on important aspects of what you have done – but this time away from work.

It can be hard to think through your personal achievements – often because we find it difficult to value the things we do.

You can use the following check-list to help you. Of course, it isn't an exhaustive list – it just gives you a flavour of the kind of things you may have achieved.

> *Personal achievements*
>
> You may have built up any of the following achievements:
>
> - been elected an officer in a club
> - managed or coached a sports team
> - played a role in a drama group
> - been awarded a medal
> - made a rescue attempt

- climbed Snowdon
- completed a marathon
- made a film
- gained a certificate for study
- been a prefect at school
- had an article published
- gained a Duke of Edinburgh award
- learned a language
- gained any award, honour, decoration, prize or distinction

References

Only this section to go and you're there. There are some golden rules for references, which are:

- Choose people who are going to give you a good reference – take no risks.

- Ensure you contact your referees first, to make sure they are happy to act as such for you.

- Make sure they are available when they need to be. There is nothing worse than choosing referees who have headed off on a round-the-world trip just at the time you need their backing.

- Choose referees who know enough about you to give a real insight into your personality and strengths. Don't use people you only know fleetingly.

- Choose referees – especially character ones – who have a good job of their own. This could help add weight to their reference.

Week Three

F R I D A Y

- Include the telephone numbers of all your referees in case the person who is advertising the job wants to ring them.

> *Choosing suitable referees*
>
> The following are just some of the people you may consider as referees. They give your CV some authority and some weight.
>
> - Bank Manager
> - Head Teacher
> - Manager or Ex-Manager
> - Personnel or Ex-Personnel Officer
> - Supervisor or Ex-Supervisor
> - Magistrate
> - Teacher
> - Tutor
> - Doctor
> - Councillor
> - Lecturer
> - Church Warden
> - Minister
> - Chartered Accountant
> - Justice of the Peace
> - Solicitor
> - Local Government Officer

Some of the books on CVs say that you should not actually put your referees in your CV and instead that you should write:

References on request.

There doesn't appear to be a good reason for doing this... unless you know better. Choose references who you are happy to have on your CV and, if it is difficult for these people to be contacted before you are interviewed, then make it clear to the company advertising the job that they can contact them after your interview. It can only help your application.

If you have a poisonous boss who you think will not give you a good reference then don't use them. Instead, choose someone else at work who does know what you are made of to act as your referee.

Summary

Today you finished putting together the first draft of your CV. You looked at how to handle the remaining sections and have ended up with enough material to make a decent job of it. It might need a bit of polishing, but you're nearly ready to send it off.

That's for tomorrow.

Week Three

SATURDAY

Getting your CV across to the employer

Today you look at presenting your CV and completing the task of getting it to the employer.

Presenting your CV

We have already touched on this but it's very important to get the presentation right.

Remember that first impressions count and if your CV looks messy, cramped, confused, complicated or massive then you won't get very far with it.

There are some pretty simple dos and don'ts when it comes to layout.

- **Do** make your CV look professional (try to produce it on a PC and print it out on a laser printer).
- **Do** keep it simple (avoid using lots of typefaces or too much underlining or emboldened text).
- **Do** keep the layout easy to follow and understand (keep a reasonable margin down the left-hand side of the page, use simple blocks of text and make sure the columns are justified – this means that the text lines up in one block).
- **Do** have plenty of white space (plenty of space makes a CV easy to read and an appealing prospect too).

SATURDAY

- **Don't** get overcomplicated and try to prepare a masterpiece of modern design with your CV, unless, of course, you are a designer.

- **Don't** cram everything on to one page if it doesn't fit easily (go onto a second page rather than cram everything onto one page).

- **Do** use clear headings on your CV. If you opt for a functional CV then choose your headings with care. They should be short and clear and punchy.

- **Do** use bullet points (this list is an example of bullet points). Bullet points allow you to pull out the punchy bits and separate your ideas clearly. They look good and professional on the page and they help people to pick out what is important.

This is how you might use headings and bullets to make your CV look good:

Jane Stevens
87 Wildwater Drive
Norwich
Norfolk
NR12 7TY

Sales
- Managed three retail outlets in Norfolk
- Coached departmental managers
- Increased turnover by 50%
- Set up staff training system and appraisal system

S A T U R D A Y

Writing that letter

When you send your CV in, the chances are you are going to write a letter in with it as well. The important thing is to keep the letter simple and professional while still giving a flavour of your unique personality.

In the letter be clear about what you want to achieve from it. Your letter should:

- Include a reference to the job you are applying for.

- Be brief. The person already knows quite a lot from your CV – if you ramble on in the letter, you will detract from your CV and may create a negative image.

- Be polite and courteous.

- Be positive but not too cocky. Avoid sign off phrases like:

    You must see me tomorrow in order to help your company get the competitive edge it needs.

- Be without spelling mistakes and be neatly typed or handwritten.

It's a letter not a book

One person who advertised a job and asked applicants for a CV and letter reports the following:

I advertised a manager's job. One person sent a good CV, but the letter was a horror. It went on for 5½ pages and just rambled. The person just threw everything in hoping something would stick.

SATURDAY
Week Three

> *The job itself required the manager to draw up reports and think clearly. I felt that the letter I received threw doubt on the applicant's ability to do this so I decided not to interview them.*

You might also use your letter to pull out one or two interesting points that relate to you and the job. It's also here that you might be able to show some of the research you did earlier. For instance, you might be able to make reference to a new factory the company has opened or an exciting new opportunity you have read about.

Here is an example of a letter. Notice that it's written in a personal and informative style and does enough to whet the employer's appetite without throwing in lots of unnecessary detail.

Week Three

SATURDAY

> Dear Mr Claymore
>
> *The Post: Clerical Assistant*
>
> I enclose my CV in response to your advertisement in *The Morning Echo* for the job of Clerical Assistant.
>
> As you can see from my CV I have five years experience of clerical work. I have completed a number of training courses, and have a computer at home that I use regularly.
>
> I was interested to read about the way your company is expanding in the local newspaper. I would like to be a part of your forward-thinking and exciting organisation. I enjoy working as part of a team and thrive on meeting tight deadlines.
>
> Feel free to contact any of my references, or indeed to phone me or write to me at home.
>
> Yours sincerely
>
> Jane Greene

Nearly there
You should now have a CV that is virtually ready to be sent. All it needs now are a few last touches... and a stamp.

The finishing touches

You have done all the hard work, and it's now just a case of getting everything ready to go.

SATURDAY

Week Three

Take time to check

The first thing to do is read everything through just one more time. If you have been working hard on your CV over the week it can often be difficult to pick up any errors that have crept in.

Basically, everyone sometimes gets a bit too close to their own work, so today give your draft CV to an understanding friend, or your partner, and ask them to read it through carefully. The chances are they may well spot the odd mistake or give you suggestions before you finally type it up. If they do, say 'thank you very much', make the changes and then print the CV out again. It will also pay you to give your CV one more read just to see if you can improve it.

Remember though, don't start fiddling with it if it is already good. With any writing there is a law of diminishing returns. You get your work to a stage you are happy with, and then any further work does not actually improve it enough to warrant the extra time spent.

Written or typed letters

So you've got your CV and you've worked out your letter. You now have to decide whether to handwrite your letter and give it a more personal touch or whether to type it. This is a decision for you to make, and will be based on your judgement of what the people will be looking for. It shouldn't be one that costs you sleep.

> *A handwritten letter:*
>
> - has the personal touch
> - feels more intimate
>
> But if your handwriting is poor then it will not do you any favours.
>
> *A typed letter:*
>
> - is more professional but less personal

When you have got everything together, put it into an envelope, and write the address neatly on the front. Stick on a first class stamp and post your CV.

You've done it. Now it's time to wait and see whether you have got that vital foot in the door to help you get the job you want.

One final clue

You have seen us stress the importance of seeing the CV process from the other person's perspective, so, if you feel brave enough, ring them up and ask them what they thought of your CV, should you get a polite refusal.

You have absolutely nothing to lose and you could pick up some really helpful information that you can use next time.

Succeeding at your Interview

ALISON STRAW
MO SHAPIRO

WEEK FOUR

CONTENTS

Week Four

Introduction		277
Sunday	The interview process	278
Monday	Do your research	286
Tuesday	Know yourself	303
Wednesday	Preparing yourself for success	317
Thursday	The interview – responding skilfully	328
Friday	Your moves	336
Saturday	Putting it all together	347

Week Four

INTRODUCTION

Have you ever wondered why some people seem to succeed almost effortlessly whenever they go for an interview? Perhaps they are just 'lucky'. We think not! Their performance, and ultimately their success, is the result of thorough personal preparation.

You too can improve your ability and success through a combination of thought, training, practice and experience. This week is your companion in this process. By setting time aside for each day, you will be guided on your route to success.

Week Four

SUNDAY

The interview process

You opened the post this morning to find you have been invited to an interview – great news! You feel good. You are high, elated and you congratulate yourself. You imagine yourself in the role; it's exciting, an ideal job for you. You read the letter again and, as the reality of the interview becomes your focus, you are bombarded with less positive feelings and thoughts, such as:

- I hate interviews
- I can't remember the last time I was interviewed
- I really want this job – I hope I don't let myself down

It is not uncommon to feel a degree of trepidation in anticipation of an interview. The trick is not to let this weigh you down.

After all, you have experienced being interviewed, not just once but many times in your career. Most career transitions such as selection, promotion or other forms of career development will have been punctuated by interviews. You are therefore experienced and familiar with the process. As interviews follow a relatively common format, you will already have some of the skills and knowledge required to make you successful.

This experience is not always reflected in your performance. The following comments from interviewers reflect common problems:

SUNDAY

Week Four

- She looked great on paper.
- I know a lot about his employer, but very little about him.
- She seemed very nervous and aggressive.
- He stumbled over all the questions related to his personality.
- I'm not sure how long he would stay.
- She seemed too good to be true.
- There was no substance in what he said.
- It was difficult to get a word in edgeways.

Think back over past interviews and answer the following question honestly: *Did I present myself in the best possible light?*

Whilst we would hope that your answer is 'yes', it is more likely to be 'no' or 'not quite'. Managers are often experienced interviewers, having undergone training on skills, techniques and questioning. They are not so skilled at being interviewed.

Week Four

SUNDAY

Having had experiences of being interviewed and being the interviewer, you will be aware that interviews often follow a tried and tested pattern. Today, we will help you focus on the known rather than the unpredictable factors, exploring questions such as why, in what way and by whom:

> *The interview process*
> - interview objectives
> - types of questions
> - interviewers

Interview objectives

If you have been invited to an interview – well done! Your invitation is based on the limited knowledge the interviewer has of you from an application, recommendation or your past achievements. They already believe that you could be the person they are looking for. The interview is therefore an opportunity for interviewers to extend their knowledge and complete their picture of you.

You will have your own agenda. The interview is an opportunity for you to discover further information about the job and the organisation. Based on that information you can reach decisions about match and suitability.

The interview is a two-way process: treat it as such.

SUNDAY

Interviewee's objectives are to:

- gain the initiative – an offer or commitment
- present yourself in the best possible light
- make known your talents and expertise
- fill gaps in knowledge about the job and organisation
- meet future colleagues/managers
- be clear about whether or not to accept the post

Interviewer's objectives are to:

- find the most suitable person
- encourage you to express yourself fully
- look for specific skills and achievements
- sell the job and organisation
- assess your initial impact and social fit
- appoint the right person

You will both have independent objectives with a degree of overlap. Spend time before the interview clarifying your objectives. You may even want to rank them; having gone through this process, you can be much clearer about whether the interview matches your objectives and, if not, for what reason.

Interview structure

The whole of the recruitment process requires careful planning. From drawing up a job description and person specification, designing the advertisement, compiling the information pack, to short-listing. The interview is no exception.

Be aware that interviewers will have clarified their objectives in general and decided on a format and a set of questions for each interviewee. No two interviews are the same. Your personality, application, CV, and experience will be different from others, as will the areas that require further exploration because they are of particular interest or concern. Whilst interviews are not the same, there are similarities, and there is a process which is common and accepted.

The process can be likened to a sandwich. It is built on some 'warm up' questions to help you both settle down and feel as comfortable as you can. The middle and main section of the interview will constitute the filling in the sandwich, where you will be asked a variety of questions, checking and clarifying match and suitability.

In the final stage there will be time for your questions, closing with a summary of the interview and an indication of what will happen next: a second interview, a meeting with other staff members, or a letter telling you the result of the interview.

Some organisations provide their interviewers with a standard form to assess certain aspects of the interviewee and their performance. They will have a points allocation for each category and make direct comparisons between candidates. Depending on the post available, they may cover the following:

Assessment categories
- skills
- knowledge
- behaviour
- motivation
- fit with team
- fit with culture
- career aspirations

Good interviewers will also be watching your reactions and body language: posture, gestures and facial expressions. You should do the same; some interviewers deliberately present an unresponsive, wooden mask. This can be because they are inexperienced or are not comfortable with the role. With practice you should be able to read and assess intentions and reactions reasonably well. You will undoubtedly also meet some ineffective interviewers.

Interviewers

Interviewers are trained, not born! Be prepared for an interviewer who:

- has not read your CV
- gets aggressive to see how you react under stress
- is constantly disturbed
- makes remarks about your previous employer or boss
- asks questions but doesn't listen to your answers

SUNDAY

Even the best training can fall on deaf ears and even the best interviewers can have a bad day. If you happen to be on the receiving end of poor interviewing, you can sometimes turn it to your advantage. You may meet interviewers who fall into the following categories.

The disorganised interviewer
Allow them time to settle down and find the papers or notes that they need. Establish your preparedness early on and, if necessary, subtly suggest an interview structure.

The unprepared interviewer
Sometimes very experienced interviewers think they can sail in on the day and don't need to prepare. You have to keep calm and be patient. It won't do your cause any good if you try to catch them out or show them up. If interviewers have a position of authority over the post, you may want to consider how you would feel working with them.

The nervous interviewer
You sense that the interviewer would rather be anywhere else than in an interview room and may even be more nervous than you are. This sometimes happens when specialist functional managers are taken out of their familiar work setting and are expected to be at ease in a more social setting. They will be grateful if you offer relevant information and loosely control the interview. Be careful not to patronise.

The aggressive interviewer
Don't allow aggressive interviewers to provoke you. Rather than apologising for the weaknesses, failings or gaps in your CV that they point out to you, give positive explanations and put over what you have prepared.

Week Four

SUNDAY

Being familiar with the process of the interview will enable you to understand the direction it is taking. If you are unclear about a question, try to assess what the reasons are for asking it and answer it accordingly.

Summary

We have begun the week with a general overview on the process of interviews, preparing you generally for what you should expect.

The interview process
- Objectives of an interview
  - interviewers' objectives
  - your objectives
- Types and styles of interviewer
  - disorganised
  - unprepared
  - nervous
  - aggressive

Remember that interviews are not a new experience for you. Learn from the past to prepare you for the future.

Week Four

MONDAY

Do your research

It is a natural human reaction to feel nervous and apprehensive going into a situation where you feel uncertain. As we suggested yesterday, interviews have common features. There are however aspects which are unique and unpredictable. No two experiences of being interviewed are likely to be the same. It is important therefore to gather as much information as you can at the earliest possible opportunity. This is easy to do and has two benefits:

- You will demonstrate to the interviewer your interest in the job.
- You will feel more confident knowing that you are well prepared.

We suggest that you research three areas:

- the interview
- the job
- the organisation

Week Four

MONDAY

By researching, you lessen the risk of feeling that you could have made a better impression or that you haven't done yourself justice. In addition, you place yourself ahead of the competition.

The interview

If you have been invited for interview, you need to know some basic facts, and if this information isn't supplied, you need to start your investigations.

> *Investigating the interview*
>
> - how to get there
> - who will interview you
> - the format of the interview

How to get there
Finding out how you get to the interview is essential before you start your journey. Once you know the location, you can decide how you will travel. Always aim to arrive early – calculate the journey time and add an hour. Whatever method of transport you choose, delays may happen which are often out of your control. Also check what security arrangements there are, as they may add time to your journey.

On larger sites, leave yourself plenty of time to get from the reception to the interview building. Some people prefer to go on a practice journey as it gives them the opportunity to view the site at close quarters without the interview looming.

On the day If you are delayed, be sure to contact the interviewers and let them know why you will be late and when you expect to arrive. Make sure you have the relevant

Week Four
MONDAY

phone number handy. They will appreciate your call as they may need to make other plans or reschedule.

On arrival Having arrived early you will have the opportunity to make last minute preparations:

- Think through your replies and questions
- Get a feel for the organisation
- Complete any further application forms
- Read through literature
- Take advantage of any other available information
- Read your CV again
- **Relax**

Who will interview you
The key information you need here is: name(s), position in the organisation and job title.

There may be a number of interviews, particularly for a senior post. The first, in-depth interview, is often held on a one-to-one basis with a recruitment consultant, line manager or member of the human resources department. It could take the form of a thorough exploration of your CV or a structured interview.

Candidates short-listed from the first interview can expect second and third interviews, which are likely to be conducted by one or more senior staff, who may have responsibility for the post or an interest in it. The objectives for these interviews are to explore any aspects still outstanding from the first interview and to assess how well your personality will blend with the team. You may meet the same interviewer more than once – so learn to pace yourself and aim to remember names.

Knowing who is going to interview you will help you prepare responses. Interviewers' interests may fit into the following categories:

Organisational role	**What they are looking for**
Functional head	qualifications/experience ability to perform tasks understanding the job/technical jargon transferable skills match with management style expectations and culture
Managing director	ability to meet targets contribution to growth and profitability adaptability aspirations

MONDAY

Peers	team working
	personality
	style
	shared experiences
	experience
Junior staff	management style
	openness
	approachability
Human resources	your background
	career patterns
	training/development needs
	salary
	benefits
	start date

Some organisations employ recruitment consultants to short-list candidates and ensure that only the most qualified go forward. They will be seeking the person who most closely matches the employer's specification, not solely in terms of experience, but also in personality and aspirations.

The format of the interview
Interviews can take many forms. The two most common are one-to-one and panel interviews. Some organisations combine different types by short-listing candidates with a telephone interview, inviting them to a panel and then asking them to return for further one-to-one interviews. Once you have found out the format, you can gear your preparation specifically to suit.

MONDAY

> *Interview formats*
> - telephone
> - one-to-one
> - panel
> - tests
> - presentation
> - socials

Telephone The informal pre-interview chat is often over the telephone. This may occur when the interviewer is uncertain whether to short-list you. For you, this call could be very important, making the difference between winning a face-to-face meeting or not. Anticipate this by keeping a checklist by the phone. Telephone screening is discussed in more detail in Week Five.

One-to-one This is the most common type of interview, and consists simply of one interviewer talking to one applicant. It is the easiest interview to arrange and conduct and, in consequence, is the type most commonly used.

However, decisions are rarely the result of one person's perceptions. It is common to hold a series of one-to-one interviews, which may be on the same day, or could extend over months.

Panel The panel (or 'selection board') may number from two members upwards. It can take many different forms, from a free for all, where all interviewers chip in with a variety of questions, to a more formal and structured approach where interviewers will take it in turn to ask questions reflecting their particular interests. At first, this style of interview may feel more threatening, but tends to be fairer and more equitable.

MONDAY

Panel interviews can be very formal. Responses and further exploratory questions are not always forthcoming because of the limitations of time. It is also more difficult to establish the same feeling of rapport as you can in a one-to-one interview.

The chair of the panel is usually the one who makes the initial introductions and the final remarks. Do not assume that they have the greatest influence in making final decisions. It is often difficult to know who to talk to –

- always look at the person questioning you
- direct your answer to the questioner
- glance around to show you are ready for the next question

Do not be unnerved by the panel; treat it as if it is a one-to-one interview concentrating your attention on the questioner at all times. Only include the other members when you are ready to continue with the next question. Do not be put off by signals between members of the panel.

MONDAY

Week Four

These probably have little to do with you personally but are more to do with matters such as time and questions.

Tests Tests are now commonly used to help assess candidates' abilities, aptitudes and personality. They are not an examination of your ability to remember facts but an extra way of gathering information. All applicants will be given the same questions, tasks and parameters. In an assessment centre format these are carried out in groups.

See Week Six for more information on all of the following.

Test type	**Measures**
Aptitude	Specific skills for the job: verbal, numerical, spatial, mechanical, clerical
Psychometric	Personality traits and preferences which may be needed to fit into team/project, temperament, disposition
Attainment	Knowledge of procedures, skills: driving, typing, technical terminology
Intelligence	General intellectual potential, problem-solving skills
Physical	Health, eyesight, colour perception, hearing acuity
Group discussions	Communication, judgement, reasoning, problem-solving, persuasiveness, listening skills, respect
Presentations	Ability to stand up and speak, arranging information, quick thinking, flexibility
Written exercises	Clarity, legibility, summarising

MONDAY

If you know there will be some form of test, remember to answer it honestly. If you attempt to paint a picture of yourself as the type of person you think they want, you will have to keep up the pretence or fail later on. Also many of the tests are sophisticated enough to detect deception.

Presentations It is increasingly common for interviews to include a formal presentation as part of the process. You may get advanced warning of this and the particular subject area you are required to present. Be sure to check what equipment will be available to you on the day, overhead projector, slide projector, laptop, software, flipchart, etc. and who will constitute your audience. You may want to make copies of your presentation or a summary to hand out.

Occasionally you receive the subject on arrival at the interview and have to prepare there and then. Think through an outline of a presentation – how and in what ways you would address the issues of the day. Then all that you need to do if you are faced with this scenario is to adapt it to the specific requirements of the topic.

Presentation content
- convince them that you are qualified and experienced
- demonstrate successes
- outline your contributions on a strategic and detailed level
- establish good relationships

Be sure to inject
- professionalism
- degree of formality
- controlled enthusiasm
- pace and drive

MONDAY
Week Four

A presentation is an ideal opportunity for you, but only if you can control your nerves and are clear about the messages you want to communicate. It is likely that this presentation will be in some way related to the job in question and most particularly to the main area of responsibility. Presentations can also be used to establish a relationship with the interviewer.

You should also consider whether it is appropriate to take a portfolio with you containing samples of your work. To be helpful, such things must be clearly relevant and be easy to handle and look at during an interview.

Socials Part of your interview day could include meeting the team or a tour of the organisation. Some organisations arrange social gatherings where you, the other candidates and sometimes partners meet together with your future employers. These may be labelled informal events, but never be off your guard; they are a part of the interview process. Use this as another opportunity to gather information. Be sure to talk to all those representing the organisation and limit your consumption of alcohol.

The job

The essential starting point for success is to know as much as you can about the job for which you have applied. There are several potential sources of information; you should use as many as possible. These include:

- preliminary discussions
- personal contacts – your network

Preliminary discussions
You will have received some information about the job which attracted you enough to make the initial contact. You may want to know more about:

- extent of duties and responsibilities
- desirable and essential qualities required
- skill levels, academic qualifications
- reporting relationships
- opportunities for training and development
- location
- hours of work
- salary and benefits

Personal contacts
You may decide to collect information about the job by talking to someone involved in the recruitment process. If you remain unsure about any particular aspects of the job or

Week Four

MONDAY

the organisation, you can save everyone's time by research. This is your opportunity to check fit and suitability – yours and theirs.

- Does your network extend into the organisation?
- Who do you know who works, or has worked, for them?

By talking to insiders you can get an 'inside' view. Remember that you will be hearing a subjective perception. Their views may be affected by personal circumstances or prejudices. So concentrate on facts rather than opinions.

The organisation

The interviewer will expect you to have some knowledge of the organisation. It is unlikely that it will be either comprehensive or complete. You need to show your interest not only in what you know but in filling in the gaps.

MONDAY

If sufficient information is not already supplied you should try to find out:

- what the organisation does
- product details
- ownership (public, private, group, independent, UK)
- size
- history
- structure (site, area or department)
- management style
- culture
- staff turnover
- outlets/factories/offices
- present degree of prosperity
- market position
- stability
- reputation
- strengths
- weaknesses
- markets
- competitors

The organisation itself and, if it is large enough, its public relations or customer services departments, are excellent starting points.

Other potential sources of information are their website and directories.

Directories

Key British Industries (Dun and Bradstreet) – basic corporate data on Britain's top 50 000 companies. Includes full contact

MONDAY

details, names and titles of executives, financial details and industry

Kompass (Reed Information Services) produces *Regional, Product and Service Directories* on over 40 000 leading companies. Includes contact names of directors, executives and department heads, nature of business, annual turnover

Who Owns Whom (Dun and Bradstreet) includes parent companies, subsidiaries and associates

Directory of Directors – lists 60 000 directors of British companies and their directorships

On-line Databases

Reuters Textline – holds up-to-date articles on companies from the UK and international press

Kompass, *Key British Industries* and *Who Owns Whom* are also available on-line *www.kompass.net*

www.dnb.com – free business directory, searching by business name or product/service

These directories and databases are available from good public and business libraries. More detailed information is available from Companies House.

Companies House
Crown Way
Cardiff, CF14 3UZ
Tel: 0870 3333636
companies–house.gov.uk

MONDAY

The Internet

The Internet is also a good source of information and many organisations now have their own home page. For further information try *The Financial Times* home page – www.ft.com.

Use your networks, arrange to talk to your contacts and if possible, borrow literature not normally given out to the public. Recruitment consultants are another good source of information; they should be able to help you access the formal information in the form of annual reports, sales literature and house magazines. They can also provide you with an insight into informal information: personalities, problems and opportunities. Use everything that is to hand.

It is more than likely that you will use the telephone for some or all of your enquiries. Be sure to have thought through and have listed in front of you the questions you propose to ask.

MONDAY

Week Four

- job for which you are being interviewed
- who will interview you – name and job title
- format of interview
- how long you will be there
- name, address and telephone number of the organisation
- name, address and telephone number of interview location
- date, day and time of the interview
- availability of car parking facilities
- security arrangements
- name and title of person who is arranging the interview
- job location
- annual reports

You may also want to ask about salary and benefits. It can save you time if you decide at this stage that you are no longer interested as the salary is too low. Although there is also a cautionary note as salaries are often negotiable within parameters, but the person on the telephone may not be aware of these parameters and the level of flexibility.

These days you may be greeted by a message rather than a person. Consider and write down what you want to say before making the call. The key information you need to leave is:

- your name
- your contact telephone number, and
- your address

- a brief message, requesting information
- your deadline if you have one
- your availability
- repeat your name and phone number

Summary

Today we have guided you through the research you need to do to prepare yourself for success. No preparation will be wasted, so invest time and energy into gathering as much information as you can at this stage. Have you:

- Researched the interview?
  - how to get there
  - who will interview you
  - the format of the interview
- Researched the job?
  - asked the questions
  - used your contacts
- Researched the organisation?
  - investigated directories
  - read Annual Report

Completing this research serves two purposes. It helps you prepare yourself for the interview so that you present yourself in the best possible light. It also helps you become clearer about your suitability.

TUESDAY

Week Four

Know yourself

Self-knowledge is an essential ingredient of your preparation for the interview.

We have already suggested that you research the interview process, the job and the organisation so that you are better informed about the process and will know what to expect. A most important ingredient in this preparation is finding out about **yourself**, so you feel comfortable in presenting yourself to the interviewer.

This idea may seem a little strange: after all, if you don't know yourself, who does?

Today we will help you to know yourself better through a process of reflection. We will give you areas to think about and guidance. Complete all the exercises and be brave, and test them out on colleagues, friends, in fact, on anyone you trust.

Week Four

TUESDAY

> *Know yourself*
>
> - you the person
> - your skills
> - your limitations
> - your strengths
> - understand your achievements
> - the essence of you

You the person

When managers are asked to describe themselves, they tend to talk about what they do rather than who they are. They think of themselves in terms of their title and describe themselves as such. Operations Manager, Personnel Manager, Finance Manager or Project Manager are on many occasions sufficient descriptions and speak for themselves. Do not expect that this will be enough at an interview. You need to understand and describe what skills make up your role and what makes you successful and different.

Being invited to attend an interview suggests you match the interviewer's specification; you are halfway to success. However, it is unlikely that you will be the only person who looks good on paper. The interview is your opportunity to stand out and be noticed. You want to convince the interviewer that you can bring enhanced benefits to their organisation as well as being able to do the job.

To be successful, you need to make a firm impression and be different. The interviewer may see many interviewees in the course of a day, so the ones they will remember are the ones who are distinctive, who have something interesting to

TUESDAY

say or who can make a unique contribution to the organisation or department.

The key to presenting yourself is to consider and understand your uniqueness. Ask yourself the following questions:

- What have I got that makes me special?
- What makes me fit?

The answers may come easily or you may have to return to these questions at the end of today when you have a clearer understanding of you. The first step in building up a picture of yourself is to appraise your skills.

Your skills

- What can you offer us?
- What are your skills?

These common interview questions, whilst apparently simple, require thought, preparation and a level of introspection and reflection. Your answer should not simply be a regurgitation of your CV, relating what you have done. It is more about when and in what contexts you have performed well and the skills and competencies, contacts and knowledge you have applied or acquired in the process.

Try to answer this question honestly and spontaneously:

- What can I do?

How comfortable would you feel about presenting these ideas to an interviewer?

Week Four

TUESDAY

It can feel strange at first to 'blow your own trumpet', but in an interview you are the only one who knows the tune.

The following list of national standards are contained in the MCI Occupational Standards for Management, they are basically a set of 'can do' statements. Look down the following list and mark whether you are:

1 Very competent

2 Competent

3 Adequate for the task

4 Undeveloped skills

Check afterwards with a colleague and see if they agree with your assessment. You may find you have been overly critical.

Week Four
TUESDAY

Maintain and improve service and product operations
- Maintain operations to meet quality standards 1 2 3 4
- Create and maintain the necessary conditions for productive work 1 2 3 4

Contribute to the implementation of change in services, products and systems
- Contribute to the evaluations of proposed changes to services, products and systems 1 2 3 4
- Implement and evaluate changes to services, products and systems 1 2 3 4

Recommend, monitor and control the use of resources
- Make recommendations for expenditure 1 2 3 4
- Monitor and control the use of resources 1 2 3 4

Contribute to the recruitment and selection of personnel
- Define future personnel requirements 1 2 3 4
- Contribute to the assessment and selection of candidates against team and organisational requirements 1 2 3 4

Develop teams, individuals and self to enhance performance
- Develop and improve teams through planning and activities 1 2 3 4
- Identify, review and improve development activities for individuals 1 2 3 4
- Develop oneself within the job role 1 2 3 4

Plan, allocate and evaluate work carried out by teams, individuals and self
- Set and update work objectives for teams and individuals 1 2 3 4
- Plan activities and determine work methods to achieve objectives 1 2 3 4

Week Four
TUESDAY

- Allocate work and evaluate teams, individuals
  and self against objectives   1 2 3 4
- Provide feedback to teams and individuals   1 2 3 4
  on their performance

Create, maintain and enhance effective working relationships
- Establish and maintain the trust and support of
  one's subordinates   1 2 3 4
- Establish and maintain the trust and support of
  one's immediate manager   1 2 3 4
- Establish and maintain relationships with
  colleagues   1 2 3 4
- Identify and minimise interpersonal conflict   1 2 3 4
- Implement disciplinary and grievance
  procedures   1 2 3 4
- Counsel staff   1 2 3 4

Seek, evaluate and organise information for action
- Obtain and evaluate information to aid
  decision-making   1 2 3 4
- Record and store information   1 2 3 4

Exchange information to solve problems and make decisions
- Lead meetings and group discussions to
  solve problems and make decisions   1 2 3 4
- Contribute to discussions to solved problems
  and make decisions   1 2 3 4
- Advise and inform others   1 2 3 4

Reproduced by kind permission of MCI

Week Four

TUESDAY

The above checklist may help to define your skills and give you the language to talk about them. The next step is to own them. People are generally poor at recognising their own skills, whilst often being good at identifying skills in others. If you are struggling with this, ask for feedback from the people you manage, or those who manage you; alternatively, think back over past appraisals and feedback you have received. Take some time to tell yourself about your skills, hear yourself saying them out loud without feeling embarrassed or apologetic. Practise in front of the mirror.

Your limitations

You are very likely to be asked about your weaknesses at the interview. We would prefer to think of them as limitations or areas for improvement and look for positive ways of presenting them. For example, you know that you can be impatient, but looked at from an alternative perspective it could be seen as an over eagerness to get things done. This is not hiding from the truth it is putting an affirmative interpretation on negative characteristics.

Your 'weaknesses' can also be listed to give you an idea of what changes you might want to make.

- What limits me?
- What has held me back in my career?
- Under what circumstances have I felt most frustrated and unhappy at work?

Week Four

TUESDAY

Your strengths

Skills are only part of the picture. They will help to show **what** you do. You have individual strengths which will dictate **how** you do things. This is what makes you unique.

The following list outlines the strengths of successful managers. Look at it and see where their talents coincide with yours.

Mark yourself on a scale of 1–4: 1 = always, 2 = frequently, 3 = sometimes, 4 = never.

                                                    1 2 3 4

- quick thinking and getting to the point
- enthusiasm
- presence
- ability to handle conflict and make decisions
- self-confidence
- strength of will
- commitment and determination
- flexibility and willingness to change
- creativity
- willingness to take responsibility
- initiative
- competitiveness
- sensitivity to people and situation
- stamina
- commercial awareness
- judgement
- being personally organised
- ability to take risks
- ability to strike the balance between big picture and detail

TUESDAY

Week Four

Using the list above for guidance, try to answer the following questions about your strengths. Be as specific as possible and add descriptions of how you utilise them.

- What are the strong points of my character and personality?
- In so far as I have succeeded, what has helped me?

Understand your achievements

The most practical way to assess yourself is to make a list of all your achievements, not solely the major ones, but everything that other people should know about. People find this process difficult, so to help you we've given you some ideas. Add any more of your own.

Week Four

TUESDAY

> *Achievements might include:*
> - a new idea
> - reducing waste
> - turning around a bad situation
> - avoiding potential problems
> - improving customer relationships
> - results which improved
> - costs you managed to cut
> - an activity simplified or improved
> - a crisis averted
> - something you made
> - a new skill mastered
> - a group you led
> - a problem solved
> - anything that had a happy ending

The essence of you

You have considered and listed your vast array of skills, strengths and achievements and examined your limitations. Now is the time to put them together to form a composite representation of yourself.

Write down a number of sentences beginning with the words 'I am', e.g. 'I am a manager'. Try to think of at least 15 of these.

Be specific
Expand these sentences to show yourself off. Add to the sentences by explaining and giving clear examples. Where

TUESDAY

Week Four

possible, angle the examples to match the post for which you will be interviewed.

Produce statements such as:
I am a good manager because I am able to motivate and develop people. In my last job I inherited a team who were bored with the weekly meetings and often strolled in late. I talked to them individually, found out their dissatisfactions and instigated a system of agenda setting that involved them all. As a result the meetings became fun and much more productive.

This is very different from saying: *I am a good manager because I have an MBA or I am a good manager because I have worked for 'x' for 20 years.*

You can see from this example that the way you describe yourself and the kind of language you use detracts from or adds to the image you portray.

As well as giving concrete illustrations, you also need to think about your language. Be confident and assertive using phrases like the following to illustrate your point positively:

Week Four

T U E S D A Y

- . . . which resulted in
- . . . so that
- . . . the benefit was
- . . . the advantage was

Dismiss all your tentative language such as:

- . . . I probably could
- . . . I think I can
- . . . I have been told
- . . . some people think I'm. . .

Summary statement
You may like to reinforce your other statements by developing a summary career statement about yourself. This has the advantage of creating the right impression in the mind of the interviewer. Produce a powerful statement about the type of person you are and the contribution you can make to the organisation. You are then able to create value in the eyes of potential employers and increase the idea of the benefits you bring.

Statements such as:

- I am a successful sales manager with a proven track record of building teams and winning high profile orders . . .
- I am a determined professional with experience across a wide range of technical products . . .

TUESDAY

This statement should be brief and powerful, highlighting all the benefits in employing you. Be sure to practise saying this statement; often statements that look good on paper do not translate to the spoken word naturally. After hearing it you may need to adapt it. Also be sure that you feel comfortable with the statement; if there is any hint of uneasiness this will show.

Try it out before the interview and validate your perceptions against another reliable source. Use a friend or work colleague who knows you well. Looking at yourself through different people's eyes can demonstrate the different facets of you. Begin by trying to share your findings with a trusted friend or colleague. Ask them what skills they think you have. Ask them what areas for development they see in you. Ask them to comment on your transferable skills.

Self-esteem

Self-esteem is essential to everyone's well being and it is something that can grow or diminish depending on what is happening in our lives.

It can be divided into two parts:

Internal self-esteem Comes from your beliefs about yourself, accepting your strengths and limitations rather than striving to be perfect. You see yourself as equal to but different from other people rather than superior or inferior.

External self-esteem Comes from interactions with others. You respond to their reactions, opinions, and how they relate to you. You let them tell you how good you are.

Many people have an over-developed need for external, reflected self-esteem because their internal self-esteem is fragile. As you increase your internal self-esteem, you will lose some of your dependence on external self-esteem.

You may find you spend time rating yourself as better in some areas and worse in others. Internal self-esteem is not dependent on comparisons. It is your own assessment of your self worth. What you have developed today is a collection of ideas that reflect your strengths and achievements.

Summary

Modesty or traditional conditioning may have made today a challenging day.

- You the person
  - what makes you special
  - what makes you fit
- Your
  - skills – what you can offer
  - strengths
  - achievements
  - limitations
- The essence of you

It may help to think of the interview and approach it as if you were preparing for a product launch. At the interview, you are the product, your challenge is to convince the other parties to invest in you. To make that decision they need to know why and what the benefits to them will be.

Week Four
WEDNESDAY

Preparing yourself for success

Some candidates see interviews as threatening situations. They worry about what limits them, about how nervous they get, about what the interviewers will think of them, and about failing to do the job if they were appointed.

For these people, what stands in the way of conveying self-respect is their overriding fear of failing themselves and their expectations. Their fear of failure overcomes their need for achievement. To some, this fear can have a paralysing effect and can completely ruin the interview.

If this is a description of you then you need to begin thinking of yourself and your approach to interviews in a more positive light.

Prepare to succeed by:
- thinking positively
- making a good impression
- looking prepared

Thinking positively

World-class athletes, amongst others, will confirm the importance of mental attitude to achieving the best performance. To give yourself the best possible chance at interview you will need to think yourself into a fully positive frame of mind. How you set about this will be a personal matter. But concentration on your strengths, and the certainty that you have the internal resources to cope with any difficulties will go a long way.

Week Four
WEDNESDAY

Some people find it helpful to relax quietly and picture their success, both at the interview and in the subsequent post. They imagine this in great and vivid detail, visualising the thoughts and sensations this will bring. Others treat them-selves to something new, ensuring that they feel good inside and out.

However you go about this, it is in many ways the most crucial phase of the whole process of preparation. You need an inner conviction that you are important to yourself. If you do not feel a sense of your own well-being and self-worth, how can you convince others that you will be an asset to their organisation?

You have to think positively before you can act positively: 'Whether you think you can or you can't, you're probably right.' Henry Ford

Compare:
- Thoughts — 'I'm sure they just asked me to make up the numbers. The others are bound to be better'
- Feelings — hopeless, inadequate, apprehensive
- Outcome — poor impression, no conviction, unsuccessful interview

With:
- Thoughts — 'They've picked me from all the applicants. I must stand a very good chance'
- Feelings — calm, confident, positive anticipation
- Outcome — assured impression, mutual fact finding, beneficial interview

Aim to direct your energy away from worrying about the interview and towards effectively preparing for it. Consider

WEDNESDAY

it as an opportunity where you are both interviewing each other, not as a one-sided test. Most importantly, remember that of all the people who applied, they have chosen you to interview.

If you are not nervous about attending interviews, then you should have little problem in this respect. Try to monitor whether you may be seen as overconfident and not taking things as seriously as you should. This is a common mistake made by interviewers who confuse confidence with arrogance.

To be just a little anxious, a little apprehensive is good; it is generally facilitative rather than inhibitive. Only when you become very anxious do you begin to harm your prospects.

Making a good impression

People make up their minds about us in minutes. Never ignore this fact, particularly at an interview when you have a relatively limited time to make an impression.

Your initial impact is vital. You don't get a second chance to make a first impression.

> *First impressions*
> - start well
> - first moves
> - appearance
> - body language
> - your voice

Start well
Whenever two people meet for the first time, they automatically start by evaluating each other on the basis of the non-verbal cues they receive. You and your interviewer

Week Four
WEDNESDAY

will be doing just that as soon as you meet, whether in the interview room or on the walk from reception. It is a subconscious 'weighing up' time.

The interviewer will often base their judgement on this initial impression and spend the remainder of the interview looking to reinforce their view. You may be judged by nothing more than how you walk across the room, the strength of your handshake, or when and how you sit.

Evidence is often sought to support initial impression. You should therefore do all you can to enter confidently, but not brashly, with a pleasant smile.

Do:
- close the door behind you
- walk forward confidently, body straight, head up
- respond to offered handshakes firmly
- wait until you are invited to sit
- remain quiet but alert to the opening moves by the interviewer

WEDNESDAY

- allow them to take the initiative
- be ready to respond appropriately

Don't:
- shuffle in, head down with hands in pockets
- carry a jumble of paper
- crash into the room pushing out your extended hand
- attempt to dominate an interview, especially in the opening stages

Appearance

It is essential that you dress the part. Your appearance reveals a great deal about your self-image, your values and your attitudes towards other people and situations. Differences in occupational status are associated with appearance, for example, the 'city' type, the 'power' dresser. More favourable qualities are often attributed to smartly dressed people. Those who are perceived to be attractive and well groomed are often treated better than those considered unattractive or inappropriately dressed.

For interviews, it is wise to find out the dominant style or accepted image of the culture you are trying to enter. If you can visit the organisation at lunchtime or the end of the day, go and see what people are wearing. If that is not possible, take a look at the organisation's literature which may contain photographs of employees and directors.

Beware of the danger of overdressing. A good benchmark is to decide how the holder of the job would be expected to dress, and go just one stage better.

WEDNESDAY

If you buy a special interview outfit, accessories or shoes do ensure that they are comfortable. There can be nothing more distracting than shoes that pinch, a jacket too long in the arms, a material that creases or generally ill-fitting new clothes.

Also be conscious of colours. More sober colours are often recommended for interviews: blues, blacks, greys with contrasting shirts and blouses. Your choice of tie, blouse or scarf is also important; any extremes of colour or pattern will make an impact. Think about the messages your appearance conveys to others.

Pay attention to the finer points of turnout: finger nails, hair, shoes and jewellery. Avoid too much perfume or aftershave. They won't be noticed if they are acceptable – only if they are not.

Avoid drinking alcohol, smoking or eating highly spiced food just before an interview. Eat mints or use a breath freshener before; be cautious.

Body language
Non-verbally you can communicate far more than you may be aware of. Although you often concentrate on *what* you are going to say – and it is important for self-confidence to do so – this must not be at the expense of *how* you say it. Research shows that:

- Words account for   35 per cent of the message
- Tone of voice   } 65 per cent of the message
- Body language

Negative thoughts and tension trigger off anxious feelings. It is possible to block them off – think about the directives 'chin up', 'stiff upper lip' and 'swallow your feelings' –

Week Four

WEDNESDAY

using our body to control them. Beware of different messages through your body that can leak out and undermine or contradict what you are saying. If you are thinking positively about yourself and the interview, then your body will give a positive impression too.

Focus your attention on the interviewer to the exclusion of everything else. Ensure that you are comfortable and relaxed in the chair provided. Whilst listening and giving the interviewer your full attention it is also important that you demonstrate this.

- sit comfortably, in an upright but relaxed posture
- rest your hands on the arms of the chair or comfortably in your lap
- look at your interviewer with an interested expression
- keep your head raised when you listen
- nod intelligently whenever the interviewer tells you something
- be relaxed

There are however things to avoid. The list below outlines some of the most common blunders that interviewees make. In some way, these all indicate a desire to escape, boredom or impatience either to speak or leave.

- fidgeting, biting your nails
- crossing arms or legs, clasping the chair or your upper arms
- leaning backwards, looking away from the interviewer
- gazing fixedly at some point in the room
- becoming distracted by the carpet or a picture

Week Four
WEDNESDAY

- pointing your body towards the door
- kicking your foot or tapping
- propping your head on the palm of your hand
- yawning
- staring blankly at the interviewer
- scribbling on paper

Your voice

Your voice is crucial to the impression you make. Many people are self-conscious about their voices and accents and, fearing they will let them down, try to mask them. Often all this does is make them unintelligible. Your voice is unique and is part of what makes you who you are. So befriend it and rather than trying to hide your accent, concentrate on being heard and understood. If you use your voice skilfully, you sound confident, knowledgeable and enthusiastic.

Always speak in a clear, steady voice. If you hesitate or stumble you will appear nervous and ill prepared. If you are

Week Four
WEDNESDAY

concerned about your voice, take care not to attempt to hide it. You will appear tense and closed up. Speak in your natural voice. Don't try to change it to impress the interviewer. Avoid bad language, slang, or annoying phrases or words such as 'you know' and 'actually', 'with respect' and 'to be honest'. Inject confidence, happiness and enthusiasm into your voice. A – v – o – i – d m – o – n – o – t – o – n – e.

Listen to your voice and get used to it. Take one of your statements from yesterday and speak it into a tape recorder. Express it as if you feel proud and positive about it and you. Vary the words you emphasise and the way you say them. See how different you can make your voice sound.

> *Do:*
> - pause and breathe deeply before speaking
> - speak slightly slower than normal
> - speak clearly, open your mouth
> - vary the tone to add interest
>
> *Don't:*
> - rattle out words 16 to the dozen
> - mumble
> - cover your mouth as you speak
> - stiffen your jaw
> - talk to your shoes

Looking prepared

You may want to consider taking a folder with you. It is useful to hold your prompt notes, statements or questions. If not overused, this will give an air of efficiency. It can also

Week Four
WEDNESDAY

help to reduce your nervousness and remind you of the two-way nature of the process.

Look and sound positive. Talk in a positive manner. If you're asked, 'Can you do this job?' – the answer must never be, 'I think so . . .' or, 'I hope so'. It should be, 'Yes . . . definitely'.

Be calm. Don't be distracted by interruptions. If the telephone rings or an interviewer's colleague enters the room, stay calm. Don't panic if you don't know the answer to a question. If you don't know, admit it. Also if your mind goes blank, don't worry. Take a deep breath and ask for clarification.

How you feel is essential to the impression you create. Use today as a practice.

Prepare yourself for success
- remember your positives
- start with a good firm handshake
- close the door behind you when you've entered the room
- walk and stand tall
- maintain eye contact with the interviewer or each interviewer in turn
- dress the part
- speak well
- indicate you are listening
- try to maintain open postures
- stay positive and calm
- remember you are interviewing them too
- relax

WEDNESDAY

Summary

Having taken you through a process of preparation, you should now be feeling and thinking more positively and enthusiastically about yourself and your ability to perform in the job. One of the other important obstacles is to be able to respond to the questions asked in a manner which demonstrates this ability in a succinct and coherent fashion.

Week Four
THURSDAY

The interview

Responding skilfully

Your preparation for the interview is now well under way. Just like a student before an exam, you should be confident that you have completed your revision, and be eagerly awaiting the big day. Continuing with the imagery, it is now time to look back over past exam papers, examine the questions asked, and plan your answers.

As you would expect, an interview is full of questions. These tend to be the same for each applicant, providing the key points for comparison. We looked at types of questions on Sunday; today we will focus on their content and give you guidelines for responding.

It is possible to anticipate and prepare for many of the questions you will be asked in advance. Interview questions have common themes. These are likely to be:

- self-assessment
- work history and experience
- the organisation
- the job
- management style
- ambitions and motivation

One of the main objectives of the interviewer is to build an impression of the interviewee not solely based on experience and history. However, criteria/competency-based interviews will expect you to present evidence of your past experience and achievements.

Week Four

THURSDAY

Where interviewers are more interested in your characteristics and how you see yourself, their questions are likely to include:

- reasons for applying for this job
- creativity and problem-solving
- adaptability
- reliability
- attitude to authority and colleagues
- motivations and aspirations

Knowing yourself is essential. Completing the exercises and answering the questions on Tuesday will have helped you to formulate your answers.

Types of questions

During your interview you will encounter a number of different types of questions. If you can recognise these and the reasons they are being asked, you can concentrate on your replies.

Week Four
THURSDAY

The better the questions, the better the interview. Questions can be categorised in the following ways:

- open
- probing
- closed
- hypothetical
- leading
- difficult
- negative
- discriminatory

Open questions
This is where interviewers give you the chance to talk. They want to hear your ideas and see how you develop an answer. Open questions usually start with:

- Who, What, Where, When, Which, Why and How

For example:
- What levels of budget responsibility have you had throughout your career?
- How did you implement Investors in People?

Questions such as these allow you the opportunity to sell yourself. They require a level of preparation on your part. Think about the key themes that are likely to be covered in the interview focusing on those which you consider will be of interest to the interviewer.

Probing
When interviewers are particularly interested in your reply and want further information, they will use probing questions to focus in on the subject:

THURSDAY

Week Four

> *For example:*
> - Tell me about your research to date.
> - How did you manage the change?
> - What made you respond in that way?

It's rather like a funnelling process where the interviewer moves from general questions to specific examples.

Closed questions
Direct questions that tend to pin you down to a factual reply or to a 'yes' or 'no' answer.

> *For example:*
> - Were you responsible for managing a budget in your last job?
> - Are you familiar with Investors in People?

Questions such as these can inhibit you and restrict your freedom in presenting information. For example, you may not have been responsible for the budget in your last post, but have had budget responsibilities in the past. If you are

Week Four
THURSDAY

not able to communicate this information it may reduce your chances of being successful. Always try to highlight relevant previous experience.

Hypothetical questions
Hypothetical questions are just that, encouraging you to imagine how you might handle the unknown. They also provide an opportunity for you to demonstrate how well you think and the quality of your judgement. The interviewer will suggest a hypothetical situation and ask how you would deal with it.

> *For example:*
> - What would you do if . . .?
> - How would you deal with . . .?
> - What would you expect from a perfect manager?

These can tend to be difficult questions to answer, especially if complex scenarios are being presented. If you are not careful you can end up tying yourself in knots, especially if you concentrate too much on trying to work out what kind of answer you think they might want. Try to relate these questions to your own experience and, if you are not clear about the complete details of the situation, ask for more information.

Leading questions
These are the opposite to hypothetical questions as here, the interviewer steers you to the kind of answer they expect. Leading questions do not give interviewers much of an idea about you, though you will have an insight into their thinking. Generally it is best not to rock the boat; go where the questions are leading and check if you are unclear.

Week Four

T H U R S D A Y

For example:
- As you have had experience of budgeting, I'm sure you wouldn't . . .
- With regard to Investors in People, you are obviously aware of the problems with . . .

Difficult questions
These take many shapes and forms. Give yourself a moment to think, rather than trying to start answering immediately. Don't be evasive; you may have some ideas about which areas of questioning are likely to cause you difficulty. Anticipate what areas interviewers might cover and be ready for them. It is important to have some kind of answer ready rather than clamming up and leaving interviewers to jump to their own, possibly incorrect, conclusions.

For example:
- I see you have a gap of 3 years in your employment; what did you do during that time?
- This job requires a professional diploma. How are you going to make up the shortfall in your qualifications?

Week Four
THURSDAY

You don't know which questions will take you by surprise. Whatever they are, take your time over them. And remember that in most cases, the interviewer is trying to give you the opportunity to put yourself forward in the best possible light, not trying to trip you up.

Negative questions
These can often reflect an interviewer's tendency to look on the more negative side of life. It may be their way of making comparisons between the best candidates.

> *For example:*
> - What are your weaknesses?
> - Why is it that you have changed jobs so often?
> - You stayed in your last job for 10 years. Why so long?

Don't fall into the trap of defending yourself, as though this were a direct attack by the interviewer. Be constructive and turn the question around to show yourself in a positive light.

Discriminatory questions
These sorts of questions may still be asked at interview, particularly of women and minority groups.

Women applying for senior jobs may be confronted with a whole battery of questions about their private lives, which male colleagues might not be asked.

> *For example:*
> - How does your husband feel about you applying for this post?
> - What effect might the increased responsibility have on your family life?
> - Are you planning to have a family?

Week Four

THURSDAY

People from minority groups may be asked:

> *For example:*
> - How would you respond to criticism from a white colleague?

These all need to be handled very carefully. You need to clarify the interviewer's intention and the relevance of the question. Ask yourself and maybe even the interviewer:

> - Is this question ever put to other candidates?
> - Would it affect my performance in the role?

It could be that the interviewer is just clumsy rather than malicious.

Employers have to demonstrate that such questions have been asked of all candidates, regardless of race and/or gender. If you feel that you have been discriminated against in your interview, you can contact the Equal Opportunities Commission who will advise you about what action to take.

Equal Opportunities Commission
Overseas House, Quay Street
Manchester M3 3HN
Tel: 0161 833 9244. Fax: 0161 835 1657
www.eoc.org.uk

As well as recognising the different types of questions, it is worth considering the order in which the questions are asked. The use of supplementary and probing questions will often suggest what is in the interviewer's mind; you should notice this and react accordingly.

Week Four

FRIDAY

Your moves

So far this week we have concentrated on the interviewee in a reactive role. Today, we will look at the interviewee from a different perspective. Identifying opportunities to be proactive, to ask your own questions or lead the discussion.

Your moves:
- ask the right questions
- keep on listening
- effective expression
- end on a top note

Ask the right questions

You will usually be given the opportunity to ask your questions towards the end of the interview. This is your chance to fill any gaps in your knowledge about the job and the organisation and clarify the next step in the interview

FRIDAY

process. Even if they do not invite questions, you should make sure that you check whatever you need to know. Few things are worse than leaving an interview thinking, 'If only I had asked such-and-such!'

Good interviewers will offer plenty of chances for you to check your understanding about the post and the organisation throughout the interview. It is still a good idea to have questions prepared that are based on your initial research and preparation. These may change or evolve as the interview develops.

The questions you ask will depend on how much information you have already collected, and your particular interests in the job. They should reflect your eagerness to work for the organisation and show evidence of thorough research. The pattern we suggest relates back to the data you collected on Monday. Your questions may relate to:

- the job
- the organisation
- the interview process

Do not bombard the interviewer. Choose one or two critical questions only. Refer back to Sunday when thinking about the types of questions you ask. Remember you are still the interviewee so watch you do not reverse roles. The interviewer does not want to be interrogated.

Work within the time left for the interview. If appropriate, check with the interviewer about time and ask no more than can reasonably be answered within that time frame. You can always ask, 'who else should I be talking to?'

Week Four

FRIDAY

The job

Your questions about the job may fall into the following categories:

- Routine and difficult aspects of the work: day-to-day responsibilities, special projects.
- Full responsibilities of the job: reporting lines (up/down/sideways), shared responsibilities.
- Support and guidance available to you: flexibility of budget, mentoring, coaching opportunities, bonus schemes, welfare.
- Amount of travel involved: relocation plans, other sites to visit.
- How often your performance will be reviewed: company appraisal scheme, performance reviews, are these pay/promotion related?
- Training and development opportunities: in-house schemes, qualifications/competence-based training, conferences.
- Promotion and career paths: company expectations, board appointments, directorships, senior appointments (internal/external).

Maintain the image you have portrayed throughout the interview. If you have focused on the fact that you are a team player, ask questions relating to the team. What are the interviewer's perceptions of its strengths and weaknesses? If you believe that you will be judged on your performance as a key factor, ask about performance indicators or the organisation's expectations over the next six months.

FRIDAY

Week Four

The following examples may help you formulate some questions:

- Why has the job become vacant?
- What will you expect from me in the next six months?
- What are the key tasks and responsibilities?
- What is the biggest challenge facing this team at the moment?
- What are the strengths and limitations within the team?
- How do you review performance?
- What development opportunities are there?
- What would my future career prospects be?
- Is promotion generally from within?

FRIDAY

The organisation

There may be some gaps in your knowledge about the organisation. Keep your questions to areas that are not sufficiently covered in the information you have previously received during the interview.

> *Topics for questions about the organisation*
>
> - Structure of the organisation: hierarchical, flat, matrix, informal structure.
> - Success of the organisation: turnover, new products/services, UK/international markets, financial health.
> - Decision-making: briefings, consultations, communications.
> - Future strategy and long-term plans: mission, strategic plan, philosophy.
> - Staffing: contraction, expansion, outsourcing.

These sorts of questions are essential to your decision-making. Is this organisation really viable in terms of profits and, if not, are funders, holding companies, bankers, etc. prepared to continue backing it for as long as it takes?

People have made bad decisions about jobs based on inaccurate information about the organisation rather than based on their suitability and the attractiveness of the job. Continue your investigations after the interview if you are still interested. Research whatever sources are available; contact suppliers, customers, professional bodies, etc.

The following examples of questions may help:

FRIDAY

Week Four

- Could you clarify for me the structure of the organisation?
- How has the market been developing for products/services?
- How are decisions made?
- What problems do you envisage for the organisation?
- What plans are there for reorganisation, expansion or retrenchment?
- What are your strategies for growth?
- How often do you update your business plan?
- What is the annual staff/financial turnover?

The interview process

You need to know what will happen once you have left the interview room. The interviewer should already have told you at the start of the interview, or the information may have been part of the advert or your invitation to the interview. If you are still not sure, ask. It is your right to have clarity about the procedure. The following examples may help:

- When will I hear from you?
- What is the next step? Further interview, medical, psychometric tests, social gathering?
- How will I be informed? Letter, phone call, fax, email?
- Is there further information you need from me?
- Is there someone else I should see in the organisation? Name, title, responsibilities?

Your prepared questions will serve you well, be sure to remember:

> - Don't ask questions about information you have already been given.
> - Don't ask questions for the sake of it.
> - Do ask supplementary questions.
> - Demonstrate you have digested the information previously given.

Keep on listening

Throughout this week we have implicitly referred to the importance of listening to and understanding what the interviewer is asking or saying to you. We believe it is equally important to keep on listening when you are asking the questions. As the interview progresses and your time to ask questions approaches, be careful not to lose concentration. Many of the worst mistakes at interviews arise from candidates who fail to hear or understand the questions or statements that are made to them. If you're not sure what the interviewer means, ask for clarification; it doesn't mean you're stupid! In fact just the opposite.

Too often, interviewees are in such a hurry to speak, usually out of nervousness, sometimes out of overconfidence, that they do not fully hear what has been said.

There is also the danger that you hear what you expect to hear rather than what is actually being said. Avoid preconceptions; let the interviewer answer your questions fully rather than prejudge the outcome or response.

Week Four

FRIDAY

Aids to listening

- Give the other person your full attention, don't fidget.
- Wait for them to finish what they are saying, don't interrupt.
- Ask open questions for more information.
- Regularly check your understanding; don't make assumptions.
- Watch your body language.
- Be open-minded, not prejudiced.

Effective expression

You want to present yourself in the best possible light throughout the interview process. This will involve effective answering of the questions asked, but also grasping any other opportunities to make your case.

Do:

- keep to the point
- be clear
- know the appropriate jargon
- speak with confidence
- keep your answers positive
- be honest and open with replies
- give plenty of concrete work-related examples
- be enthusiastic
- weigh them up

Keep to the point
It is essential that you keep your questions and answers brief. In a short interview, aim to take no longer than two minutes with each. Also be clear to answer only the questions you have been asked and ensure your answer is relevant.

Structure your statements to ensure that your message is clear. You can achieve this in a number of ways. To make the most impact, limit your reply to one subject at a time; the more you try to include in your answer, the less the interviewer will get from it. So take time to think about which subject is most relevant to the job, organisation or the interviewer.

Be clear
Clarity in reasoning and expression is a skill which can be developed. Your aim should be to present your responses in an interesting and intelligible way, so that the interviewers are not left confused or uncertain. Be specific and talk about examples; always ask for precise details.

Know the appropriate jargon

Be careful not to talk in technical, functional or organisational shorthand that may lose the interviewer. We tend to assume the same knowledge base as those to whom we talk. At an interview this can be dangerous.

But, be familiar with any jargon connected with the job or the industry so that the interviewer doesn't leave you behind.

Speak with confidence
Be confident in all that you present. If you are not confident it will show. Let your body language reinforce your words. Be natural, let them see and appreciate the real you.

Be enthusiastic
Enthusiasm is a wonderful quality; it is a combination of energy and determination. Enthusiastic people are those who enjoy what they are doing and convey this to their companions. They are free from self-consciousness and are more in control of themselves.

Weigh them up
An interview must, to succeed, be a two-way process. The interviewer will be trying (whether consciously or unconsciously) to find out how good the 'chemistry' or the rapport is likely to be. You should do the same from your side; few jobs are worth having if you are unable to get on with your boss. You should be alert for indications of honesty, efficiency, friendliness, and the other characteristics you want from your manager.

Week Four

FRIDAY

End on a top note

Do not assume the interview has ended until the interviewer makes it clear that it has.

Last impressions linger longer
There is a danger of relaxing too soon when the interview appears to be over and the interviewer is conducting you to the door. Fix in your mind the picture of yourself that you want the interviewer to keep and maintain, if you want to be sure that those last impressions are favourable. You should leave the interview room as you arrived, confidently but not brashly, shaking hands firmly and with a smile.

If you are still interested in the job, a short letter to the person you met is invaluable. You can thank them for the time they took to tell you about the job and the organisation. Remind them of the key benefit you would bring to the company and briefly restate your reasons for wanting to work there.

Summary

Be spontaneous but in control at the interview. It will help having completed the preparation. Remember to:

- maintain eye contact
- take your leave as smoothly and politely as possible
- do not add any afterthoughts
- try to resolve any outstanding issues
- shake the interviewer's hand
- thank them for giving you their time
- follow-up letter with your key benefit

S A T U R D A Y

Week Four

Putting it all together

We have come to the end of the week and your preparations are nearly complete. By this stage you should be feeling more confident about how best to present yourself in the interview. An interview is, after all, your chance to shine.

Throughout the week we have focused on areas such as, what to say, how to say it and what to do. Today, we will aim to bring it all together. When you first learn a skill or technique such as driving, word processing or chairing meetings, you are anything but natural. But with practice, these skills become natural extensions of you. Interviewing skills are no different.

Today we will focus on helping to remove *all* the blocks that prevent you from being yourself. After all your *unique selling* point is ***you***.

Week Four
SATURDAY

> *Putting it all together*
> - objectives
> - rehearsal
> - readiness
> - review
> - feedback

Objectives

As we discussed on Sunday, interviewers will have set their objectives before the interview and will have planned how these will be achieved. An interviewer's key objective is to find the right person for the job. Other objectives will reflect the stage of the interview; for example, in the final stages there will be greater emphasis on fit rather than skills.

As an interviewee, you should also set objectives. Your main objective is to be offered the job. However, there will be secondary objectives ranging from presenting yourself in a positive light, through to exploring the real culture of the organisation.

These objectives should help you become more concrete in preparing for the interview and clearer in the messages you should concentrate on *communicating*. This will help you make the impression that will bring attention to you as **the** candidate for the job rather than just another runner.

Rehearsal

No-one ever taught you how to be interviewed. If you are lucky, you may have attended a workshop on the subject or received some feedback on how you present yourself. It is more likely that the only experience you have had of interviews has been the real thing, for real jobs. You don't have the time to experiment; only poor performers get lots of interview practice. So you need to rehearse:

- entrance
- body language
- voice
- answers to questions
- the benefits you bring
- asking your questions
- taking feedback

Don't let the success of your future depend on trying to find out how you interview on the day. Take time to practise. Practice develops performance in most things; interviews are no exception.

Ask a colleague, your partner, anyone whose opinion you value or trust, to act as the interviewer then role-play the situation and take feedback. Before you participate in the 'interview' with them, show them your objectives, the job description and a prepared list of the kinds of questions you expect to be asked. Encourage them to ask their own questions too. Then you can see how you handle the unexpected.

Decide whether you wish to record this practice using either a video or tape recorder. You will learn more this way and much of it will be positive learning. The better the rehearsal, the better the performance.

Your entrance
Have the person in the role of interviewer meet you and invite you to sit down. Don't tell them the image you want to create; check their perception later. Even at rehearsal it is quite likely you will feel nervous. This is fine; you will feel less anxious on the day.

Your body language
We would encourage you to breathe deeply and relax in your own way. Sit upright in a comfortable position and look attentive. You are likely to be attentive if your body is. If you appear uneasy, the interviewer will pick that up through your body language and not hear your excellent responses. Here you can find out whether you have any nervous and distracting mannerisms to change.

Your voice
Can your 'interviewer' hear you clearly? Do you sound convincing and interesting? To which questions do you give most energetic answers? This can give you an idea of where your key interests lie. Listen to the rhythm in your voice; work at not being monotone.

SATURDAY

Answers to questions
Experiment with the time you take to answer the questions. Just how long are the silences between the questions and your responses? Make sure to listen right to the end of the question and make your reply clear and specific.

The benefits you bring
It is important to reassure the interviewer throughout the interview that you are the person they seek. Introduce examples and case-studies that reinforce your positive statements. Remember to turn any weaknesses into strengths and learning points.

Asking your questions
You will have some questions you prepared earlier; use the rehearsal to practise asking unprepared questions too. How clear and thoughtful are they? Be sure to keep them specifically related to that job or company.

Feedback
After the rehearsal make sure you have plenty of time to play back and discuss what happened. Listen carefully.

Week Four
SATURDAY

What can you improve? Also accept where you are strong and feel confident about it. Keep practising if you can. Draw up a checklist of the things you wish to rehearse and ask your interviewer for comments and suggestions on it.

Readiness

Here are a few questions you might want to ask yourself just before you go to the interview:

> *Am I ready?*
>
> - Are my clothes and shoes clean, neat and tidy?
> - Is my hair tidy?
> - Am I clear what image I want to project?
> - Have I decided how to project that image?
> - Can I be heard clearly?
> - Am I walking/standing/sitting tall?
> - Am I relaxed?
> - Do I feel confident to answer the questions?
> - Have I structured my answers for the best impact?
> - Have I prepared a sheet of prompts/questions?

Review

By analysing and reviewing your performance after the interview, you can see where you might need to improve and so develop the necessary skills. This review should take place as soon as possible after the interview. It will help you to identify areas you need to strengthen if you are attending any more interviews. One of the most important questions to ask yourself is the one which began the week.

SATURDAY
Week Four

Answer this honestly: *Did I present myself in the best possible light?*

The following list will help you to review your interview performance systematically in more detail:

Did I:

- Arrive on time?
- Speak confidently to all employees you met?
- Handle the opening moments well?
- Feel and look relaxed?
- Maintain appropriate eye contact?
- Use the full range of your voice to convey your message?
- Stay cool and calm?
- Answer all the questions well?
- Expand your answers?
- Refer to your strengths?
- Listen carefully to the questions?
- Understand the questions before you replied?
- Work out in advance the points you wanted to make?
- Volunteer information when given the chance?
- Capture and hold the interviewer's attention?
- Impress the interviewer?
- Demonstrate your knowledge of the job and company?
- Ask good questions?
- Adapt and adjust your questions?
- Deal with the closing moments well?
- End on a confident, optimistic note?

Week Four

SATURDAY

These questions will give you an idea of what you need to improve. If your answer is 'no' to any of the questions, try to explore the reasons why and particularly how you could improve. Answer the following questions:

- What impression did I create?
- Which questions did I find it difficult to answer?
- Did I say all I wanted to say?
- What will I do differently?

The more you know about yourself, through this form of review and other forms of feedback, the better equipped you are to present yourself to others.

Interviews are so complex and artificial a process for all parties that no matter how thoroughly you prepare, some may not turn out as you hope or expect. Don't dwell on the interviews that don't go well, understand why and learn from them. Focus on success and success will come to you.

Feedback

You should also not be afraid to ask for comments from the interviewer. If they are not forthcoming request them. If there are areas that you suspect, or are told, consistently let you down, seek help or a second opinion. Investigate your local sources of help, such as:

- Colleges/adult education centres
- Business schools/universities
- Correspondence courses
- Learning and Skills Councils (LSCs)
- Guidance organisations
- Professional institutes: The Chartered Management Institute
- Videos and books
- Careers counsellors

Don't be afraid to ask. Educational establishments are responsive to their customers and if you have a need, approach them with it. If nothing currently exists then why not set something up, or organise an event through your local professional institute or with a group of colleagues. Practice is never wasted. Feedback and development are essential to your future success.

Above all enjoy the experience. The most valuable interviews are frank open discussions involving facts, ideas and opinions. By following a simple pattern you can achieve the success you want at interviews.

Week Four

SATURDAY

Simple steps to success:

- do your research
- know yourself
- prepare yourself for success
- respond skilfully
- practise
- review

As you are very well prepared, all you now need are our best wishes – good luck!

Tackling Interview Questions

MO SHAPIRO
ALISON STRAW

WEEK FIVE

CONTENTS

Week Five

Introduction		359
Sunday	What's involved?	360
Monday	Are you sitting comfortably?	370
Tuesday	What have you done so far?	379
Wednesday	Who are you?	393
Thursday	How will you do the job?	409
Friday	Will you fit?	421
Saturday	Are you ready?	434

Week Five
INTRODUCTION

By the end of the week you should feel better informed about the process of *Tackling Interview Questions*– the content, style and motivations behind questions – as well as feeling more confident about presenting your experience, your knowledge, your skills and your abilities.

We would like you to think of this week as your companion and your guide through what can be uncharted waters. Your challenge is to apply this learning to yourself and the situations you face. Use the examples to develop a language and method of talking about yourself. This will lead to easy, flowing answers you can access even under pressure.

Remember that your interviewer is interested in you, not how you believe you should respond. Many interviewers are becoming wise to, and wary of, textbooks answers. So work on responses that will differentiate you from the other candidates and think about how to hold the interviewer's attention.

Week Five

SUNDAY

What's involved?

Today we will begin by summarising what's involved – what you are likely to encounter on your journey to the interview. We want to set the scene so that you are ready to concentrate on the questions that follow during the rest of the week.

> *What's involved?*
> - Objectives.
> - First steps.
> - Telephone screening.
> - Assessment centres.
> - What makes a question tough?

Objectives

Throughout the week you will have the opportunity to reflect on the reasoning behind the different kinds of questions you are asked. You will be able to consider your own aims. It is amazing how many interviewees expect the interviewer to be so in charge of the interview that they disempower themselves by not having their own clear plan and set of objectives. If you don't know specifically what you want from a job, how will you know when you achieve it?

Week Five

SUNDAY

Today's objectives relate to overall considerations of what's involved for both parties in the lead-in to the interview itself.

Interviewer's objectives	**Interviewee's objectives**
To get the right person for the job with: • key interpersonal skills • relevant qualifications • high energy • a record of quality results • initiative	*To find the job I want by:* • creating a positive impression from the start • being prepared mentally and physically • getting to know the organisation • anticipating questions • having something to say • feeling confident

Week Five

SUNDAY

It is vitally important that the interviewer selects the right person the first time, otherwise they might upset the balance of the team, have to look over their shoulder at a rival, or, at worst, have to suffer the expense in terms of time and cost of re-advertising and recruiting anew. Interviewers are also aware that the interview process itself is flawed so the process is often made up of different steps.

First steps

Good interviewers will have invested a significant amount of time in the planning process – scoping the role, allocating a budget, talking to the stakeholders, defining the competencies and the person specification, planning the advertisement and briefing headhunters or recruitment consultants. After receiving applications, the tasks are far from over. The interviewer, or someone else in the organisation, has to arrange the first steps:

- long listing
- short listing
- first interviews – sometimes telephone
- second interviews
- assessments
- meeting the stakeholders

Be aware that the more responsible the role, the more involved the key stakeholders will be. This may mean greater demands on your time because it may involve a series of meetings.

Week Five

SUNDAY

Telephone screening

The route to receiving an invitation to an interview can differ from organisation to organisation. Letters of application accompanied by CVs are the preferred way to present yourself and give information on your qualifications, experience and career to date. Increasingly this information is acceptable on-line. Your aim is to sell yourself in no more than two pages, giving the reader what they need to make their decision. Refer back to Week Three for more help with your CV. Some organisations use application forms, and the same applies to an application form as applies to a CV. Don't forget to sell yourself, even though your style may be cramped by the space available or questions asked – be creative.

Many organisations screen their long list of applicants by using a telephone interview. The purpose of the conversation is to create a realistic short list for the next stage. Only a small number of the candidates will progress beyond this stage so don't underestimate the importance of this conversation.

Often a screening interview will be unannounced: don't be put off by this. The interviewer normally asks whether it is convenient to talk so you can always buy some time and ring the person back. Your preparation is essential – you will need to think through what you say, how you say it and what you want the interviewer to remember. Also consider the limits of time; whilst we know of screening interviews that have lasted over an hour, it is more likely that you have under 20 minutes. Check whom exactly you are speaking to and don't make any assumptions.

Week Five
SUNDAY

> *Case history*: One senior manager screening applicants for a key post in her team, rang an applicant to discuss certain aspects of his CV. He was unable to talk immediately. When she answered the phone, he assumed he was speaking to an administrative assistant and was both sharp and dismissive. Once he realised he was talking to his potential boss, his manner changed. But it was too late and there was no way he was going through to the next stage.

Pre-screening is one of the most challenging stages as making an impact with only your voice is extremely difficult. When you listen to an interview on the radio or have a telephone conversation, you probably only listen to a small amount of the conversation. Who do you listen to and why? What is it about their conversation that holds your attention? It's then up to you to build these techniques into your conversation with the interviewer! Use pace and tone to punctuate what you are saying. Think about what makes a voice attractive to you. Relax your jaw and mouth by repeating the sounds 'me – you' a number of times to help. If nothing else it will make you laugh which in turn will relieve any tension.

Be prepared – what you say

- which parts of your CV to highlight
- make it interesting
- relate what you say to the role

Be prepared – how you say it

- speak up and out
- use tone and pace
- be relaxed
- smile

Some organisations are now using video conferencing for this screening and you are asked to attend an anonymous office with what looks like a computer screen. Don't be put off by the technology. Arrive early and become familiar with the surroundings. In global organisations this is as commonplace as a telephone link.

If you are one of those lucky people who receive headhunters calls on a regular basis, treat all these seriously. They may lead to the opportunity you are looking for.

What makes a question tough?

The concept of a tough question is usually a matter of personal interpretation. Sometimes an interviewer will deliberately ask what they consider to be a tough question; on other occasions they may hit your Achilles' heel without intent.

Week Five

SUNDAY

You may already have a clear idea of your 'tricky' areas. If so, it is a good idea to think about them now instead of hoping they might be missed. Compile a table like the one below to help you.

What constitutes a tough question?	Why?	How will I combat this?
Gaps in employment	....	....
Industry/technical knowledge	....	....
Health problems	....	....
Why I am leaving	....	....

If the question is tough because it is a surprise either in content or timing, take a deep breath, and think about what you have been asked. You can't prepare for the content of a surprise question, but you can prepare a general response. Practise the skill of checking with the interviewer that you

SUNDAY

have understood what has just been asked without simply echoing their question. *'Let me be clear – you are asking me . . . So you want to know how precisely I would . . .'* This is a useful technique if the question requires you to go to a level of explanation that feels uncomfortable to you. This buys you some thinking time, too. Watch politicians, they are expert at this technique.

Why do interviewers ask 'tough' questions? In many cases they want to gain a deeper understanding in a particular area – either a greater insight of you or to check the extent of your knowledge and expertise. They may need to test your response to the types of pressure demanded by the job.

The way to answer tough questions is to be confident that if you have done your preparation you will have a reasonable answer somewhere in your repertoire. Go for that rather than struggling to find a 'perfect' answer; just like the 'perfect' question they don't exist! While every question the interviewer asks has a purpose, it is unwise to answer until you know:

- the reason for the question
- the most appropriate answer
- how to reply positively

Over the next few days, notice whether your automatic responses to any questions tend to be framed in positive or negative language. When you use negative words like 'trouble', 'problem' and 'disaster', you base your thinking in a negative framework.

Week Five

SUNDAY

The interviewer will join you there and be in a negative set too. If you use language in a positive vein, then you will feel more confident and can expect the interviewer to respond in a more friendly and co-operative manner. Use words like 'opportunity', 'challenge' and 'learning'. Consider the different impacts and choose to be more positive.

Summary

Today we have considered interviews and their part in the recruitment process. Whilst the other tools that organisations use are either organisation or role specific, the preparation you do for interview is essential to your success. Here are some simple rules to help you.

- stay calm
- listen to the question
- speak clearly and steadily
- tell the truth
- avoid talking too much
- make it relevant

You need to understand the interviewer, and by simply listening and reflecting back the language and pace of the interviewer you can demonstrate this understanding. Before you jump in with your response you need to think about the question, considering why it has been asked and what the interviewer wants to find out. If you understand this, then you are able to answer the question comprehensively, presenting yourself well and leaving the interviewer with no need to ask you any supplementary questions.

SUNDAY

By doing your research well, you should also have picked up some of the language from company reports, or any information you are given about the job, department and organisation.

Tomorrow we will ensure that you are ready to make a positive first impression.

Week Five

MONDAY

Are you sitting comfortably?

You've passed the first stage of the recruitment process – well done! Your application and responses suggest that you could do the job and fit in. You've successfully answered the screening questions or passed the tests giving the right mix of content and style to help with the decision making process. Your task now is to influence the interviewer from thinking you 'could' do the job, to thinking you 'can' and 'will' do it successfully. Whatever the next stage, it is important that you feel comfortable enough to succeed by:

- presenting yourself well
- meeting and greeting with ease
- establishing relationships
- opening moves

If you have done your homework and prepared yourself well, you will be setting yourself up for success right from the start. Even before you meet the person who is going to interview you, you will be party to a mutual weighing up. The opening stages of the interview can be very influential, as both you and the interviewer want to impress each other.

Interviewer's objectives	Interviewee's objectives
• Did they impress all the people they met?	• Do I create a good impression?
• Do they look the part?	• Can I do myself justice?
• Will they settle in quickly?	• Does the place feel and look good?
• Can they be easily understood?	• Did they make me feel 'at home'?

Week Five

MONDAY

You may have been invited to attend an informal interview. Beware, there is no such thing as an informal interview, and every meeting should be treated with careful thought and consideration.

Presenting yourself well

First impressions
First impressions are important, so how you sit, how you make eye contact with whoever approaches you, the quality of your handshake and how you look will all make an impact. Interviewers will notice uncleaned shoes, dirty fingernails, style and mannerisms. For most jobs, the impressions we make on our colleagues, clients and managers matter. How you look at the interview will be taken to indicate how you would look and conduct yourself when working.

MONDAY

You can anticipate their first words and prepare your responses accordingly. That way you can avoid blurting out something nonsensical such as 'Goodnight' or 'Sorry'. If you know that you suffer from either verbal diarrhoea or paralysis when you're nervous, a few practised responses will stand you in good stead. Only continue your conversation with the receptionist or secretary if you get a favourable response. If the reception is busy, then the replies will be limited and you need to show your awareness of this.

Your first challenge is to introduce yourself and make polite and interesting conversation before you even start the interview. Make sure you have thought about your opening remarks in advance. If you have a number of comments ready at the beginning, their familiarity will calm you down. The earlier you can say your name, the better. It's something you know very well and because you don't have to think about it, you will be able to start with your 'normal' voice rather than a nervous, high pitched squeak.

Your first words

- Hello, I'm . . . I've come for an interview with . . .
- What's the agenda for the day?
- How do most people travel into work?
- What a fascinating building. How long have you been based here?
- How does it compare with your offices at . . .?
- Do you have any company brochures I can read while I'm waiting?

Meeting and greeting with ease
When you enter the room, the interview is ready to begin – well nearly. Sitting down and getting comfortable are

Week Five

MONDAY

important. It is likely that the room has been set out for an interview, but sometimes you will be interviewed from behind a desk. If you are not directed to a chair, it is appropriate to say, when invited to sit down. *Will this be OK?*

Be careful not to sit in direct sunlight otherwise your squint or frown caused by the bright light may be misinterpreted as your normal expression. You may be asked if you want a drink. Do remember that juggling with a drink when you are talking may be difficult. Asking for water is the safest option, particularly as you can expect to be doing most of the talking for up to an hour.

If there is more than one interviewer, you should, at this stage, be introduced to all of them. A simple: *Yes, we've spoken*, or *Pleased to meet you*, gives you the chance to talk and keep your voice loosened. The interviewer may then describe the interview process, where this stage fits and what comes next. They may also describe the role you've applied for in the context of the organisation. You may be asked at the end of this section whether everything is clear. A brief *Yes, thanks*, is all that's needed to signal that you're both ready to start. If you're unclear, ask for clarification.

The interviewer may then go through some of the same questions you have already been asked, so you will be well practised at answering these: *How was your journey? Did you get here Ok?*

These questions are simply breaking the ice, so be careful not to go into a long monologue about transport, and resist the temptation to say the obvious or be sarcastic. This is not an opportunity to talk about the amount of traffic on the roads, how you hate commuting or the state of the public transport system. Your answers should be short but warm. If any conversation is to develop from this, make it positive. *Fine. The roads were clear and your map was a great help. I enjoy my travel time as it gives me time to plan.*

How long did it take you?
If this is the office base you will be working from, they will be interested in your commute. Research shows that because of the uncertainty surrounding employment, more people are establishing a base and travelling to wherever there work is. Some families now have more than one home to help them manage their commute. Most organisations, however, prefer that their employees live within a certain radius of their place of work and some even stipulate it. This question, whilst simple on the surface, may have an underlying query about your flexibility: *The train only took 35 minutes and I took advantage of that time.*

Establishing relationships

At this point your intention is to relax and keep your voice active and loosened up. As well as settling yourself down, you want to get into the rhythm of the person with whom you are speaking. Research suggests that people tend to like people who are like them. If you make the effort to be like someone else, they will feel more comfortable in their dealings with you. (On Friday we will consider how this relates to the question, Will you fit?)

Notice the pace at which the interviewer speaks, and try to speed up or slow down to match. Once you are synchronised, you may be able to lead them to a pace that better suits you.

Week Five

MONDAY

Opening moves

What follows are a range of questions to warm you up, get you talking, giving both of you time to settle into the interview. Some of the toughest questions are those that give you enormous scope, such as:

- Talk me through your career to date.
- What are the highlights of your career?
- Take me through your CV/résumé.

Most readers will have experienced questions such as these. They are used early in the interview to see how you cope and whether you are able to give a lucid and relevant response. Your interviewer wants to know how you present yourself in relation to your career. Your answer to these questions should give them clues to your suitability and the areas they may want to expand later on.

MONDAY

Don't panic when you hear these questions. You should be well prepared, in control and able to respond effectively. In preparing for the interview you will have thought about your personality and strengths, picking out the qualities which show that you are well matched to the organisation and job, thus allowing you to describe how you are the ideal employee to be recruited.

You may choose to ask them: *Is there a particular part of my background that interests you?* Be aware of questions in response to questions, as they often do not give you the answers you want. They may respond by: *The parts which equip you for this role!* The question, *Would you prefer a chronological or skills-based review?* may elicit the response: *Whichever will give us the best overview of you.*

One other cautionary note is that this is a warm-up question; it is not intended to take the whole of the interview. Do not focus on every role, project and conversation you have had. The interviewer is still settling down and giving you something you can easily talk about to get the interview going.

Choose what you say carefully – your description of your career should be entertaining and no longer than four minutes. You may decide to start by saying:

I see the start of my career as when I had to make choices at school and university as these have influenced all my future experiences.

I was clear what I wanted to do from an early stage and have followed that through a, b, c, whilst developing my skills . . ., to the point that I reach today. I am now seeking an opportunity to stretch and develop myself further.

MONDAY

Week Five

There are two significant themes in my career – my skills and the environments in which I have worked. I have developed my skills which are . . . and my success has depended on them. The environments in which I have applied them are diverse . . . I enjoy working in different environments.

I started my career at . . . as I was seeking to . . . I then sought to develop both my skills and knowledge by moving companies and chose to join . . . because of their reputation for . . . This has been the pattern throughout my career.

Whatever you say, you should demonstrate or refer to one or more of your key behavioural attributes. Your interviewers will want to know what you have done in addition to how you have done it. It will help them if you can look back to describe past achievements and then project forward to say how they will apply and benefit this post.

You may, depending on the context, want to refer to:

- improvements
- turnover
- people managed
- projects completed
- savings instigated
- budgets managed

This is a time for you to shine, so don't discuss problems you had with previous employers or managers. Take some time to think about yourself. These questions are not easy to answer off the cuff, but you can prepare for them.

MONDAY

Once you have safely navigated your way around these early questions you can be confident and ready to concentrate on the more weighty ones that will undoubtedly follow.

Summary

Remember, in the opening stages:

- start well
- everyone you meet may be asked for an opinion
- there is no such thing as an informal interview
- be relaxed
- sit comfortably
- use your warm-up questions to your advantage

Tomorrow we will focus on the questions surrounding *What have you done so far?* This will help the interviewer to understand that you can do the job!

TUESDAY

What have you done so far?

The introductions are over. You are in the interview room. Your interviewer has talked you through the role, the organisation and what to expect. You sense that the interview for real is about to begin.

Interviewer's objectives	Interviewee's objectives
	To demonstrate that:
• Can you do the job?	• I could do the job given the opportunity.
• Do you have the skills and experience?	• I have what you need.
• Do you match your CV?	• I am articulate.
• Are you qualified?	• My achievements speak for themselves.
• Do you match our competencies?	• I could add value.

Today we will focus on the following areas:

- work history and experience
- training and qualifications
- competence.

Normally this phase of the interview is not populated by the toughest questions. The interviewer is wanting factual answers, but don't waste an opportunity – tell your interviewers not just what your goals were, but how you achieved them, and what this has taught you for the future.

TUESDAY

Work history and experience

Your jobs, projects, experience, achievements and career choices are of interest to the interviewer at this stage. Do you have what they need to do the job? They will ask:

- What have you done?
- What have you achieved?
- In what ways have you achieved your goals?
- Why did you leave?

What have you done?

Your response to questions in this section should recognise the interviewer's motivation for asking them. They are not wanting a regurgitation of your job titles or organisations; they want to go below the surface to hear about how you have contributed to the success of the team, department,

TUESDAY

company or group. Their questions may reflect this, but even if they don't, your answers should!

Talke me through your career to date?
This question is asked for a variety of reasons. As we mentioned yesterday, it can be used as a warm up, or it can be used to reacquaint them with your CV. Your interviewer should already have read through your CV so in this question they want a 'whistle-stop' tour of what you've done. We emphasise the whistle-stop, so be succinct and precise! Make sure your words match what you have put on paper, and beware of too much detail such as dates, who you reported to, responsibilities.

My career has spanned four different organisations and has been about acquiring knowledge and skills and applying these to each different role. Each role has contributed to the person I am today and supports the contribution I can make to your company.

Your interviewer may ask the question, *What brings you here?* in a variety of different ways. This question indicates your interviewer is interested in the choices you have made in your career, and how your skills have developed through your different roles and organisations. You have to be selective in your answers and choose the elements that demonstrate individual and organisation benefits.

I have enjoyed a successful and varied career. My first job gave me an opportunity to develop my people management and leadership skills. I managed a team of 40 on three different sites, establishing set procedures and monitoring the service level. I then moved on to develop more specialist skills in a sister organisation, managing projects and achieving the deadlines set, always coming in under budget and always on target. I am now seeking an opportunity in which I can bring together both these sets of skills and develop them.

Tell me about your responsibilities in your present job?
This is not an opportunity to recite the twenty responsibilities outlined in your job description or your competencies. It's an opportunity to blow your own trumpet. Wherever possible, summarise your responsibilities. The more you can describe them in terms of the benefits they bring to the organisation, the better.

I have four main responsibilities . . . Balancing these and setting targets to ensure my team achieves them has been a challenge, particularly in a climate of managing a reduced cost base. I have been successful and my success in the role has been due to my ability to manage and control the work of the team.

What have you achieved?

This style of question is relatively easy to respond to, if you have prepared.

How is your effectiveness in your present post measured?
Measures are important to most organisations. Even if your role isn't formally measured you should think about how you quantify your success. It gives the interviewer some ideas of the scope of your role, what you have achieved and the potential contribution you could make to their organisation.

The principal measure is the business review process. I have both a cost and a revenue budget for which I am fully accountable. The bottom line is what counts most. Apart from this, I have the

Week Five

TUESDAY

freedom to make decisions. I enjoy being measured as I can always focus my attention on identifying and working towards improvements.

Tell me about a recent project. What aspects of it gave you the most satisfaction?

Pick a good example. Don't just go for personal satisfaction, although that is the essence of the question. Also focus on the immediate- and long-term benefits.

They asked me to reorganise a department. I did my research, reading and talking to the key stakeholders. I identified four key improvements which could save over £10,000 a year and implemented them over the next two months.

Week Five
TUESDAY

Have you done the best work you are capable of?
Say 'yes' and the interviewer will think you're a 'has been'. Your focus on this question should be on how you could apply and develop your skills further.

I'm proud of my work achievements to date. But I believe the best is yet to come. I'm always motivated to give my best efforts and in this job there are always opportunities to contribute and improve.

In what ways has your job prepared you to take on greater responsibility?
The interviewer is looking for examples of professional development, perhaps to judge your future growth potential, so you must tell a story that demonstrates this.

When I first started, my boss would brief me daily. I made mistakes, learnt a lot and met all my deadlines. As time went by I took on greater responsibilities. Now I meet with her weekly to discuss any strategic changes so that she can keep management informed. I think that demonstrates not only my growth but also the confidence my manager has in my judgement and ability to perform consistently above standard.

In what ways have you achieved your goals?

What has made you successful in your current position?
Here the interviewer is trying to find out not just what, but how. You may want to talk about your influencing skills, your persistence, your understanding of the business needs, timing or whatever else has made you successful.

I believe my success is due to my ability to recognise who it is I need to get on my side. I then start to influence them by identifying the business benefits and get them to sponsor the

TUESDAY
Week Five

project at the highest level. I keep these people constantly updated on progress, giving them an opportunity to continue to contribute by challenging the blocks I experience.

What problems have you met in relationships with your present colleagues and what techniques have you developed to overcome them?

We only achieve things in organisations through other people, but often we do experience blocks of some kind. This doesn't mean that the interviewer expects problems with the role or your relationships; it means they are trying to uncover what strategies you have for dealing with disappointments, blocks, obstacles or the culture of the organisation in which you have worked. You should be honest and positive about how you have tackled these; you may want to include a bit about your learning.

My role was about change and I knew there would be resistance. The resistance I experienced was subtle – it involved only giving me a part of the story, not following through on actions and undermining me with colleagues. The best technique I found for dealing with this was by recording on paper all key conversations where decisions were made, giving timescales for action. I would then distribute them to all the other key stakeholders. It seemed to work. My colleagues understood that I would not lie down and accept their behaviour and they changed. This isn't my preferred style but I adapted my style to the people and the situation.

What are the most difficult decisions you have made in the last six months? What made them difficult?

Your interviewer is interested in what you find difficult and wherever possible you should balance this with a strength. You may want to talk about managing people, or others'

Week Five
TUESDAY

expectations or that you have stretch goals and this challenges you in terms of prioritising.

Due to the cost of savings which had to be achieved, I needed to make a member of my team redundant. It was a very tough decision as she made a valuable contribution to the team, but I just needed to find a more cost-effective way to deliver. My biggest challenge was to communicate this to her in a way she understood and was not too damaging. I think I achieved this through careful planning and preparation.

How do you feel about your progress to date?
This question is not only about your progress but also asks you to rate your self-esteem. Be positive. Help the interviewer believe you see each day as an opportunity to learn and contribute. That you see their organisation's environment being conducive to your best efforts.

In looking back over my career I am very pleased about my progress, I have achieved all that I have set myself and more. I have identified opportunities that would stretch and develop me and been pleased with my achievements. I am now seeking to maintain this momentum.

Why did you leave?

Questions on the decisions you made that prompted you to seek a change in your role or organisation should be answered with a degree of caution. Many people, when answering these questions fall into the trap of focusing on what wasn't right rather than what was. Focus on the 'pulls' (what drove you forward) rather than the 'pushes' (what made you want to leave).

TUESDAY

Week Five

Pull factors

- seeking fresh challenge
- new organisation/ products
- working with new people
- belief in vision

Push factors

- boredom
- relationship with boss
- asked to resign
- redundancy

What made you leave – after 10 years with them?
Here the underlying question is 'what went wrong?'
Organisations are now looking for a mixture of loyalty and exposure to different environments, cultures, projects and people. In answering this question you have to walk the fine line between demonstrating this loyalty and commitment whilst seeking fresh challenges and being flexible and adaptable. Make sure that you also pace

Week Five
TUESDAY

whatever moves you have made within a context of a long term strategy, even if it didn't feel that at the time – every move should be seen as moving towards a career goal.

I wanted a position that would give me more responsibility, a position in which I could put into practice what I had been learning. I recognised that this wasn't available to me at . . .

What do you want from your next job that isn't in your current position?
This question has a slight twist in its tail. It should always be answered positively and be tailored to the position you are applying for.

An opportunity to apply my . . . skills in a new team, with a different set of customers and in a different environment. The challenge will come from all those changes. I know I can make a contribution and from what you've been describing, it sounds even more exciting.

Why have you applied for this job?
This is one question you should expect, if it doesn't come in this form, it may be couched in *why* . . . (the organisation)? You need to be sure of 'why' as it will be obvious from your body language if you are not convinced, committed or clear. Your reasons may be opportunity, challenge, and association.

From all I know about the role, it is exactly what I am looking for. My knowledge of your organization from talking to employees and reading the literature you sent, tells me it is somewhere I would fit in particularly well.

Week Five
TUESDAY

> *Case history* – One candidate when asked why he wanted to be an accountant, responded, 'Well, I don't really, but I've been told it's a good profession and it pays well. I think you're a good company to work for'. He didn't get the job!

Training and qualifications

Interviewers tend not to make assumptions on the basis of people's qualifications because they are more interested in people's competence. Competence relates to the skills, knowledge and behaviours which, combined, produce the required results. This generally reflects a shift from the concept of education to the concept of learning: from input (classroom-based learning) to outputs (self-paced learning, coaching); from becoming qualified to continuous professional development. You will probably be asked less about the institutions or courses you've attended, and more about how you have applied your learning.

What have you done since you first qualified to keep your knowledge up to date?

The interviewer is keen to understand how you are continually updating yourself to the external environment. You can demonstrate this in a range of ways – books, coaching, shadowing, conferences, project groups, training courses, professional associations, journals, the Internet. Make sure you give a balanced response. Present yourself as someone who has taken responsibility for their own development and seeks regular opportunities to learn.

I read journals and papers. I attend workshops through the Institute. I seek opportunities to work alongside people I feel I can learn from and attend courses and conferences.

TUESDAY

Which of your qualifications do you see as relevant to this post, and how?
In answering this question you need to think carefully about what skills this role requires. If it's a technical role, then you should refer to your technical qualifications and experience. If it's more a management role, then refer to whatever training or qualifications you have. Do not be put off if you don't have formal qualifications. Talk through your learning.

My degree, whilst some time ago, has given me a good grounding in the principles, models and practice of . . . Whilst I have studied for my Masters and a Diploma in Management Studies, the qualifications most relevant to the role are not so much of the accredited type, but more to do with 10 years of success in the role with achievements both personal and professional.

Whtat important changes are taking place in your field? Do you consider them to be good or bad?
This question tests how up to date you are, so you may want to clarify it in terms of your function or sector. They are also asking for your opinion, which is a little more tricky; all you can do is be honest. Your interviewer is not wanting someone who sits on the fence, but if there are good and bad points you should state them. Think about what 'good' and 'bad' means to you, and what they might mean to the interviewer.

Competence

As we mentioned previously, competencies are now commonplace in most organisations. They don't simply focus on *what* you do, but *how* you do it.

Week Five
TUESDAY

Competencies make the interview process much more focused and less dependent on the intuition and gut reaction of the interviewer. The competencies for the role are normally available to applicants. If you haven't received these then do request them as they are an essential part of your preparation. By reading them, you will get an idea of the culture and what is important to the organisation. You can then frame your answers to reflect this.

Competencies may also include characteristics such as resilience and influence. The questions you may be asked in order to uncover these areas of competence may be:

Resilience

- How do you bounce back after a setback?
- How would I know you were under pressure?
- In what ways has your boss disappointed you?
- What does resilience mean to you?
- When have you demonstrated resilience?

Relate your answers to your own experience and related aspects of your work, not how you recovered after having a puncture on the way to an airport.

Influencing

- Describe a time when you got the solution you wanted.
- Whose support have you found elusive and why?
- How do you influence others?
- Tell me when you persuaded someone senior to do something they were unwilling to do.
- How would I know you were trying to change my mind? I have a preferred candidate for this role – change my mind.
- Which areas of influence challenge you most?

TUESDAY

Summary

Today, we have concentrated on the questions concerned with: *Can you do the job?* Think about what you've done and how you've applied your learning:

- Sell yourself.
- Make sure your words complement what you have said on paper.
- Present your career in a logical, planned and progressive manner.
- Convince the interviewer that you can do the job.
- Present your learning in terms of competence, not solely formal qualifications.
- Use transferable skills.

These questions offer you an opportunity to sell yourself to the organisation. Be focused and clear, and sell yourself as just the person they are seeking. Tomorrow we will begin to help you understand how best to answer more personal questions.

WEDNESDAY

Week Five

Who are you?

You should now be confident about describing what you have done in your career, and be able to talk convincingly about your experience, skills, competence and qualifications. Today considers who you are in terms of:

- self assessment
- personality
- achievements
- strengths and weaknesses
- perceptions
- leisure

Interviewers want you to bring to life the person you presented in your CV or application letter. Depending on the type of job, they will need to know if you are a team player or a loner, a concrete thinker or an ideas person.

WEDNESDAY

They will be constantly asking themselves – is this the kind of person we need for the post?

Interviewer's objectives	Interviewee's objectives
• Are you easy to get to know? • Can you talk about yourself? • Does your personality fit?	• Be honest and open. • Be able to describe myself succinctly. • Portray my personality accurately.

We would encourage you to give an assessment of yourself which shows a confident and informed individual. Dependent on the post, this is also the chance to describe your life outside the job. Be intuitive: put yourself in the interviewer's shoes. You want the interviewer to feel that you can get along with them and their organisation. This is your opportunity to make the most of yourself. The skill is to get the balance right. The way you talk about yourself and your work; your team's and your organisation's achievements, your work and leisure.

Self assessment

Self knowledge is increasingly important in the world of work. You are expected to know yourself – your skills, characteristics and limitations. You are expected to understand what impact these may have on your performance and, of course, be seeking to develop and improve. The interviewer will be interested in how you manage self-assessment questions. For your part you need to think about the *you* you want to present. Some people find all the questions that ask them to describe themselves *tough*. If this is you, it is well worth spending some time analysing your anxiety and working out ways to combat it. The key to overcoming anxiety is planning and practice, so think about your responses in advance and practise saying them out loud.

Anxiety	**Solution**
Once I start talking, I won't know when to stop.	Write the main points and time yourself as you say them – aim for no more than 2 minutes.
I've nothing to say about myself.	Complete the sentence 'I am . . .' at least 50 times and then assess your responses.
How can I know what they want?	Go back to your earlier research and note the type of person you would be looking for to fill the post. Pick out what relates to you.
They will think I am being arrogant.	They want you to be confident about yourself and aware of who you are. Select truthful evidence.

It is certain that these kinds of questions will emerge at some stage during the interview, so overcome your anxiety if it exists. Be proud of who you are, and what you have achieved, and present it in a way that convinces the interviewer. Use every source of information to inform your preparation. Ask colleagues for feedback, look over the

WEDNESDAY

comments from your appraisals, think about projects you were particularly proud of or enjoyed. If you have completed tests, these may help. All these sources say something about who you are. Also think about examples to back up statements, as your interviewers will be interested in how you present the evidence. Self-assessment questions come in a variety of forms, the most common ones are:

- Tell me about yourself.
- How would you describe yourself?
- What are you like as a person?
- How would your colleagues describe you?

It is worth experimenting with different statements to describe who you are. Take a couple of sentences from your 'I am' list and play around with them: *I am an ideas person . . . I am easy going . . . I am in charge of the catering outlet . . . I enjoy challenges . . .*

Now start to flesh out your statements with examples that demonstrate how they relate to the job and the organisation. Create a sense of your value to the potential employer and the benefits you can offer. Prepare a statement that is powerful, accurate and that demonstrates what differentiates you from other candidates:

I am creative and identify unconventional ways of tackling a situation. At . . ., I often put forward suggestions that saved the company time and money, whilst preserving the company image.

Answers to these questions will flow with practice. The skill is to make them relevant to your role and your interviewer.

Week Five

WEDNESDAY

Personality

You may be asked some questions that relate to specific personality types and traits which are considered necessary for the post. For example, if you are applying to manage a remote location, you will need to have a degree of independence; for a customer relations post, you will need to demonstrate tolerance and patience. Consider how the personality traits on the next page apply to you and the jobs you want.

However you describe your personality, be sure to have substantive examples and, wherever possible, give times and benefits:

I pride myself on my ability to act on my own initiative. We were keen to take on a project to assess waste management. There was no spare money to do this so I spoke to various local organisations to arrange a sponsorship programme.

Week Five
WEDNESDAY

Personality traits

Independence	Making decisions without supervision or reference.
Patience	Calm and prepared to wait for the right time and place.
Integrity	Takes responsibility for own actions, good and poor.
Judgement	Evaluates data and courses of action rationally.
Adaptability	Responds effectively to change.
Compliance	Adheres to company policy/procedures.
Tenacity	Demonstrates staying power in challenging situations.
Commitment	Belief in job/role and its value to the company.
Decisive	Readiness to take actions and make decisions.
Dependability	Staying power and stamina.
Confidence	Calmly aware and comfortable with who you are.

Here are some other questions to think through.

What are your likes?
This is a rather vague question, but it may be chosen in contrast to what you are like as a person to see how you respond.

I like challenges. I always set personal goals to try and push myself that bit further and to feel I've achieved something.

WEDNESDAY — Week Five

What are your dislikes?
This inevitably follows 'what are your likes'. The interviewer may be wanting to know how compatible your personal values are with the role.

Be wary of criticising your former boss and colleagues, or implying that you were unhappy about working hard, doing boring tasks or dealing with the less pleasant aspects of your work. Also steer clear of launching into a tirade about dislikes of pot noodles and other trivia.

I try to be honest and act with integrity. I dislike it when others lie, blame or don't show the same commitment to the task or the company as I do.

How have you benefited from your disappointments?
Disappointments are different from failures. It is an intelligent interviewer who asks this question. The question itself is very positive – it enables you to talk about what you have learnt from your setbacks and how it has changed your approach.

I treat disappointments as learning: I look at what has happened, why it happened and how I would do things differently at each stage should I face the same situation again.

Be yourself when you are answering these questions. After all, it's not just what you say, it's the way that you say it. Part of your personality will shine through as you utter your response. Notice whether your body language complements or refutes your descriptions. It is no good suggesting that patience is one of your qualities if your foot is tapping in anticipation of the next question or, when talking about your energy and enthusiasm, you talk into your chest with a sullen expression.

Week Five
WEDNESDAY

Strengths and limitations

It is well recognised that people have both strengths and limitations. There will be parts of your personality that support you and other parts that trip you up. Interviewers ask about strengths and limitations as another way of assessing your knowledge of yourself, your honesty and your objectivity. They may also talk about weaknesses, areas for improvement or personal development.

Before the interview you should spend some time thinking about the characteristics that you make successful in everything you undertake. What has contributed to making you who you are today? It helps enormously if you can portray a sense of self worth and confidence in what you do well. If you can excite the interviewer with your enthusiasm, they will assume you can do the same with their internal and external customers.

Week Five
WEDNESDAY

I pride myself on being able to build rapport quickly with new people. In fact at . . . I was often asked to take visitors around the plant because the MD knew I would make them feel welcome and important.

Think through examples of your strengths balanced against the expectations for the job. For example, a manager might be expected to have strengths in planning, delegating, budgeting, time management, influencing people and managing relationships.

The interviewer will also expect you to give examples of how you are working to improve your limitations. Think about how you might have held yourself back in your career and your achievements. What has led you to feel frustrated and unhappy at work? You may come across some familiar areas for development that you can usefully admit to in an interview. Do remember that limitations can simply be the reverse side of a strength:

My eye for detail can be a great strength in designing copy, but a limitation when I'm managing people as I need to be convinced that everything is as it should be.

You have choices in presenting your limitations – you could focus on those strictly related to the post:
I am not familiar with the software you use. I became proficient with our present scheme in about 3 weeks and I'm sure I could do so with yours.

Or you can relate to your personality:
I am very particular about the way work goes out to clients. In my last appraisal we discussed the way this sometimes slows down output. We also agreed that without such attention to detail our

Week Five
WEDNESDAY

consistency and accuracy could be affected. I am working on finding a more balanced approach.

Some questions refer indirectly to strengths and limitations:

- Tell me about the last time you didn't delegate work to a subordinate and you were left handling a disproportionate amount of the workload?
- How did you feel about it?
- How did you handle the situation differently next time?

What are the most difficult situations you've faced?
How do you define 'difficult'? You must have a story ready for this one in which the situation was both tough and flexible enough to allow you to show yourself in a good light. Avoid talking about matters to do with other people. You can talk about a difficult decision to fire someone, but emphasise that once you had examined the problem and reached a conclusion you acted quickly and professionally, with the best interests of the company at heart.

What do you not have that we need for this post?
This is an easy response.
I think my skills match your requirements. I need more detailed product knowledge and experience of the company procedure.

Achievements

Achievements should be easy to identify. There is always something in our careers or lives that we feel particularly proud of: a project completed on time and budget against all odds; a crisis averted, people you managed, a bid that you won, a person you influenced. In fact, anything that

WEDNESDAY

Week Five

had a happy ending. You should judge the merits of sticking to job-related accomplishments or whether it is appropriate to expand into your life outside the workplace.

I was proud to be part of the team that successfully guided the company towards a quality award.

I raised £ . . . for charity running in the London Marathon. I also picked up some business from my fellow runners along the way.

What has been your most creative achievement at work?

Although I feel my biggest achievements are still ahead of me, I am proud of my involvement in . . . with . . . I made my contribution as part of that team and learned a lot in the process. We succeeded through hard work, concentration and an eye for the bottom line.

What makes you stand out from the crowd?
A simple question, but it requires some thought. You can answer it in terms of increased revenues, decreased

operational costs, streamlined work flow. You may also want to think in terms of your characteristics.

I have a great track record for assuming responsibilities above and beyond the call of duty and I'm always willing to go the extra mile to get the job done well.

This reveals focus, direction, a sense of strength and determination. There are many different styles of 'achievement' questions: *Tell me about some of the toughest groups that you have had to get co-operation from. Did you have any formal authority? What did you do?*

Perceptions

Once you have given an account of your ideas about yourself, you are likely to be asked what other people think of you. Take care not to be flippant or to regurgitate what you have already said. Also be mindful that some of the people mentioned may have written, or be about to write, your references. It is important to be consistent. Ideally it would be good to check with your referees what they might write. Where that is not possible try to recall conversations and appraisal discussions you have had with them. You may be asked a selection of the following questions:

- How might your current colleagues describe you?
- What would your boss tell me about you?
- What is likely to be in your references?
- How would your staff describe you?
- How might one of your closest friends describe you?
- How might your worst enemy describe your character?

WEDNESDAY

Week Five

In my last appraisal my manager said how much he appreciated my candidness. He knows that I think very carefully before giving feedback and then do so in a professional way.

My staff know that I represent them positively in any organisational issues that may concern them. I know from feedback at appraisals that they trust me to keep their interests at the top of my agenda.

We can never underestimate the power of perceptions. Remember our comments from Monday that the perception people have of you will count. Anxiety can create the wrong impression, so by managing your anxiety you should be better able to manage perceptions.

Leisure

Leisure is a very important part of who you are. Because of the nature of the commitment that work now demands, interviewers are wanting to hear about the balance you strive for, to preserve your energy, or simply recuperate and switch off from the challenges of the day. It also gives the interviewer a fuller picture of who you are outside work. The following questions are a selection of those you may be asked:

- If you were on a desert island, what book would you take and why?
- What was the last book you read/film you saw and how did it affect you?
- How do you relax?
- What do you do for your holidays?
- What do you do in the evenings and weekends?

Week Five
WEDNESDAY

Be prepared for these questions. It makes sense to decide before the interview whether there is a particular film or book you want to mention because it says something about you that you want to convey.

Do you escape into thrillers and spy stories, or immerse yourself in science fiction? You may be a fan of the classics or poetry, romance, politics or sport.

Many people enjoy personal development books or tapes – there are no right or wrong answers, and these are not trick questions. Having said that, it is crucial that you have read or seen whatever you discuss so that you can talk about it with knowledge and enthusiasm.

> *Case history:* We spoke to one candidate who, at interview, enthused about *Pride and Prejudice* and was asked if they had read *Middlemarch*. They replied honestly, 'no', and were relieved when the interviewer suggested that it was a book they thought the candidate would thoroughly enjoy. Imagine the embarrassment if they had said 'yes', and then been expected to discuss it.

How do you wind down after a busy and pressured time at work? With increasing awareness of the long-term effects of stress, enlightened employers are recognising the importance of recovery time for their staff. It is important to demonstrate that you know how to look after yourself and keep yourself mentally and physically agile.

I work away a lot and take care that I either go for a swim, a sauna or a long walk around the hotel to make a break from the office environment.

WEDNESDAY

Whatever you do or choose to refer to, make sure it involves doing something constructive and worthwhile, and wherever possible focus on transferable skills.

Summary

Today focuses on all the dimensions that make you unique. It is your opportunity to be proud of your achievements and honest about where there is room for improvement. Feel free to talk about your ambitions and ideas for the future. They won't be used against you, they help to understand you as a person rather than just another job applicant.

Start to collect comments that people make about you and notice how you feel about yourself in a structured way. Create a portfolio of ideas that would fit into this part of the interview. Read through it regularly and think what it says about you. That way you will have material from which to select appropriately, whatever interview you attend.

Who are you?

- Present yourself confidently.
- Write a profile statement and practise saying it.
- Prepare for questions, which are about you the person.
- Identify what makes you different – your unique selling point.
- Think through your achievements.
- Research how other people perceive you.
- How do you relax?

Week Five
WEDNESDAY

Whilst today has been focused on what makes you tick, tomorrow is more work related: why do you want the job and how will you do it?

Week Five

THURSDAY

How will you do the job?

Yesterday we concentrated on giving the interviewer an impression of *who you are*. We hope that you are feeling more confident about the more intimate aspects of yourself. Today we will take this a step further. It is not just you or your skills, experience and knowledge that the interviewer is interested in, they are also interested in how these interrelate – *how do you do the job*. You may have experienced situations when you've planned something well – all the component parts are great – but when you mix them together, things go disastrously wrong. You may be a brilliant candidate, with all the essential and desirable characteristics and experience, but your interviewer may sense your methods of working do not mach those of your prospective boss or department. Where this type of conflict is not constructive, it can be costly.

Interviewer's objectives	Interviewee's objectives
• What is your management style? • What motivates you? • How do you motivate others? • How does this fit with the culture? • What blocks might you experience? • How does your style complement others?	• Articulate my style with examples. • Clearly state what I want from work. • Demonstrate how I manage my team. • Express how I could add value. • Describe my fit and flexibility. • Show how my style complements others.

Week Five

THURSDAY

Today we will guide you through the relevant questions:

- Why this job?
- What motivates you?
- What is your management style?
- How will you do the job?

Why this job?

Why do you want this job? is a predictable interview question. It may not be quite so direct but at some point during the interview it will emerge. Consider the different ways of answering it.

Because it ...

- was advertised
- matches my skills
- is the right time to be moving
- appealed to me

I was ...

- excited by the advertisement
- seeking a challenge
- planning my next move

The 'because it' column has more of the 'push' factors that we mentioned on Tuesday; the 'I was' column contains more of the 'pull' factors. There is only a slight difference in the response, but if you choose your words carefully you sound planned, focused and proactive.

This only becomes a tough question when you haven't thought through your response. Is it a question you have ever seriously asked yourself? This is a good opportunity to work out what makes a job appealing to you and what

THURSDAY

Week Five

might lessen its attraction. We are suggesting three key areas for you to think about:

- identity
- values
- preferred environment

Identity

We often frame our understanding of our identity around what we do, rather than who we are. This is why yesterday we took you through a step-by-step approach to understanding yourself. When you describe yourself to a stranger you may say: *I'm a team leader, a programmer, a manager*. Much of our status comes from our title. We like shorthand ways to describe ourselves but this only conveys a part of the picture – the what rather than the how. There is a huge difference between identifying yourself as a project manager or as the central coordinator for large-scale capital projects. Think through how you would respond to the following questions:

Week Five

THURSDAY

- How would you describe yourself?
- Who do you want to be when you are at work?
- Which are your favourite roles?

Companies have identities, too, and these give employees and customers a clear idea of what to expect from them. Where there is a strong figurehead as founder, that person often incorporates their identity and values into the organisation. Take care to check that the external identity which attracts you to an organisation is applied to the staff too. For example, it would be inconsistent of an educational organisation to advocate strongly the importance of lifelong learning whilst blocking its staff from attending development courses for themselves. You should work on a snappy response to the question *What kind of organisation do you want to work with?* Think broader than *I want to work in pharmaceuticals* or *I want to work in retailing* as there are many companies to choose from. What differentiates them surrounds the *how* questions – the way in which they achieve their objectives. *I want to work in a company that recognises and rewards a job well done.*

Values

Your values relate to what is important to you when you are at work. A key value might be security. If this describes you, then an organisation with a low staff turnover and good pension may suit you. If you value variety, then a job that sends you around the world to buy products may appeal to you. It may be that what matters most to you is a sense of 'celebrity', and so the opportunity to represent your organisation at a national level would be exciting and

Week Five

THURSDAY

stimulating. Conversely, if this doesn't fit, you will be thrown into panic, anxiety or sheer terror at the thought of working in that environment. Think through the answers to the following questions:

- What matters to you when you are at work?
- Why do you go to work?

Whatever your values, you will enjoy your job much more if they are matched at work.

Preferred environment

This refers to where you are and who you are with. The comfort and safety of your surroundings make a big difference to job satisfaction and achievement. Think about what effect different work environments have had on you and which aspects you would like in any future jobs. Is it important to be able to work in natural light or more significant to have your own desk or office? You may also want to consider any environmental factors, such as transport, housing and schooling that affects you and your family.

Now you have a clear idea of what you are looking for in a job, you can start to form some answers to the following questions.

Why do you want to work for us? What makes you think you're right for the job? What makes this the right job for you?

I want to work for an organisation that is committed to staff involvement at all levels. I know that you have installed a rigorous 360° appraisal scheme and that you have acted positively on the feedback you have received.

Week Five
THURSDAY

When I rang your department for the annual figures, I was impressed by the friendliness of the administrator I spoke to. I rang back for some fairly obscure data and felt that my request was treated seriously. That is just one example of the way I like to deal with people. I feel I would fit into this organisation.

In the examples above you are reinforcing how you do your job by talking about what you know about the organisation. In a very subtle way you have communicated aspects of yourself. At the same time, with this as with the following question, we would always advocate honesty.

What is most important to you in a job? What would make the ideal employer for you?

The most important aspect of a job is that I am able to work at my own pace and in my own space. I am a specialist in my commercial field and I have learned over the years to trust my intuition. My work is highly regarded throughout the industry and I wish to stay pre-eminent. It follows that my ideal employer would be someone prepared to nurture my creativity and appreciate my need for space. I enjoy working in organisations where my thoroughness is valued and appreciated.

Management styles

Management style has changed over the last decade. There are many terms used to describe recent management style, including the following:

- Coaching – let's find a solution together.
- Organic – change as a process rather than event.
- Empowerment – working with, accountability, responsibility.
- Quality – how can we improve?
- Customer focus – listening, understanding, responding.
- Learning company – acquiring new knowledge and skills.

For most organisations, language such as *do as I say* is now abhorrent. Change is something which is embraced, rather than opposed, and the quality of working relationships is seen as the key to achievement. From your research you should have some idea about the organisation's style of management:

- How do they describe their management style?
- What do they refer to in their competencies?
- What do you pick up through their literature?

It is quite normal to have a series of questions about your management style. However, interviewers are not interested in your theoretical perspective but how you put the theory

Week Five

THURSDAY

into practice. So prepare your answers. If you talk about empowerment, tell them how you do it and with what results.

What kind of people do you find it difficult to work with? How have you worked successfully with these difficult people?
Watch out for these! There could be an assumption that you have some difficulties in your people management skills. It would be foolish to suggest that you never have challenges with people. Here you need to demonstrate tact, understanding and diplomacy without being sidetracked into a lengthy discussion of certain types of people.

Everyone had lost patience with one member of the team who always came up with why something wasn't good enough or couldn't possibly work. When I spent some time with her and told her that it appeared as if she was always putting our ideas down, she was horrified. She explained that she thought the team was working brilliantly and she wanted to use her attention to detail as a final checkpoint. We agreed that she would point out all the positives she associated with our projects and we would give her five minutes at the end of every team meeting to air her concerns. After that no one could have hoped for a more committed team member.

You have been given a project that required you to interact at different levels within the organisation. How do you do this? What levels are you most comfortable with?
This is a two-part question that probes communication and self-confidence. The first part indirectly asks how you interact with senior staff and motivate those working with and for you on a project. The second part of the question is saying: *Tell me whom you regard as your peer group – help me categorise you.*

Week Five
THURSDAY

Which management thinker has influenced your practice?
Be honest with this question. If the answer is 'no one' then state it. You may not be a great reader but something will have influenced your practice. You could interpret this question and talk about a manager you respect.

I have been most influenced by . . . their work had the most significant effect on my understanding of how I could make the difference and how I always needed to have my goal in mind.

I am not a great reader of management books. I have worked for many people who have influenced my practice, and through observation and discussion I have come to understand what goes on in their heads, and I have applied this to myself.

You may also be asked for your definitions of terms such as: 'co-operation', 'management' etc. You should have some definitions up your sleeve for this type of question. Avoid sounding textbook-based and wherever possible give examples.

Motivation

Questions about motivation are trying to uncover which forces determine what you want and need from your working life. These are sometimes referred to as 'drivers' and are sources of energy and direction that become obvious as people study the shape of their working lives. Research has identified nine distinct career drivers that can act as key motivators.

THURSDAY

Key drivers	Seeking
Power/influence	To be in control of people and resources.
Affiliation	To be part of the group, being popular.
Expertise	A high level of accomplishment in a specialised field.
Material rewards	Possessions, wealth and a high standard of living.
Creativity	To innovate and be identified with original work.
Autonomy	To be independent and able to make key decisions.
Security	A solid and predictable future.
Search for meaning	Doing things you believe are valuable for their own sake.
Status	To be recognised, admired and respected.

Adapted from Schein's career drivers

Take some time to think about which of these have motivated you in your career choices and decisions to date. How do they fit in with the opportunities offered by the types of jobs and organisations you are considering at present? Then think about the following set of questions.

What motivates you to put in your greatest effort at work?
What are the most important rewards you want from your career?

It is important to me that my work makes a positive contribution to the wider community. I want to work on issues that are important and do more than just promoting my career.

THURSDAY

Week Five

I want my products to have my 'name' on them and I want to be genuinely innovative in my work.

What was your least favourite position? What role did your boss play in your career at that point?

Here the interviewer is trying to uncover style-related issues, how you cope with a negatively-framed question and how you constructively criticise both your boss and the organisation. Be careful not to lay blame.

What I disliked most about my former company was the fact that it offered very little risk and reward. It was a very mature company with exceptionally long staff tenure. Working for the Sales Director had the most challenges. We worked very well together personally, but he needed to be much more proactive in terms of anticipating the workload. He prided himself in putting out fires. My style, conversely, was to forecast potential problems before they arose. It got very tiring after a while and took most of the fun out of coming to work every day.

Week Five

THURSDAY

You should also be prepared for questions along the lines of: *What is more important to you, pay or the type of job you are doing?* If you are applying for a job with a high element of commission, then you will do well with a 'materials reward' driver. If you are going for a more vocational type of job then 'search for meaning' or 'affiliation' is likely to be stronger.

Summary

Today, we have taken you through the questions relating to how you will do the job. We have given you some exercises to help you clarify and understand what matters to you at work and how you want to achieve it.

> **Why this job?**
> - identity
> - values
> - environment
>
> **What is your management style?**
> - theoretical understanding
> - examples of good practice
>
> **What motivates you?**
> - your driving forces

Tomorrow you will be looking at one of the most difficult issues to define, that of fit.

FRIDAY

Will you fit?

So you have convinced the interviewer that you can do the job. You have the necessary skills, knowledge, experience, training and, given the opportunity your behaviours, motivators, style and characteristics would help you do the job. The important question now is *Will you fit?*

Today, we will focus on convincing the interviewer that you will. The question of *fit* is being assessed from your very first exchange: from the style and language in your letter, your choice of clothes, your handshake, through to your degree of articulation and your understanding of the questions. Whilst this is, to some degree, a subconscious process, it is probably the most influential in decision making.

Will you fit?

- Scenarios.
- How long will you stay?.
- How much are you worth?.
- How does this role fit?.
- How do they fit? – your questions.

This is a key area for the interviewer to get right. In the main, they want to recommend the appointment of someone who will benefit the organisation, work well with the existing staff and embrace the culture. Sometimes, of course, they want just the opposite. You may be applying for a job that involves reducing staffing and making a unit mean, lean and cost effective. If that is so, make sure it fits you.

FRIDAY

The interviewer needs to achieve a good fit between the job role and the organisation's expectations. Someone with the personal and professional ability that matches the organisation's policies and management style. The better the fit, the more harmonious and effective the professional relationship.

Interviewer's objectives

- Do you fit the company image?
- How will you adapt to the culture?
- Would our clients want you at their meetings?
- Will you blend with the team?
- Could you represent us?

Interviewee's objectives

- Would I feel proud to be with this company?
- Will I want to talk about where I work?
- Will I wear the uniform with pride?
- Do I feel comfortable here?
- Could I represent them?

FRIDAY

These are probably the most important questions for the interviewer to find answers to as a wrong decision can be costly to the organisation in terms of time, energy, lost opportunities, internal and external relationship breakdowns. This is the final balancing act for the interviewer.

You must have been exposed to someone in your career who didn't fit, so you will understand at first hand what this feels like and the disruption it can cause. Therefore, the judgement of fit is the part of the interview process that interviewers are most cautious about. There are some sophisticated questions and situations that have been devised to gauge fit, but much of this part of the process remains instinctive. Decisions are often made on a 'gut' reaction or discussions that rest on perception rather than evidence. If there is ever a part of the process that interviewers will discuss at length, disagree on and even get second opinions on, it is fit.

In some cases it is obvious: the interviewer will know you will fit. Sometimes, they may make comments such as:

- . . . there was something about them . . .
- . . . I'm sure they could do the job . . .
- . . . I can't put my finger on it . . . or even
- . . . I'm not sure how they would fit . . .

As fit is so difficult to gauge, companies have devised their own sets of questions to help uncover whether your style, manner and character match theirs.

FRIDAY

> *Case history*: One of the companies we advised was receiving many complaints about the style and attitude of a senior manager. He was rude and unfeeling, with no interest in staff concerns. When he was employed, this organisation was overstaffed and running at a loss. He was brought in to stop the downward spiral. There was no room for sentiment and he achieved his objectives. Once the rot had stopped, his skills were inconsistent with the organisation's needs. Eventually he moved on to another 'troubleshooting' job. He no longer fitted in and rather than change his style, he moved on – a pattern he will often follow.

Scenarios

Increasingly, interviewers are making use of real life, relevant situations to check how you fit with their organisation. Most of the colleagues we talked to agreed that their most challenging and revealing questions were ones which asked the candidate to declare how they would react in a given scenario.

What would you do? questions can fall into two categories: hypothetical or real. They focus on how you would cope. The interviewer does not want to hear the answer *it depends* – they already know that. They want to know how you process information, what your first actions would be, who you would talk to . . . the list goes on. You have to think on your feet and put yourself in the interviewer's shoes. The context of their question should give you some understanding of what are they interested in so you can give them what they are looking for.

FRIDAY

Week Five

It's 8.00 a.m., your most prestigious client is due to arrive at 9.00 a.m. and the computer equipment for your presentation hasn't arrived. What do you do?

I think we've all faced situations like this. I always try to plan against anything like this happening by setting up presentations in advance and not leaving things to chance. But given this situation I would have the contact numbers for the people bringing the equipment. Then I could contact them and, if necessary, arrange for other equipment to be delivered.

What would you do? questions often bring a similar level of anxiety as the real situations. Don't slip into the easy trap of saying *panic* in reply. You may be thinking that, and many of these situations do create a level of anxiety, but remember your interviewer wants to hear how you would cope, what you would do and how you would deliver given the uncertainty and ambiguity that happens in everyday situations.

Every company has its own quirks. How dysfunctional was your last company, and how would you deal with a company's shortcomings and inconsistencies?

When we came across this question, from sample questions used by a large multinational company, it stopped us in our tracks. Remember, this is a *What would you do?* question. Beware of these questions as they are there to test your ability to remain objective and positive about your last organisation, and your interpretation of dysfunction – what it means to you, how you tackle organisational development issues. The list is endless, but your answer must remain succinct – so think carefully.

Week Five

FRIDAY

My last company was open about its dysfunctionality as it was the flip side of its effectiveness. The passion with which it attacked the business created a high degree of emotion in all functions. This led to a need to react very quickly when messages or changes were interpreted wrongly to prevent them spiralling out of control. In one case, for example, I called everyone to a short meeting to explain what had and hadn't already been decided by senior management.

You are chairing the monthly interdepartmental meeting. All is going well – except for the head of operations, a bright and ambitious woman. She keeps looking at her watch, sighing and whispering 'hurry up' when someone else speaks. Eventually she cracks and suggests you speed the meeting up – she has places to go, people to see.

I would want to tackle this in two ways. Firstly at the meeting by acknowledging her urgency and asking for her patience to listen to all contributions. I would also remind her of our agreed timings and that we would finish on time. My next step would be to talk to her alone outside the meeting, challenge her behaviour and ask for her ideas about reaching a workable solution.

Your success in answering all the *What would you do?* questions is to think about the interviewer's objectives and respond to these directly. Be honest, succinct, direct and help them understand how this relates to you generally.

How long will you stay?

Whilst interviewers have a current need, they will also be thinking about the future. The investment in the interview process or in consultant costs needs to demonstrate some return. So the questions which relate to how long will you stay or what you want to do next are important to the interviewer. A good fit is likely to encourage you to stay, and be a greater return on the investment.

How long will you stay with the organisation?
If the interviewer asks this question, they may be thinking of offering you a job. So build on this. You may want to end your answer with a question of your own that really puts the ball back in the interviewer's court.

I would really like an opportunity to make a contribution to the success of the organisation and could see where I could add value. I can operationalise strategies and love to learn. As long as I am growing professionally and challenged, there is no reason for me to make a move. How long do you think I would be challenged here?

Week Five
FRIDAY

Where do you see yourself in ten years time?
Questions such as this don't require you to make a long-term commitment to the organisation. They are probing your career ambitions and goals. Most managers would be expected to have thought through their career plans so that they could at least articulate a goal, although it is surprising how few can. This question is difficult to answer in terms of a role, but it's not asking that. It's asking you to consider where do you see yourself in terms of responsibilities, contribution to an organisation, work style etc.

Ten years ought to give me time to grow within an organisation like yours which provides the right nourishment, such as training and good management. I am ambitious and would be keen to reach my full potential which would be . . .

You may want to add: *It is reasonable to expect that other exciting opportunities will crop up in the meantime and I am always keen to apply my skills in different environments.*

The question may also be asked in the following way:

How would this post fit into your long-term career plans?

My plans have always been influenced by experiences and opportunities. I believe this post would be just right. I could use the skills I have developed and be sufficiently challenged to develop whilst learning from new people, processes and clients. I could then look forward to what opportunities my success in this role would bring.

How much do you think you are worth?

It is not uncommon to be asked to put a price on your head. You can quantify worth in many ways:

- the value you add
- your market value
- what you are paid at the moment, or
- how much the organisation is prepared to pay

Our advice would be start with a high figure and don't be afraid of negotiation. Many people find they undersell themselves because they are not ready for such a direct question, so don't fall into that trap. Be bold. It is not unreasonable to ask for 10–20% more than your current package – always quantify all your benefits: discounts, healthcare, pension, car allowance, shares, etc. when negotiating salary, as these could be worth more than you imagine.

FRIDAY

What salary do you require?

I am looking for something in the range of £x–£y. You don't need to go into any more detail than this. Do not answer this question with a question, such as *How much are you prepared to pay?*

How does this role fit?

You may be faced with questions you feel are only asked of you because of your gender, disability, ethnicity or sexual orientation. These are some of the more difficult questions to deal with as they challenge your fit, not on the basis of skills, experience or behaviour but because of who you are. The key to these questions is to understand the reason they are asked.

In the interviewee's seat it may feel as if you are being discriminated against; in the interviewer's seat it may be they genuinely want to know if you are a good person in whom to invest their time, training and money.

Keeping the interviewer's underlying question in mind, you will have some guidelines on how to answer. If you want the job, then you have to answer the question in a way that says: *yes, I am a good bet or a low risk.*

This style of question is disappearing, but every so often you will be faced with one that can 'wobble' you, not just for the duration of the question but beyond. You may also want to consider whether you would want to work for an employer that asks such questions as:

Week Five

FRIDAY

- What is your marital status?
- Are you in a long-term relationship?
- Whom do you live with?
- Do you plan to have a family? When?
- How many children do you have?
- What are your childcare arrangements?

For example, in response to the question: *What are your childcare arrangements?* you may choose to respond: *If you are asking would I be willing and able to travel as needed by the job, the answer is 'yes', I would just need some notice to make the necessary arrangements . . . I am willing to work overtime and have often stayed late to complete tasks.* This can come across better than a direct: *Would you ask that question of a man?*

Also, don't be surprised if you are asked for your birth certificate, passport, proof of qualifications, or any document containing your national insurance number. Legislative changes require employers to establish that each new employee, at whatever level, can legally work in the country. Every employee, even those at the most senior level, should be asked to produce evidence.

Do they fit? – your questions

The last time you bought a car or a house, did you ask about the financing, have it valued or investigate its reliability? We would hope that you did! We would suggest that your next carer move is at least as important. So if you want to impress your potential manager with your grasp of the position and knowledge of the organisation, it makes sense to draw up a list of questions. Asking good questions at an interview helps you get the information you need to make an intelligent decision; it also shows the interviewer that you've done your homework and are in a position to discuss the job's potential opportunities and challenges. Here are just a few questions you may want to think of asking:

Organisation

- What are the long-range plans?
- I consider your competitors to be . . . what do you think?
- What did you wish you knew about the organisation before you started?
- What values are sacred to the organisation?
- How are decisions made?
- What is the organisation's philosophy towards employees?

Success and measurement

- Could you give me examples of the best results the previous holders of this position have attained?
- What is your biggest problem and what role would I have in solving it?

Development opportunities

- What opportunities of advancement are there for me?
- How are staff developed from this post?
- Why did this post become vacant?

The interviewer

- What are your key selection criteria for the post?
- How long have you worked here? In what capacities?
- How do you allocate and review work?

FRIDAY

Asking articulate and well-thought-through questions leaves a good impression on your interviewer. It's a great opportunity to professionally challenge the interviewer and be remembered. Try to avoid going over old information and remember this is not the appropriate place to talk through terms and conditions – this leaves the interviewer with the impression that this is all you are interested in.

Summary

Today we have addressed the issue of *fit*. The interviewer wants to find out if you are the right person for the job not just in terms of what you can do but how you do it. You also want to assess how they and the organisation fit your needs and requirements.

- How could you fit into their scenarios?
- Are you a worthwhile investment?
- Do they meet your requirements?

So far this week we have developed your understanding of how to respond to tough interview questions. Tomorrow we will help you put the finishing touches to your preparation by focusing on you.

Week Five

SATURDAY

Are you ready?

At this stage of the week we expect you to feel more confident about tackling tough interview questions. Only you will understand what makes you feel supremely confident. We have attempted to prepare you by looking at the interview from different perspectives. Perhaps the most important perspective is to put yourself in the shoes of the interviewer, to understand their motives for asking the questions, and to respond appropriately. Remember, your interviewer thinks you can do the job and they want to help you bring your application to life.

Today is about bringing all your preparation together and harnessing all your inner resources to ensure that you are ready and raring to go when the next interview arrives.

Are you ready?
- Rehearsing your responses.
- Preparing your thoughts.
- Focusing on your outcome.
- Relaxing before the event.
- Is this the job for you?
- Tackling tough interview questions.

We have focused throughout the week on your responses to tough interview questions. Preparing what you are going to say and how you are going to say it are equally important.

Have you ever been in a situation in which you've wanted to listen to someone because they know their subject or you respect their opinions? Try as you might, you've been unable to give them your full attention. Their delivery has undermined the message. This could happen to you, too. You can prevent this happening to you by spending time rehearsing. Prepare yourself so that every aspect of what you say convinces and engages your audience.

Your objectives

- get myself as ready as i can
- put all my preparation into practice
- imagine and rehearse my success
- draw on and recognise all my resources

Rehearsing your responses

What makes a great performance? Whatever the context in which you practice sport, art, craft, business, there are some essential components: skill, understanding the criteria for

Week Five
SATURDAY

success, practice and learning. The interview is just the same. Whilst our comments this week have focused on developing your skills and understanding the criteria for success, do not underestimate the importance of practice, feedback and learning.

Saying your responses out loud, asking a trusted friend to be your interviewer, working with a coach, taping yourself, can all help. Physically saying the words will give you a sense of their impact, as some of your answers may look better than they sound! Rehearsal takes planning and effort, so be sure to give yourself time and don't be put off by the fact that it may be embarrassing. It's better to be embarrassed in front of a colleague or friend, where the cost is personal, than in front of the interviewer where the cost may include prospects and earning potential. We like the notion: *The more I practice the luckier I get*, a response golfer Gary Player made to a shout of *lucky shot*.

Often, a bad day experience, when broken down into its component parts, does not seem so bad after all. A bad experience can affect you and it can leave you expecting the worst to happen. This can send your self-esteem plummeting, with far reaching consequences. If you're struggling with some of these thoughts, you need to exorcise them by exposing them to the light of rational thought. Balance your thoughts on what could go wrong with what will go right. When you think positively, you behave positively and it shows.

Week Five
SATURDAY

The following questions may help your rehearsal:

	Worst interview to date	**Best interview to date**
How did you prepare?	....	....
What did you feel about the job?	....	....
What did you notice on arrival?	....	....
What did you do well?	....	....
What could you have done differently?	....	....

Preparing your thoughts

Many of our comments this week have been based on logical, practical and analytical assumptions. Some commentators refer to this as 'left brain' activity. Whilst it's likely that much of an interview will also be based there, remember the other side, your right brain activity. This is the source of your imagination and creativity. Your ability to demonstrate your creativity is as important to your success. It's part of your uniqueness. You can also harness your imagination to create the interview in which you feel at your best.

Think for a moment about the notion of beginner's luck. No one has told them how difficult it is to succeed and they have no prior memory of doing it well or badly. In fact if they believe in beginner's luck, they will expect to do well the first time. Then, depending on their beliefs, they go on and build on their success – or they become gradually worse. Our ability to achieve excellence or perform well is dependent on how well we believe we can do.

Poor performers

- It was a fluke
- It won't last
- I always mess up

Good performers

- I can make this a success
- I can keep doing this well
- I always do well

You can make or break an interview just by talking to yourself in the above way. You know what you say to yourself and how to mentally prepare yourself for the task ahead. We would recommend the following:

- encourage yourself
- tell yourself you can do it
- think about previous successes
- focus on what success could bring

SATURDAY

It may help you to develop affirmations: short, positively-focused statements that introduce and reinforce the way you want to be. They are always stated in the present or present continuous tense as if they already exist. They work on the premise that thoughts create experience and keep the mind programmed in the positive. As you repeat them regularly, so you will believe them and your mind will focus on what you want.

Write and repeat your own affirmations about the interview and the new post you are aiming for:

Example affirmations:

- I always do well at interview.
- I enjoy the opportunity to tackle tough interview questions.
- Every day brings a new and welcome challenge.

Also remind yourself that the interviewer doesn't hold all the trump cards. Put yourself in their shoes and you'll realise that they have as much at stake in the interview as you. What if they appoint the wrong person? They are probably under as much pressure as you are because they can't afford to make a bad decision.

Focus on your outcome

There are examples from many walks of life which suggest that if you focus on your outcome and imagine yourself having succeeded or being successful you will achieve whatever you set out to achieve. Setting goals focuses your attention and action. With clear goals you are more likely to engage in purposeful behaviour. When you know what you want, you are more likely to pursue it. With realistic and

Week Five

SATURDAY

specific goals you know what you are aiming for; with no goals you have no target.

So start this process by thinking what you want your outcome to be and create some affirmations to achieve it.

Exercise

- Find a place where you can sit or lie down for a few uninterrupted minutes.
- Close your eyes and create your ideal interview.
- Start from the night before. See and feel yourself relaxed and sleeping well.
- Wake up feeling energetic and keen to be there.
- Imagine yourself arriving for the interview.
- Feel calm and confident as you enter the building.
- Tell yourself how well prepared you are and ready to enjoy the interview.
- You are treated with respect and feel comfortable.
- You know you are performing well.
- Experience the interview going the way you want.
- See yourself leave the interview with a sense of satisfaction and achievement.
- Open your eyes and enjoy your positivity.

SATURDAY

Relaxing before the event

We would encourage everyone reading this book to take or create some form of relaxation before an interview. How you relax is your choice. You will know what works for you. For some this may mean activity: a visit to the gym, swimming, a round of golf, gardening, walking the dog. For others it may mean inactivity, stopping the round of activities which make up a normal day and spending time with family, friends or partners. Or taking time on your own to read, listen to music, write letters or do nothing. What matters is that you do something that relaxes you.

When you are relaxed and not overly tired, you are much more able to deal with situations as they emerge. You are much less likely to make mistakes as you will be alert. Your words and actions will support rather than contradict each other. Also decide how you approach the interview, otherwise all your preparation and relaxation would be in vain. Picture the two scenes below:

Scene 1	Scene 2
• Work until midnight the night before.	• Complete preparation the previous day.
• Haven't received a map.	• Ring to check details – location.
• Decide to set off, will ring on approach.	• Decide to travel by train.
• Arrive in town with just 15 minutes to spare.	• Plan to arrive with hour to spare.
• Car park is 10 minute walk.	• Have lunch on site.
• A queue at security of 20 people.	• Meet employees, talk about company.

Which scene would you prefer? Just reading Scene 1 can raise your anxiety. Imagine how you would fare walking into an interview with that as your build up. Creating your own Scene 2 is not about luck, it is down to planning and preparation and if you want to do well, don't leave it to chance! We would encourage you to leave time to relax and not to be distracted by tasks or people. This time is important to your success.

Is this the job for you?

As we saw yesterday, the fit issue affects both parties. You may be ideal for the company, but are they the perfect match for you?

> **Will they**
>
> - support your development?
> - look good on your CV?
> - offer good prospects for the future?
> - fit with your style?
>
> **Will the job**
>
> - be sufficiently challenging?
>
> **How will you**
>
> - complement the team?
> - add value?

If your answers to any of the above questions are not clear then you should check your goals and motivation. One of the major factors that can influence whether the job is for

SATURDAY
Week Five

you will be your relationship with your boss. We would recommend that you never accept a position without an interview with your immediate manager. No one has more impact on your career. Their performance, feedback, attitude, expectations and style will have an effect on your performance and the way you feel about your job. In turn, their conversations with their boss can colour higher management's long-term perceptions of you.

Before you accept a job, get to know your boss. Ask probing questions:

- What are the key indicators of success for you in this role?
- What do you expect from me personally?
- How could I influence you?
- How would I know your opinion of my performance?
- How would you describe your style?

You need to determine whether your work styles, goals and philosophies are compatible. Decide if this is someone you could admire. If they prove not to be, perhaps you should look for another job, managed by a person who more closely mirrors your image of a good manager.

By reading company literature, and by active listening, you can uncover what their values are. By looking at pictures or examples used when answering your questions, you will get a feel of how the company likes to see itself. One word of caution: if you find yourself at variance with your potential employer's value system, you would do well to consider any job offer very carefully. It is difficult to be

Week Five
SATURDAY

successful in a culture in which you feel an outsider. If you sense that the fit is not right from your perspective, then we would suggest that you don't pursue the opportunity. If the company is embarking on a major change, be sure of where the motivation and commitment for the change comes from. Are you being appointed as one of the change agents? There is nothing more de-skilling than being in a company where you don't fit and there should be signs of this almost immediately. If your gut reaction tells you no, listen to it and try to analyse why.

If you think you are close to a job offer that you want to accept, this may be the time to talk about the practicalities. Even if you don't discuss these in the interview, they are worth considering when you are negotiating from the strong position of having a job offer.

Practicalities

- Will you need a medical?
- Preferred start date
- Pension details
- Salary review – independent of appraisal, how often?
- Private healthcare scheme
- Car scheme details
- Insurance company and personal
- Expected job and company growth
- Potential career paths
- Leave allocation
- Profit sharing

SATURDAY

Week Five

Tackling interview questions

This week was designed to give you an insight into the world of the selection interview. An interview is a discussion with a clear purpose: the interviewer wants to know how you will bring benefits to them and the company. They are seeking someone who can fill a vacancy with minimum upheaval. You want a new job, a new challenge or a change. You also want to get there as calmly as possible.

Our advice throughout the week relates to the preparation and thought required to develop a script for your answers. But remember, if you are too staged in your responses then your interviewer will detect this. The words you use need to be yours, not ours, or they will sound affected and unconvincing. Of course the interviewer wants to know that you are taking the process seriously and have done the necessary preparation. They also want to know how you deal with the unexpected and how you might respond in the real world where not everything goes according to plan. Remember to think of your interview as a discussion rather than a test. Even if a panel of people interview you, they are only asking one question at a time. That is what you need to concentrate on.

Tackling tough interviews

- Identify your tough questions
- Establish rapport with everyone you meet
- Your education, skill and competencies
- You and your personality
- What makes you tick?
- What would you do if . . .?
- Prepare creatively

Week Five
SATURDAY

We wish you well in whatever types of interview you attend. You can now go to them knowing you are prepared and that you have all the resources you need to answer whatever you are asked. Now you've read this week, you should be saying:

Tough questions? I don't know what you mean!

Assessment Centres & Pyschometric Tests

JOHN SPONTON
STEWART WRIGHT

WEEK SIX

CONTENTS

Week Six

Introduction		450
Sunday	The Assessment Centre process	452
Monday	Competency based interviews	458
Tuesday	Preparing for Group Exercises	470
Wednesday	Preparing for psychometric tests and questionnaires	479
Thursday	Preparing for Presentation Exercises	494
Friday	Preparing for Analysis Exercises	505
Saturday	Pulling it all together	514
Appendices		521

Acknowledgements

Reproduction of test materials

The publishers and authors would like to thank the following for their kind permission to reproduce materials:

SHL (UK) Limted, The Pavilion, 1 Atwell Place, Thames Ditton, Surrey KT7 0NE. Tel: 0870 070 8000.
Website: www.shlgroup.com

ASE, Chiswick Centre, 414 Chiswick High Road, London W4 5TF. Tel: 020 8996 3337.
Website: www.ase-solutions.co.uk

Week Six

INTRODUCTION

It is Sunday morning, and you have had a sleepless night. You have covered the whole range of emotions in your restless mind. Somehow, you just do not fancy your usual bowl of cornflakes today. Yesterday a key letter came in the post, the job of your dreams is within reach – or you thought it was!

The letter said that, following your recent job interview, you have been invited to an 'Assessment Centre'. You were initially delighted that you had been successful at the interview, but now you are starting to think more about the next hurdle – the Assessment Centre.

You have heard a mixture of stories about Assessment Centres, sometimes also called Assessment Events, Selection Days, or Extended Interviews. It is true that employers are increasingly using them, but for some candidates the thought of attending causes anxiety and may lead them to drop out of the process and miss a great career opportunity. This is a great pity, because the employer inviting you to an Assessment Centre clearly feels you may have the skills that they are looking for. They just want to find out more about you, and to let you find out more about them.

Perhaps attending an Assessment Centre will be a new experience for you. Alternatively, you may have been to one before, but you realise that your performance could be improved with the benefit of some hints and tips on preparing for the day. Either way, this book is for you and will help you to succeed at an Assessment Centre.

You have already taken the first step by opening this book. Well done! Preparation in advance and an anticipation of situations that might occur are key skills that employers

Week Six
INTRODUCTION

value – particularly in Assessment Centres. Alongside that preparation, a greater familiarity with the workings of an Assessment Centre will also ensure that you are ahead of the game on the day.

In this week we will look in more detail at the type of exercises that you are likely to encounter. There will be plenty of practical hints and tips to help you give your best on that all-important Assessment Centre day.

SUNDAY

The Assessment Centre process

What is an Assessment Centre?

An Assessment Centre is not a new phenomenon, but they have been used more and more frequently since the late 1980s onwards. They are often the final hurdle in the selection process and tend to occur after an initial interview or series of interviews, and after an assessment of your application documents. The Assessment Centre is used to build up a picture of your key strengths against a 'template' of what is required to do the job well.

Assessment Centres consist of a series of different selection exercises. They also involve a number of different assessors or interviewers. These assessors are often managers, human resources (HR) or personnel staff and possibly even external consultants, hired by the employer to help out on the day.

Assessment Centres vary in length. They range from around half a day up to two days' duration, depending on the role and its seniority. On average, most events tend to be around one day in duration. You may find that the Assessment Centre is held at the employer's premises, or alternatively off-site at a hotel or another similar venue.

So far so good. One thing you will quickly notice is that other candidates who also applied for the role(s) will be attending the Assessment Centre at the same time as you. You may feel this is awkward or off-putting. Don't worry; we will give some useful hints and tips on this. In the meantime, the key thing to focus upon is that the other candidates will feel the same. Show them the common courtesies and be yourself. Also, remember that other candidates are usually always

Week Six

SUNDAY

present in any recruitment process – you just do not always meet them!

Why have Assessment Centres become more popular?

The key reasons behind the increasing popularity of Assessment Centres are their accuracy, objectivity and fairness.

Week Six

SUNDAY

What are employers looking for?

By the time you attend an Assessment Centre, the employer will have thought carefully beforehand about the job in question, the tasks involved and the objectives of the role. This will help them to think about the type of person they need to perform the job well. They will have created a picture of the ideal person to perform the job, defined by the person's experience, knowledge, skills, personality style and other attributes.

This collection of qualities – experience, knowledge, skills, personality style and other characteristics – are often developed into 'Competencies'. Each Competency is written down as precisely as possible, and in such a way that an assessor knows exactly what to look for when assessing a particular candidate.

For example, part of a definition for a Competency called 'Communication' might include the phrase, 'speaks clearly and concisely'. In an Assessment Centre, the assessors will be looking for evidence of a candidate's ability to speak clearly and concisely, as well as any other aspect of the definition, during the various exercises.

A fuller example of how some employers may define a related Competency called 'Oral communication' is shown below:

Week Six

SUNDAY

> **Competency – Oral communication**
> **Positive indicators:**
>
> - Speaks clearly and concisely.
> - Speaks confidently on both a one-to-one and group level.
> - Utilises facts and information to influence others.
> - Promotes own ideas.
> - Convinces others and wins them round to own point of view.

It is, however, important to note that the exact definitions of Competencies do differ across employers and from level to level. Competencies for the same level of role can be defined very differently across employers, often reflecting the diversity of their businesses. Nevertheless, an example of a broad Competency 'menu' – applicable for a range of professional and managerial roles – can be found in Appendix 1.

You will now appreciate how important it is to have as much information as you can about the job, and in particular the Competencies required to perform the job well. A key aspect of preparing for an Assessment Centre is to gather as much of this information as you can. On Saturday we will spell out the key information you need to obtain to help you in this process.

What typical exercises can I expect?

Employers have a very wide range of exercises upon which they can draw in order to get information about the different

Week Six
SUNDAY

Competency areas. They will choose the methods that they feel are most relevant to the job and that are most likely to give you the opportunity to display the Competencies.

In the list below, you can see the most commonly used exercises. However, do not panic! It is *extremely unlikely* that you would be asked to undertake all of these in one Assessment Centre. Instead, you will probably be asked to undertake a minimum of two exercises, and probably no more than half a dozen.

Each and every one of the exercises will be discussed in more detail during the course of the week.

- Interviews: based around your track record, your experience and/or key Competency areas.
- Group exercises: a team activity based around a practical task or discussion exercise.
- Psychometric tests: standardised tests proven to measure as accurately as possible specific skills and abilities, such as numerical reasoning.
- Personality questionnaires: also standardised, but measuring personality characteristics.
- Presentation exercises: where you are asked to present on a given topic to assessors.
- Analysis exercises: structured exercises where you are given particular scenarios or problems to work through under timed conditions.

Summary

We have begun the week with a general overview about what an Assessment Centre is. We have looked at its history, reasons for its popularity, what employers are often looking for in terms of 'Competencies', and the types of exercises that you are likely to encounter.

The following days of the week will focus on the individual exercises you are most likely to encounter in the Assessment Centres that you attend. These will include plenty of suggestions to ensure that you give your best on the day and avoid some common pitfalls.

You have taken the first key step to preparing yourself for an Assessment Centre. Preparation is invaluable to performing well at an Assessment Centre. You are already on the path to success!

… MONDAY …

Competency based interviews

Introduction to the interview

As discussed on Sunday, Assessment Centres consist of a number of different exercises and events. An integral part of an Assessment Centre, however, is still the interview. Why is this, when employers have so many other exercises to choose from?

Interviews retain their importance, both in Assessment Centres and elsewhere as a recruitment tool, because:

- They are an effective information gathering tool for the recruiting organisation when conducted professionally.
- They are also an important information gathering tool for you.
- For both a potential employer and employee, an interview fulfills that very human need to meet each other and communicate face to face.

An opportunity, not a threat

The interview, then, is your opportunity to display your relevant experience and Competencies. It is also an opportunity for you to find out what you need to know about the organisation and the role. However, interviews can often create anxiety. Perhaps this is because they come in so many different shapes and forms, and you may not know which style you will be facing until it begins.

MONDAY

Week Six

The style of interviews can vary considerably in terms of the degree of formality adopted. Some interviews seem to have a less formal flavour, taking place around a low table or when interviewers and interviewees are seated in easy chairs. Others may seem more intimidating, with the interviewers sitting on the other side of a desk, and with a generally more formal setting. Even the number of interviews and interviewers can vary.

In addition, during the same interview, you will find that the style of questions frequently changes. Some questions 'open up' a particular topic (e.g. 'What did you enjoy most about that role?'). Other questions are more searching and ask for further elaboration or detail on a topic (e.g. 'Tell me more about that'). Finally, some questions seek specific clarification of details and facts (e.g. 'When exactly did you leave that role?').

Comments frequently heard from interviewees are:

'I got asked to give an example and my mind went blank.'

Week Six

MONDAY

'When the time came for me to ask my questions I felt I let myself down.'

'When I was asked to initially "paint a picture of myself", I felt I could have given a better first impression.'

It need not be like this. Preparation combined with a sound interview technique on the day will turn your interview experience from something to be endured into a real opportunity to shine.

To begin this day of the week, let's look in turn at:

- The questions you are likely to face and top tips to help you prepare.
- Questions you can ask to get the information you need, and at the same time create a positive impression.
- Finally, your general interview technique which pulls it all together.

Week Six

MONDAY

Questions you are likely to face and top tips on how you can prepare

What we will look at now is the different types of questions you are likely to be asked in an interview within an Assessment Centre, and how you can prepare for them and make the most of the opportunities they present.

Preparation for the different types of questions will be critical to your success. These different types of questions can be summarised as follows:

- questions about your career track record and experience
- questions about Competencies relevant to the role

Refer back to Week Five for more ideas of questions you might face.

Questions about your career track record and experience

These questions look at the length and nature of your work experience. In particular, interviewers will be keen to explore the positions that you have held, the responsibilities that you had, and the depth of your technical knowledge and expertise in key areas. They will also be looking to fully account for any apparent gaps or breaks in your career history.

Questions in this area can cover four themes:

1 Your career direction
These questions focus on your career path to date and where you would like it to go. Typical questions include:

Week Six

MONDAY

'Tell me a bit about yourself.'

'Where do you see your career heading?'

'What were you doing between (a particular gap in your employment record)?'

'What attracted you to that role?'

'Why did you leave the previous role?'

Top tips

Plan your responses to these and related questions about where you have come from and where you want to go in your career.

Pay particular attention in your preparation to your important 'lifeline junctions', such as career changes, and to any employment breaks – particularly in the last 10 years.

However, career paths, like train journeys, do not always proceed smoothly. At times they do not go as planned and to schedule! The key is to talk comfortably about the choices you have made, and the lessons and skills you have learned, and the positive aspects of the experience.

In preparation for a question along the lines of 'Tell me about yourself?', have in your mind a *short* (maximum 2 minutes) summary of yourself, covering your key experiences, key strengths, and the main reason why you are applying for the role, identifying how it fits in with your overall career goals.

2 Positions and responsibilities you have held

These questions focus more specifically on the positions themselves and their responsibilities. They will tend to focus on your more recent roles, but an earlier position may be explored more fully if it is felt to be particularly relevant to the job in question. Typical questions include:

'What were your main responsibilities in that role?'

'What was the purpose of the role?'

'Who did you report to?'

'What were you accountable for?'

Top tips
Plan your responses to these questions, particularly for your last three roles or for the last 10 years (whichever is the shorter). Differentiate clearly between the purpose of the job (why it existed) and the tasks you did.

3 Your technical knowledge and skills
These questions focus on the depth of your technical knowledge and skills in relevant areas. For example, an Office Manager may require technical knowledge about Microsoft Office and a Personnel Manager will be expected to have knowledge of employment legislation. Typical questions include:

'What are your technical strengths and limitations?'

'How do you keep your technical knowledge up to date?'

'What professional publications do you read on a regular basis?'

'What would you see as the key technical demands of this role?'

Top tips
Plan your responses to these questions. Be clear about your areas of strength and how you can tackle/are tackling any areas where you are not as strong.

Week Six
MONDAY

If appropriate, ensure that your professional memberships are up to date and keep yourself abreast of any relevant stories in newspapers/journals relating to technical products/processes in your areas of relevant expertise.

4 Your achievements and successes

These questions focus on your key achievements to date and the particular successes that you have had in relevant areas. It is less about the roles you have held and the tasks you performed (which are covered in questions about your position and responsibilities), but more about how successfully you did it and what you achieved.

It is worth noting that candidates often sell themselves short in this area. This is a pity, because employers are looking for people who can replicate their previous successes in a new setting. Typical questions include:

'What are your key achievements to date?'

'What were your main successes in that role?'

'What challenges did you face in the role of . . . ?'

MONDAY

Top tips:

Plan your responses to these questions, and in particular try to have at least *two* achievements for your last *two* roles clear in your mind.

Focus on *your* achievements: avoid the royal 'we'!

Make your achievements as relevant as you can to the role you are applying for.

Be specific if you can, and quantify your achievements as much as possible, for example:

'I improved the company's financial performance by 10 per cent.'

'I reduced staff turnover by 20 per cent.'

'I was sales representative of the year.'

'I successfully passed my professional exams whilst studying part-time over those 2 years.'

Make sure your achievements are justifiable, because you are likely to have further questions on them during the interview. Your achievements may also be verified with your referees.

Questions about Competencies

These questions look at when you have demonstrated the required Competencies in the past. As discussed yesterday,

Week Six

MONDAY

a Competency – such as 'Planning and organising' – is a clearly defined grouping of qualities which is required to perform a job effectively.

When assessing your Competencies, interviewers are still working on the premise that the best gauge of future performance is past performance. However, the focus here is very much on 'how' people have done things (the Competencies they used and clearly demonstrated) rather than 'what' they necessarily achieved.

Competency questions will vary, but they often follow a particular pattern that you can use to good effect to help your preparation. Have a look at the example question below for the Competency of Planning and organising:

> **Opening question**
> *'Talk us through an example of when you planned a particular project . . .'*
>
> **Follow-up question 1**
> *'What was the situation?'*
>
> **Follow-up question 2**
> *'What tasks had to be done?'*
>
> **Follow-up question 3**
> *'What actions did you take to plan the project?'*
>
> **Follow-up question 4**
> *'What was the result?'*

Top tips
As you can see, a Competency-based interview question asks you to describe a particular example or event. You are

MONDAY

Week Six

then often asked a series of follow-up questions to expand on the situation, what you did and what the outcome was.

Candidates who have not had the opportunity to prepare can often find these questions very demanding. This is because you are having to talk through real events and in some detail. Preparation really pays dividends in this area.

The preparation you will need to do for any Competency interview is to consider firstly what likely Competencies are required for the role. If possible, try to get the Competencies, or at least information indicating what they are likely to be, from the employer (such as the Person/Job Specification). If you cannot do this, don't worry, use our Competency definitions in Appendix 1 to inform your choice and predictions.

Not all the Competencies in Appendix 1 will be relevant for every role. Look to identify the ones which you feel would be the most important. Work on around a maximum of nine for any one role.

Having identified the Competencies, plan your preparation using the acronym STAR:

- **S** is the **Situation** that sets the scene for the particular Competency – this needs to be a real life example that you experienced personally.
- **T** is the **Tasks** that needed to be undertaken to resolve the situation or problem represented above.
- **A** is the **Action** or activity clearly taken, by you, in response to the situation.
- **R** is the **Result** – think of it as the happy ending arising from the Actions you demonstrated above!

MONDAY

As you can see, this acronym mirrors the follow-up questions asked in the earlier example.

In Appendix 2, you will find a template that you can use for each Competency that you prepare.

Ideally, draw upon a mix of recent examples (preferably from approximately the last 2–3 years, because these are easier to recall in detail) that cover different situations from your career to date. Also, feel free to include noteworthy examples from outside of work.

In the interview itself, listen carefully to the phrasing of the exact question that you are given. Clarify the question if you are unsure, and take your time before answering.

Be concise and focused – try to use no more than a couple of sentences on each STAR element. Remember to describe what you did rather than what the team did – do not fall into the trap of being too modest!

MONDAY

A good way to practice this is either to talk through your evidence with a friend, record it on tape or talk to yourself in a mirror. We suggest you do the latter in a private rather than public place! The key is to become comfortable when articulating your examples.

Questions you can ask

It is important during the interview, and during other appropriate opportunities in the Assessment Centre, that you ask questions that you really want answered – rather than just asking questions for the sake of it. Refer back to Week Five for more information on how to tackle this issue.

Preparing for Group Exercises

Introduction to Group Exercises

Another important and often used element within an Assessment Centre is the Group Exercise. By a Group Exercise, we mean:

- You are one of a number of individuals working together as a group.
- A task is given to the 'group' to complete, often under timed conditions.
- Assessors are present to observe: whether the group completes the task; how the group approaches the task; and your individual contribution in relation to the Competencies.

Group Exercises have been used ever since Assessment Centres came on the scene and they fall into a category of exercises called 'simulation exercises'.

TUESDAY

Week Six

A 'simulation exercise' is different to an interview. In an interview, it is ultimately about you saying what skills you can offer, or talking about what motivates you, and so on. A Group Exercise is about what you do in a 'live' setting. A Group Exercise gives an opportunity for the assessors to observe you 'in action' – what you say, how you react to the task and, indeed, to the other candidates.

Typical Competencies assessed by Group Exercises

The evidence that the assessors collect from the Group Exercise is as likely to come from your approach to the task, as from whether you complete it.

Remember from Sunday that exact Competency definitions will vary from organisation to organisation and from role to role. The more you can find out about the Competencies the better. However, the following Competencies are more likely to be assessed during Group Exercises.

- **Leadership**
- **Relating to others**
- **Persuasive communications**
- **Self-motivation and resilience**

For each of these four Competencies, refer to the fuller descriptions in Appendix 1. Think also about how you could make the most of your strengths in a Group Exercise.

Week Six

TUESDAY

Different types of Group Exercises

Broadly speaking, Group Exercises fall into two categories:

- *Discussion based*: where the group is asked to debate and often reach consensus and conclusions on a topic or on topics.
- *Practical tasks*: where the group is asked to design and physically construct something.

Discussion based
Discussion-based Group Exercises are the most commonly used type in an Assessment Centre.

Individuals tend to be seated around a table in a group size of between four to six. There will tend to be two to three assessors in the room, set back from the group.

Depending on the seniority of the role, Group Exercises will tend to last between 30–90 minutes. However, not all of that time will be taken up with discussion. It may include time for individuals to review the materials before the discussion formally begins.

The actual topic(s) may be completely unrelated to the work setting. For example, you may be asked to assume that you are all in a hot air balloon that is slowly losing height over the ocean. The group has to agree which items they need to discard, and in what order, so that height can be maintained until landfall is reached. At the other end of the scale, the topics will be work related and tailored specifically to the role being assessed. Here you are likely to find more complex briefing materials.

TUESDAY

You may find that you and each of the other candidates are given different briefing materials or asked to play a particular role in the discussion (e.g. someone is representing Finance, someone else Marketing etc.).

The topics may have no simple – or indeed single – answer and the candidates have to reach a consensus on the course of action.

Practical tasks
Practical task Group Exercises, though less widely used, do still occur in Assessment Centres. These types of exercises have moved on considerably from their military origins. The military made use of planks of wood, oil drums and ropes and still do!

The principle underpinning the use of the practical task, however, remains the same. Their purpose is to place all candidates on an even footing by reducing the advantages of prior job knowledge and experience. The types of practical tasks that you are more likely to face in today's Assessment Centres are indoor exercises involving equipment such as:

- Table-top plastic construction kits (often using K'nex and Lego style materials).
- Larger versions of the above requiring a reasonable amount of floor space for design and construction activities.

The task will often require you to design and construct a particular object (car, bridge, chair etc.) within certain time and material constraints.

Week Six

TUESDAY

Common concerns and top tips

Common concerns specific to Group Exercises are captured by the following questions:

How can I prepare beforehand?

As with interview preparation, try to find out the exact Competency definitions used by the recruiting organisation. These will give a steer on the type of style required for effective performance in the role. If you cannot, do not worry – use the Competency definitions in Appendix 1.

For each of the Competencies, reflect upon your strengths and your developmental 'blind spots' (which we all have) – particularly those which might show when you are in meetings and when working with others.

For example, you are aware that you could do more to acknowledge the contributions of others in your day-to-day working. Write a short action plan of things to do more of when you are undertaking the Group Exercise. By doing this, you will see benefit, not just at an Assessment Centre, but on a day-to-day basis.

If you are in a Group Exercise where individual preparation time has been allocated, allow yourself sufficient time to familiarise yourself with all the materials. Ensure that you have reviewed all of the material by the end of the allocated time, even if this is just at a 'surface' level.

How should I act?

The key tip here is – do not act. You will find it difficult to sustain a role for the duration of a Group Exercise, let alone for the whole Assessment Centre. Rather, be yourself and

TUESDAY

work on making the most of your strengths and showing them to best effect on the day.

What are the common pitfalls to avoid?

It is easy in a Group Exercise to forget about the common courtesies that we would all expect to see displayed in group situations.

Do:

- Address others by their names.
- Invite others to contribute – particularly those who seem reticent or quiet.
- Listen to others; actively acknowledge their contributions.
- Be clear on what the task is before you start, and try your best to complete it.
- Throw yourself in to the task and contribute fully.
- Accept the constraints placed on you by the exercise instructions.
- Check the resources available to you – these may be physical things like a flip chart, a computer and calculators.
- Be prepared to respond positively and appropriately to any unexpected changes that the assessors make to the exercise brief.

TUESDAY

> Do not:
>
> - Interrupt others.
> - Become aggressive or argumentative.
> - Monopolise the 'airtime'.
> - Be frightened to ask questions of assessors and fellow participants.
> - Forget to monitor the time.
> - Be put off by the presence of the assessors – once the exercise begins, most people soon forget they are there.

How should I behave with the other candidates?

Remember you are working as a team to complete the task. Do not try to score 'points' against the other candidates.

Should I become the Timekeeper, the Note-taker or 'the Person at the flip chart'?

Some candidates jump in very quickly to adopt these roles. If you feel comfortable performing any of these roles, that is fine – but ensure the roles do not get in the way of allowing you to contribute in other ways.

How do I tackle a very dominant candidate?

Very dominant candidates are unlikely to be doing themselves a service by behaving in this way. If leadership is being assessed, it tends to be defined in more consultative or collaborative terms these days. Useful questions to manage the situation include:

'Shall we see what others think about this approach before we rush in . . .?'

TUESDAY

'Can we just check we are all happy with this?'

However, it is critical that your voice is heard – and this is not about shouting! Politely stand your ground and, if you are talked over, be prepared to repeat your point.

What do I do if one candidate is extremely quiet?

When working as a group, it is important to ensure that all members of the group contribute. If you aware that a candidate is very quiet, ask an open question like, 'What do we all think about this?' If the individual does not take up this opportunity, a little later address them by name as follows, '(first name), what are your thoughts?'

I have heard that sometimes the instructions change half-way through. What do I do?

You may encounter changes to the exercise remit – in just the same way that the goalposts change in all the jobs we have. These changes can take the form of extra information, changes to the instructions, changes of time-scale and so on. The key is not to complain and not to challenge them! Just go with the flow. Ask aloud, 'Based on this development, what changes do we need to make?'

If I am assigned a specific role in a group discussion exercise, what should I do?

As mentioned earlier, you could be given a specific role to play in a group discussion that would include having reference materials unique to you. A key point is to accept the role and any constraints placed upon you – remember that the other candidates will have to do exactly the same.

TUESDAY

Look to strike a balance between being true to yourself, and incorporating the approach required by someone performing the role. For example, if your role was to act as the company accountant in the Group Exercise, try to convey the importance of financial considerations in the subsequent discussion.

Are there any particular tips for practical exercises?

All the tips given above apply to both practical and discussion-based exercises, but there are two extra considerations:

1 Make sure that you are wearing smart but practical clothing appropriate to the exercise. Assessors will often notify you in advance if they are planning to run a practical exercise. Dress code for practical exercises tends to be less formal, reflecting the need to work with physical materials on the floor and to 'roll up your sleeves'.
2 The issue of special requirements will be covered in more detail on Saturday. It is worth stressing here the importance of making the assessors aware of any special requirements specific to an exercise of a more practical nature (e.g. mobility).

Summary

Today we have looked at Group Exercises. Specifically, we have discussed the type of exercises you are likely to encounter and top tips to help you during this important element of an Assessment Centre.

Preparing for psychometric tests and questionnaires

Introduction to psychometric assessment

Psychometric assessment often plays an important part in an Assessment Centre – but for candidates, it is often one of the most dreaded parts of the day. For many, even the term itself smacks of some unpleasant psychological scrutiny and gives rise to feelings of worry about what the exercises might unearth. Today we will 'demystify' the process for you and give you some top tips to ensure that you do yourself justice on the day.

Definition

So what does the term 'Psychometrics' actually mean? It is literally 'measurement of the mind'. In reality, it means measuring a broad range of characteristics, skills, abilities and behaviours governed by our mind.

From your perspective, it is important to differentiate between the two broad types of psychometric instruments that you are likely to encounter within the context of an Assessment Centre, namely tests and questionnaires.

- *Tests* have right and wrong answers (as do educational exams). This is because they are looking at specific skills and abilities.

Week Six
WEDNESDAY

> • *Questionnaires* do not have right or wrong answers. Instead they look at how you describe your style, interests or motivation, and how this picture of yourself relates to the requirements of the job and the organisation.

Background

Psychometrics is not a new science. The first commercially available tests were published in the early part of the last century. Particular growth periods occurred during the two world wars, when psychometric assessment significantly assisted with matching the large volume of individuals to different roles within the military, as well as identifying Officer potential.

Their popularity grew rapidly in the post-war years, as employers increasingly saw the benefits that well-designed and professionally administered and interpreted tests and questionnaires brought to their recruitment processes, namely:

> • Consistent and dependable results through careful standardisation of the way the exercises are administered and used (candidates who have been through tests and questionnaires in recent years often comment upon the classroom style in which the exercises are sat).
> • The objectivity of test or questionnaire results.
> • The accuracy with which tests or questionnaires predict specific characteristics and skills in the workplace.

WEDNESDAY

Range of tests and questionnaires

It may come as a surprise to know that there are several thousand commercially available psychometric tests and questionnaires in the UK. Some of these are for use in non-work settings, such as clinical and educational applications. Even if we focus solely on those tests and questionnaires designed specifically for use in the workplace, we are still left with several hundred commercially available products.

However, as an individual applying for a graduate, professional or managerial role at an Assessment Centre, the reality is that you are most likely to encounter the following:

- Ability Tests
- Personality Questionnaires

As mentioned on Sunday, Assessment Centre formats vary, and you may be asked to complete several tests or questionnaires drawn from the above areas. Alternatively, you may not have to complete any!

Today we will focus upon these two categories of exercises and provide you with examples of each to aid your understanding and preparation.

Different ways to complete tests and questionnaires

This has been an area of significant development since the early 1990s. There are now three main ways of completing psychometric tests and questionnaires:

WEDNESDAY

- Online – via the internet.
- On-screen – via desktop PCs/laptops and also by using hand-held technology such as pocket PCs.
- Paper and pencil – under the supervision of a trained Test Administrator in a 'classroom' style setting.

Ability Tests

Ability Tests can be either tests of a general nature which look to measure 'general intelligence', or they can focus on specific abilities such as verbal ability and numerical ability.

There are many different types of tests available in each category; the exact type that you may encounter will depend on the specific level of job you are applying for – some tests are pitched specifically at very senior levels.

For the rest of today we will focus on 'specific Ability Tests' as these are more commonly used within Assessment Centres. There are many Ability Tests available which cover a wide range of verbal, numerical, abstract, spatial and mechanical abilities. However, for the majority of graduate, professional and managerial vacancies, the Ability Tests that you are more likely to encounter are abstract, verbal and numerical reasoning.

In these three areas a typical test would tend to take between 25–45 minutes. Examples of these are shown below:

Week Six

WEDNESDAY

Graduate and Managerial Assessment

The GMA consists of three tests which cover Abstract, Verbal and Numerical Reasoning respectively.

There follows one example of each of these tests for you to gain a feel for the product.

Abstract reasoning

This is a test of your skill at finding similarities and differences in groups of patterns. All the patterns in group A are in some way similar to each other, and all those in group B are similar to each other.

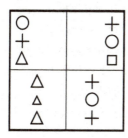

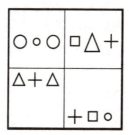

A   B

Below, you will find five separate boxes with patterns in them. Your task is to decide if each box:

i) belongs to group A
ii) belongs to group B
iii) belongs to neither group

Week Six

WEDNESDAY

Answers:

first is group A
second is group B
third is neither group
fourth is neither group
fifth is group A

Verbal reasoning

This is a test of your skill at making sense of reports which cannot be relied on to be objective, truthful or even consistent. The test consists of a series of short passages, each of which includes a number of short statements intended to convey information or persuade the reader of a point of view.

Each passage is accompanied by four statements relating to the information or arguments it contains. Assume that what is stated is true; even if it contradicts what you know or believe to be the case in reality. Decide on this assumption whether the statement is:

a) true,
b) false,
c) you cannot tell and need more information.

In recent years it has become clear that man's use of fossil fuels is likely to have a major impact on the world's climate. As a result of this, increased concentrations of 'greenhouse' gasses such as carbon dioxide and methane will lead to global warming; an overall small increase in average temperatures; whose impact is difficult to predict.

WEDNESDAY

Week Six

Whilst some scientists predict melting of the polar icecaps, and so a rise in sea levels, others think this will be balanced by increased precipitation at the poles.

1. If we go on using fossil fuels at the present rate, we must expect climatic change.
   TRUE : FALSE : CAN'T TELL

2. Depletion of the ozone layer will result in global warming.
   TRUE : FALSE : **CAN'T TELL**

3. Scientists are all agreed that use of fossil fuels will eventually lead to a rise in sea levels.
   TRUE : **FALSE** : CAN'T TELL

4. The burning of fossil fuels increases the concentration of methane in the atmosphere.
   TRUE : FALSE : CAN'T TELL

Numerical reasoning

This is a test of your skill at reasoning with numbers. First you are given some information in a variety of forms – text, tables or graphs – followed by three related questions. For each question, choose what you think is the correct answer from the possible answers A to P.

An insurance scheme pays benefits to its members who are sick for extended periods of time at the following rates

1st month:	nil
2nd–4th months:	50% of normal salary
5th and succeeding months:	25% of normal salary

Week Six
WEDNESDAY

on the first £24,000 p.a. of salary for each month in which the member is sick and is not paid by the employer. How much does the scheme pay to:

1. John, who is off work for two months, whose salary is £12,000 p.a., and who gets no sick pay?

2. Pat, who is ill for six months, but who is paid normally for the first two months and whose salary is £18,000 p.a.?

3. Hilary, whose salary is £30,000 p.a., who gets 3 months sick pay from her employer, and who has to take nine months off?

A) £250	B) £500	C) £750	D) £1000
E) £1125	F) £1500	G) £1765	H) £2125
I) £2250	J) £2350	K) £2500	L) £3125
M) £3750	N) £4000	O) £5000	P) £5625

Answers:

1. Answer B is correct. John gets £500.00 (1 month at half his usual monthly salary)

2. Answer I is correct. Pat gets £2250 (3 months at half her usual monthly salary)

3. Answer N is correct. Hilary gets £4000 (3 months at half of a monthly salary of £2,000 plus 2 months at a quarter of a monthly salary of £2,000)

GMA – A Test Taker's Guide © 1992 S.F. Blinkhorn. Reproduced with permission of the publishers, ASE, Chiswick Centre, 414 Chiswick High Road, London W4 5TF a division of nfer Nelson, Tel +44(0) 208 996 3337. Email contact@ase-solutions.co.uk. Website www.ase-solutions.co.uk

Personality Questionnaires

Personality Questionnaires look at your typical 'style' of behaviour and not your ability. In other words, how you prefer to do things typically, such as the way you relate to others or how you approach tasks and solve problems.

A Personality Questionnaire is essentially a structured form of self-assessment and it tends to be completed without any time constraints.

There are a number of well-established work-based Personality Questionnaires used in the UK. Personality characteristics that are normally assessed include social confidence, anxiety levels and preferences for making speedy decisions. Questionnaires will vary in the number of personality characteristics that they look to measure – some will measure 5, some 16, and some 32.

Personality Questionnaires will also have different ways of asking their questions. Examples of two common styles of question format are shown below:

Personality Questionnaires

Here are some examples of the types of questions that might be asked.

1 Rating Statements

In this example you are asked to rate yourself on a number of phrases or statements. After reading each statement mark your answer according to the following rules:

Week Six

WEDNESDAY

Fill in circle 1 If you strongly disagree with the statement
Fill in circle 2 If you disagree with the statement
Fill in circle 3 If you are unsure
Fill in circle 4 If you agree with the statement
Fill in circle 5 If you strongly agree with the statement

The first statement has already been completed for you. The person has agreed that 'I enjoy meeting new people' is an accurate description of him/herself.

Now try questions 2 to 6 for yourself by completely filling in the circle that is most true for you.

	Strongly disagree	Disagree	Unsure	Agree	Strongly agree
1 I enjoy meeting new people	①	②	③	●	⑤
2 I like helping people	①	②	③	④	⑤
3 I sometimes make mistakes	①	②	③	④	⑤
4 I don't mind taking risks	①	②	③	④	⑤
5 I'm easily disappointed	①	②	③	④	⑤
6 I enjoy repairing things	①	②	③	④	⑤

Week Six

WEDNESDAY

2 Making Choices

In this example you are given a block of four statements: A, B, C and D. Your task is to choose the statement which you think is most true or typical of you in your everyday behaviour and then choose the one which is least true or typical of you. Indicate your choices by filling in the appropriate circle in the row marked 'M' (for Most) and in the next row 'L' (for Least).

The first block has been completed for you. The person has chosen, 'Enjoys organising people' as most true (or typical) and 'Seeks variety' as being least true (or typical) of him/herself. Now try questions 2, 3 and 4 yourself.

I am the sort of person who . . .

1. A Has a wide circle of friends
   B Enjoys organising people
   C Relaxes easily
   D Seeks variety

2. A Helps people with their problems
   B Develops new approaches
   C Has lots of energy
   D Enjoys social activities

3. A Has lots of new ideas
   B Feels calm
   C Likes to understand things
   D Is easy to get on with

Week Six

WEDNESDAY

> **4** A Enjoys organising events
> B Sometimes gets angry
> C Is talkative
> D Resolves conflicts at work
>
>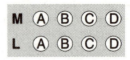
>
> © SHL Group plc

How your results are interpreted

So how are your results interpreted from tests and questionnaires? The key principle with both tests and questionnaires is that they do not look only at how you completed the assessment, but at how your score compares to a large sample of people who have taken the assessment previously.

Imagine that you have just completed a Personality Questionnaire at an Assessment Centre. Your responses to the questions are then compared to the responses of a group of people who took the questionnaire previously, for example, 'UK Managers and Professionals'. This will give an indication of how strong your preferences/characteristics are relative to that group, and what this is likely to mean in terms of how you 'behave'.

With Ability Tests, the principle remains the same. The organisation is interested in relating your test performance to individuals of a relevant background for the role in question – do you perform in the top 25 per cent, the bottom 25 per cent, or is your performance typical of most managers?

Week Six

WEDNESDAY

Common concerns and top tips

What can I do beforehand to help me with tests?

Once advised that you will be completing an Ability Test, ask if you will be sent practice leaflets. If specific practice leaflets are not available, useful websites that provide a selection of online practice questions and information are:

www.shlgroup.com/candidate/default.htm

www.ase-solutions.co.uk/support.asp?id=63

Do yourself justice by practising the relevant skill areas. For example, in order to brush up on your numerical reasoning skills, read financial reports in newspapers, practise studying and interpreting information presented in a numerical format, and refresh your memory about straightforward calculations, such as percentages.

Finally, if you are going to complete a numerical test, take your own calculator. If you are allowed to use calculators, it will normally be acceptable for you to use your own.

What can I do beforehand to help me with questionnaires?

Fairly limited, but once advised that you will be completing a Personality Questionnaire, ask if you will be sent a practice leaflet or any further information on the questionnaire.

What should I remember if I am completing a questionnaire online?

If you are completing the questionnaire over the internet, ensure that you give yourself quality time for its completion, i.e. sufficient time, and time free from distractions or interruptions.

WEDNESDAY

In addition, if you have been asked to complete more than one questionnaire, consider taking a break between each questionnaire.

What can I do during the session to help me with tests?

Listen carefully to the instructions. Do not be afraid to ask questions – the other candidates are likely to be thinking the same! Make the most of any practice questions; they are there to help you and to prompt questions from you. Read each question carefully before answering.

Unless instructed otherwise, if you are unsure of an answer, mark your best choice, then move on to the next question. You may not necessarily be expected to fully complete all the questions in the test. Work quickly, but not so quickly that your accuracy is potentially undermined. Most of the tests will be timed, therefore, monitor your time.

I have special requirements. What should I do?

If you have any special requirements, contact the organisation. If you wear glasses, contact lenses, hearing aids etc., ensure you take them with you.

What can I do during the session to help me with questionnaires?

With most questionnaires, you are asked to consider how you typically behave in a work setting. If this is the case, think about yourself in a work rather than home or leisure setting.

WEDNESDAY

Work through the questions at a comfortable pace, but do not ponder too long over any one question. The questionnaire is about how you see yourself now, so ensure that your self-assessment is up to date!

Do not try to create an 'unreal' image; be honest about how you see yourself rather than presenting how you would like to be.

How can I find out more?

Go to the websites listed earlier, or consult the Further Reading section at the back of this book. Moreover, if you have been to an Assessment Centre that involves completing tests and questionnaires – ask for feedback. This will help you to find out more about the process, as well as about yourself!

Summary

Today we have discussed psychometric assessment. We have looked at the more widely-used psychometric tests and questionnaires that you may encounter, and given examples of the more common formats. We have provided top tips to help you before and during the assessment sessions.

Preparing for Presentation Exercises

Introduction to Presentation Exercises

Candidates are often asked to give a presentation in an Assessment Centre. The presentation element has a number of distinct phases, each of which requires a particular approach to get the best out of the exercise. Today we will look in more detail at each of these phases and the issues you need to consider. For each phase we will give you top tips to ensure that your presentation will be a success.

The phases

- *Preparation for the presentation, in response to the topic you have been given*: the topic may be given to you a number of days before the Assessment Centre is due to take place. Alternatively, you may not be given the topic until the very day of the Assessment Centre, and in these circumstances clearly your preparation time is going to be far more limited.
- *Delivering an effective presentation*: your presentation may be delivered to any number of assessors, from just one person to a very large audience. Sometimes the other candidates at the Assessment Centre are also invited to listen to your presentation and sit with the assessors. A more commonly adopted approach is that your presentation (and subsequent 'questions and answers') is delivered to a small panel of assessors, who then immediately follow the presentation with an interview.

THURSDAY
Week Six

- *Dealing with any questions from the audience arising from your presentation*: often the panel has set aside a number of minutes for the specific purpose of asking you questions about the presentation you have made.

Of course, assessors are often particularly interested in presentation performance when the post itself requires the job-holder to make presentations in the course of their duties, for example, a Sales Manager having to make sales pitches.

Candidates often find making presentations very stressful, particularly when the success (or otherwise) of their application depends upon it. Even experienced presenters rarely fully overcome their nerves – and some argue that nerves in moderation can be a good thing to keep you 'on your toes'.

As with other elements of an Assessment Centre, the key is to be familiar with how presentations are assessed and, through a combination of preparation, practice, and some useful practical hints, to ensure that you do yourself justice on the day.

An effective presentation is rather like being on the stage. For a few minutes you have complete control of the audience. They are, literally, all ears, waiting on your every word.

Take heart – even if public speaking concerns you, presentation performance can be massively improved by preparation and the application of just a few key tactics.

Week Six
THURSDAY

Typical Competencies assessed by Presentation Exercises

As you know from Sunday, the goal in any assessment process is to provide an opportunity for candidates to display the relevant Competencies. You will remember that exact Competency definitions will vary from organisation to organisation and from role to role. The more you can find out about the Competencies, the better. Below are some Competencies that will tend to be assessed during Presentation Exercises.

The assessment will be based around how you delivered your presentation; how you dealt with subsequent questions from the assessors; and, depending upon how technical the topic is, what you said.

- **Planning and organising**
- **Persuasive communications**
- **Self-motivation and resilience**

THURSDAY

Week Six

For each of these three Competencies, refer to the fuller descriptions in Appendix 1. Think also about how you could make the most of your strengths in a Presentation Exercise.

The above Competencies (or something very similar, depending upon the organisation's precise definition) will tend to be assessed regardless of the exact topic of the Presentation. Other Competencies may or may not be assessed depending upon how 'technical' the topic is.

Different types of topic

By 'technical' topics, we mean whether the topic you have been given relates directly to knowledge and/or experience required in the role.

If 'non-technical', the topic may be of much less importance to the assessors, and the content of what you say is simply the means by which, for instance, your communication skills are assessed.

Sample 'non-technical' topics that you might be given could include:

- my finest moment
- my greatest achievement

Week Six

THURSDAY

Common concerns and top tips

Some of the most commonly asked questions and our top tips are shown below.

I have just been given the topic. How can I prepare beforehand?

As with interview and Group Exercise preparation, try to find out the exact Competency definitions used by the recruiting organisation. These will give a steer to the style required for effective performance in the role. If you cannot, do not worry – use the Competency definitions in Appendix 1.

If the topic is 'technical', look for clues in the Job Description and Person Specification to any important themes or issues that you might wish to cover in your presentation. Think about what other Competencies (maximum three) from our Appendix might be assessed, such as Analysing and solving problems.

Check the information that you have been given. Make sure that you know how long you have to present, and what resources are available to you in the form of an overhead projector, flip chart facility or a computer-based projector. If you are using the latter, and it is being supplied by the organisation, ensure that you know exactly what version and release of software you are going to be using on the day to avoid compatibility problems.

Look carefully at the topic you have been given. Check that you understand exactly what is being sought. Even if you think you do, check with a trusted friend or family member what they think the topic is all about. If anything requires clarification – contact the organisation.

THURSDAY

Draft out the key points that you want to get across in your presentation, but pay careful attention to the time that you have been allocated. A common trap is to try to cover too much.

Think carefully too about the audience. Make sure that the content of your presentation is pitched at the right tone and level for them.

Plan out how long you have until the presentation and how much time you will need to allow for your preparation, not forgetting things like preparing slides and hand-outs.

For a pre-prepared presentation, we recommend that you allow a ratio of *10 minutes' preparation time for each minute of delivery time*.

If you can – stop at this point in your preparation! Put your work away and go and do something different. Come back later and look again at the topic and your earlier work – you will be surprised how, in the intervening time, your brain has come up with some new or alternative ideas.

When you are comfortable with the content of your presentation, do a draft of your slides and hand-outs. Keep the slides simple – just headings covering key points. Aim for a maximum of one slide for each 45 seconds or one minute of delivery time – less if you are particularly confident at delivering presentations with minimal supporting materials.

Week Six

THURSDAY

Now, do a draft of what you are going to say, either written out on small index cards, or on the computer in note form – these are prompts for your eyes only. If you can, avoid putting too much detail down – you do not want to be seen simply reading off cards or notes in your presentation.

Make sure that the presentation has a proper introduction and a conclusion. Try to leave 'on a high' – make the last point upbeat and positive, and then recap on the whole content with a conclusion. A clear conclusion is particularly important – you *must* revisit the main points you have made.

Rehearse your presentation. Inflict it mercilessly on members of your family, a supportive friend, to yourself in a mirror, even to the pet cat or dog – they generally do not complain. The key, of course, is to feel relaxed and comfortable with the content. Remember to speak a little more slowly than normal to ensure that the audience has time to absorb the content.

Invite honest feedback – unless it is your pet (in our view, dogs tend to say everything is perfect and cats tend to be too critical). In particular, check how you fared against the time you have been given – was the presentation too long or short? Does the message clearly address the topic you were given? Was the language and tone you used relevant to the level of the audience?

Remember to make backups, particularly if you are using a computer-based projector. As a minimum you should have spare hard copies of any slides, notes and hand-outs that you are intending to use, as well as a backup disc.

I have been told I won't get the topic until the day of the Assessment Centre.

All the above principles apply, but our '10 to 1' rule may not be possible. You may not have much time to practise or the luxury of being able to leave your first draft workings and come back to them later. Instead, planning your preparation activity will become particularly critical.

As a rough guide, allow 60 per cent of your total preparation time to developing the content of what you want to say; 20 per cent to preparing the presentation; and 20 per cent to a final rehearsal and fine-tuning.

Week Six
THURSDAY

What about delivering the presentation itself?

Check that all the materials you need are to hand, and any technology you are about to use has been tested before you begin.

Make sure that you have a glass of water in case your voice gets dry.

Speak clearly, and a little more slowly than normal speaking speed. Use pauses effectively to emphasise key points and when moving on from one content area to another.

Vary your voice and pitch to give your delivery some richness and depth.

Speak loudly enough so that those in the back of the room can hear you adequately, though try not to shout.

Use hand movements effectively but sparingly to emphasise key points.

It is important to develop eye contact with the audience. Move your eyes over the entire audience, but do not linger too long over any one individual.

If you can, try to take a step or two occasionally from the podium or your 'base point' towards the audience. This can be a very powerful way of retaining audience attention, particularly if you time it to coincide with an important point in your presentation. In these instances, it helps to have index card notes so that you are not too tied to the computer for your prompts.

Avoid unconscious, repetitive mannerisms (common ones are slight swaying or using certain phrases on too many

T H U R S D A Y

occasions), if you possibly can. The honest feedback you sought from your rehearsal audience should have alerted your attention to these.

Keep an eye on the time. Make some quick decisions about whether you need to speed up or slow down your delivery.

As a final quality check to your delivery, concentrate upon the following:

S is for **Start at the start** – outline what you intend to cover.

I is for **Inject** a positive and confident style.

M is for **Monitor** the time.

P is for **Project with some passion** in your voice.

L is for go **Light on laughter** and **Leave it** to comedians, unless you are a very confident and experienced presenter who can gauge the mood of his or her audience well. Humour can backfire or fall very flat.

E is for **End at the end** – summarise your main points in a succinct conclusion.

How do I deal with difficult assessors' questions?

You can 'buy' yourself some valuable seconds of thinking time by using one or more of the following: pausing for a few seconds before answering (it will seem like a lifetime to you but it will not be nearly so noticeable to the audience); taking a short sip of water; and repeating back the main essence of the question before you respond.

Reflect on any questions your practice audience raised with you when you did your 'dummy run', and roughly plan your responses should the same themes be raised by the assessors.

Week Six

THURSDAY

I feel very rusty on my presentation technique. Can you give me some practice topics?

Have a look again at the two topics that were mentioned as examples of 'non-technical' topics:

- my finest moment
- my greatest achievement

For each, think about STAR – what was the situation? What did I do? What happened? What was the outcome?

Convey in your presentation what was so special to you about the events that you are describing. The STAR format will assist with the structure of your delivery.

Other topics (of a semi-technical nature) to practice include:

- If appointed to this job, what would you hope to achieve during the first 3 months in the role?
- What are the main opportunities and challenges facing our organisation?
- How do you measure your success at work?
- How do you get the best out of other people at work?

Summary

Today we have looked at Presentation Exercises. We have reviewed how presentations consist of three phases – preparation, delivery, and subsequent questions. You can equip yourself to deal with the challenges of each part. We have shown that keeping your delivery SIMPLE can help you to present well at this crucial part of an Assessment Centre.

FRIDAY
Week Six

Preparing for Analysis Exercises

Introduction to Analysis Exercises

Analysis Exercises feature regularly in Assessment Centres and are not necessarily restricted to appointments for more senior roles.

Like interviews, Analysis Exercises can take many different shapes and forms. Unlike interviews and presentations, however, your scope for preparation may be quite limited. Instead, the key to your success will lie with your approach to the particular exercise on the day.

Today we will look at the different types of Analysis Exercises that you may be asked to complete in an Assessment Centre and our top tips will enable you to perform to the best of your ability.

What exactly is an Analysis Exercise?

In an Analysis Exercise, you are given a specific 'bundle' of information, and you are set a task relating to that information.

The information
This is usually in the form of documents such as memos, notes, correspondence and/or a general background briefing on a fictitious situation.

The information overall sets a particular scene, or 'simulation', rather like we discussed with Group Exercises on Tuesday, which may or may not bear a resemblance to the role for which you are applying.

FRIDAY

Often you are asked to imagine that you are a member of the management team (sometimes stepping in at short notice to cover for an ill or absent colleague), or that you are a Consultant who advises a fictitious organisation.

The amount and complexity of the information will depend upon the level of role for which you are applying, and the Competencies which are being assessed. Increasingly these days, the information includes print-outs of e-mails, and the information itself may be presented on a computer screen.

The task

Again this will vary, but you may be asked to do one or a combination of the following:

1 To prioritise the issues represented within the information, distinguishing between what may be of relevance and importance from that which is less so.
2 To analyse the information and arrive at some judgements or conclusions based upon it.
3 To propose particular actions based upon your analysis.
4 To present some sort of summary or report on your findings, either in a written form and/or as a presentation; look upon whatever is being submitted and assessed as your 'key output(s)'.

Analysis Exercises come by many different names and forms, and their length can vary from approximately 45 minutes to 2–3 hours (for the most senior roles).

Look out in the timetable for phrases such as 'In-Tray Exercise' or 'In-Basket Exercise'. These both refer to the same type of exercise, in which a file of notes, memos and documents needs to be 'processed' in whatever way the instructions state. Key outputs here, for example, may be to prioritise the items and make a list of action points. Other commonly used formats are 'Analysis-Report Writing Exercise' and 'Analysis-Presentation Exercise', reflecting the different key outputs which can be sought: a report or a presentation.

Typical Competencies assessed by Analysis Exercises

You will remember from Sunday that the exercises in an Assessment Centre are selected to provide an opportunity for candidates to display the relevant Competencies. We outlined that exact Competency definitions will vary from organisation to organisation and from role to role, and that the more you can find out about the Competencies, the Job and Person Specification, the better. If you cannot get hold of that information, do not lose heart – below are some Competencies that may be assessed during Analysis Exercises.

The assessment is likely to be based upon: how you analysed or responded to the content of the Analysis Exercise, bearing in mind that there may not be a single 'right' or 'wrong' answer; how well and how clearly you delivered those responses; and how much you got done within the time constraints imposed upon you.

Week Six

F R I D A Y

- **Planning and organising**
- **Persuasive communications**
- **Analysing and solving problems**

For each of these three Competencies, refer to the fuller descriptions in Appendix 1.

The above Competencies will tend to be assessed regardless of the exact content of the Analysis Exercise. Other Competencies may or may not be assessed, depending upon how 'technical' or 'high level' the material or task is. For example, senior managerial Analysis Exercises may well include a 'Strategic thinking' Competency.

Common concerns and top tips

Some of the most commonly asked questions and our top tips are shown below:

You said that the preparation I can do is limited. Is there anything, though, which I can do beforehand to help me on the day?

Firstly, think about any general skills gaps you may have. For example, some Analysis Exercises include numerical data as an element of the briefing information. If working with numbers is not your strongest point, try to brush up on things like working with percentages, ratios and fractions so that these do not trip you up on the day.

FRIDAY

Week Six

In addition, take a closer look at any statistical tables, graphs and basic accounting information that you can get your hands on, particularly where these are accompanied by supporting narrative information. The business supplements in the quality Sunday papers, magazines such as the Economist, and sets of accounts are all good sources.

Identify any knowledge gaps you may have which could be exposed by a 'technical' Analysis Exercise – namely, an exercise that may be based upon technical or professional knowledge underpinning the job that you have applied for. Perhaps this would be a good time to get a 'refresher' text down from your bookshelf.

What tips can you give me to help me do the Analysis Exercise once it begins?

Before you begin, make sure you know the answers to the following:

FRIDAY

- What are you expected to do?
- What exactly is being assessed – for example, is it just the report you have been asked to do? Or will your supporting or 'rough' workings also be looked at?
- What Competencies/technical areas are you being assessed against in this Exercise?
- How long do you have?
- Can you split up, or mark/highlight the briefing papers to help you?

If you have any doubts – ask before the exercise begins.

Regardless of the exact nature of the key outputs sought – whether a report or a presentation, for example – you will need to manage yourself effectively through planning your work, familiarisation with the materials and then meeting those 'key outputs'.

Planning
Once the exercise begins, plan out what you need to do. Allocate time to the key elements, ensuring that you leave long enough to actually meet the key outputs, whether writing a report, submitting action points etc.

Once you have allocated your time – stick to it! It is crucial to allow enough time to do justice to the key outputs. An all-too-common trap is to spend too long familiarising yourself with the materials. The key is to stick to the timings you set yourself.

FRIDAY

Week Six

Familiarisation

If you need to familiarise yourself with a particularly large collection of briefing materials, make sure you at least 'skim-sift' all the materials first. Remember, all the important or priority issues are unlikely to be in the very first few items you read. Therefore, do not spend too long reading the lower-priority items and concentrate instead on the more important areas.

As you become more familiar with the materials, identify any links and connections in the data, perhaps making a rough note of these as you think of them, remembering to communicate your awareness of the relevant ones in your key outputs.

Meeting the key outputs

If you are being asked to supply specific action points in response to issues, be as specific as you can. Tell the assessor who exactly you would involve, to what purpose, and why. Avoid comments that are unspecific such as 'Have a meeting to discuss' or 'File'.

Try to communicate to the assessor that you feel a real sense of responsibility and controlled urgency towards resolving the major issues in question, and that you are aware of the implications of your proposed actions.

Clearly flag up to the assessors in your submitted work if you feel that you have had to make particular assumptions about the materials.

Avoid wasting time on overly lengthy or unfocused 'scene setting' in your final report or presentation – but make sure that you have a proper introduction and a clear conclusion.

Give appropriate rationale to support or explain your conclusions or findings. This need only be brief, focused explanatory comment, integrated into your work. However, having an identifiable 'trail' linking the material to your findings will help the assessor to appreciate your train of thought on particular points, and to assess your submissions fairly.

As a closing thought, if you can drive, can you remember your driving test when you had to make those slightly exaggerated movements of 'mirror – signal – manoeuvre'? It is the same with Analysis Exercises – not just being competent, but doing what you can to help the assessor to *see* your competence!

FRIDAY

Summary

Today we have concentrated on Analysis Exercises. We have seen that, although Analysis Exercises can vary greatly in terms of length and content, you can make a real difference by using our top tips for successful familiarisation, planning and delivery in an Assessment Centre.

Week Six

SATURDAY

Pulling it all together

It is Saturday morning and what a week it has been! All the fears and concerns of the unknown have disappeared. Your appetite has returned with a vengeance – and the cornflakes taste great!

You look again at the letter inviting you to the Assessment Centre. With your preparation for each individual exercise under way, it is now time to pull it all together with the following thoughts:

- What general hints and tips should you follow before the Assessment Centre takes place?
- What general hints and tips should you follow during the Assessment Centre?
- What general hints and tips should you follow after the Assessment Centre?

General hints and tips before the Assessment Centre

I've just received my invite to an Assessment Centre. What should I do first?

First and foremost, check to see if a briefing or information pack is included with the letter. If not, ask if further information will be forwarded.

Read the pack carefully, and make sure you are clear on the following points:

- What exercises can I expect?
- What Competencies are being assessed?
- Where and when is the Assessment Centre?
- What is the dress code?

Also, action any requests, for example, confirming attendance or forwarding information in advance (such as certificates). Then, make a very clear check-list of which exercises and activities you need to prepare for in advance of the Assessment Centre, as covered previously in this week.

If not covered in the information pack, make an educated guess about the Competencies that you are likely to be assessed on and the exercises you can expect on the day. Remember, if you feel that you require more information or clarification – ask.

I have special requirements – what should I do?

If you have any special requirements – including disability, dietary or other – contact the organisation. Organisations will look to make any adjustments that are reasonable, in

SATURDAY

order to ensure that no one is at a disadvantage. If you wear glasses, contact lenses, hearing aids etc. – bring them.

What should I take to the Assessment Centre?

If there is a numerical element to the day, pack your calculator (check if it needs a new battery).

Always take along a spare CV and a copy of your original application. You may meet assessors who would find it helpful to see your documents on the day.

Always take a watch – time is a critical issue at an Assessment Centre.

Have some spare paper or a small reporter's notepad to write down key names, times and learning points that you want to record for the future.

What advice can you give me about the travel arrangements?

Find out exactly where the event will be held and ensure that you get there in plenty of time. Remember to allow extra time if the venue is in a town centre, or is on a Monday morning, or if you are generally unfamiliar with the location.

If your journey is a particularly long one, ask the organisation if they are prepared to consider overnight accommodation for you.

If you are driving, make sure that you know where to park and if parking spaces are available.

What about the night before?

Try to get a good night's sleep!

SATURDAY
Week Six

General hints and tips during the Assessment Centre

What if I'm not clear about something during the day?

Do not be afraid to ask questions if you are unclear about any points – understanding the instructions is not part of the assessment!

I've heard stories that there might be 'hidden assessment' during Assessment Centres.

Be aware that you may be assessed throughout the day. This could take place over coffee, lunch or dinner, and even during a site tour.

Whenever you are in the presence of an assessor or a member of staff there is the potential for being assessed. Be on your best behaviour from the moment you walk through the door, until you leave the site at the end of the day.

How can I do my best to 'look the part' during the day?

Be alert throughout the day to your body language – your facial expressions, eye contact and mannerisms. Are they communicating what you would want them to communicate?

Dress code should be covered in the briefing pack. However, if not, phone to ask. In the event that you are unable to ascertain the dress code, always opt for normal but comfortable business attire.

SATURDAY

Any final advice?

No matter how unfamiliar the exercises may appear, always enter into the spirit of the day. Remember, the Assessment Centre is an opportunity for you to show your capabilities. Make sure you make the most of it.

Do not try to play an unnatural role during the day that you would be unable to sustain. Instead, trust in the preparation you have done and feel confident in the skills you can offer.

Try not to panic if an exercise does not go as well as you would like. Remember it is the whole day that will be taken into account. Moreover it is a well-known fact that no one is perfect! Instead, make a note on your pad (or commit to memory) the areas where you feel you could do better next time.

Finally, switch your mobile phone off!

General hints and tips after the Assessment Centre

How can I get the most from my Assessment Centre experience?

Look back over any notes that you may have taken (written down or in your memory). Consider each exercise and think about:

- What did I do well?
- What could I do even better next time?

Also reflect on how the other candidates performed and what you could learn from their approach to the day overall, and in specific exercises.

Finally, ask for feedback from the organisation, regardless of whether you were ultimately successful or not. Compare their observations on your performance with your own notes from the day.

In closing

Assessment Centres offer a great opportunity for you to give your best, as well as to find out more about the organisation and the role. In just one week, you have done all of the preparation necessary to ensure that you are ready to succeed at an Assessment Centre.

The only final ingredient we would add is – best wishes and good luck!

Useful addresses

The British Psychological Society (BPS), 48 Princess Road East, Leicester LE1 7DR. Tel: 0116 254 9568.

The Chartered Institute of Personnel and Development (CIPD), CIPD House, Camp Road, London, SW19 4UX. Tel: 020 8971 9000.

The Chartered Management Institute, Management House, Cottingham Road, Corby, Northants NN17 1TT. Tel: 01536-204 222.

APPENDIX 1

Professional and Managerial Competency definitions

Analysing and solving problems

Positive indicators:

- Identifies the core issues of a problem
- Accurately analyses facts and figures
- Explores a range of options/solutions to the problem
- Anticipates potential obstacles
- Makes logical judgments

Commercial awareness

Positive indicators:

- Understands and applies core financial management principles (i.e. cashflow, revenue, margins, return on investment, and debtors)
- Is customer-orientated in everything they do
- Knows who the competitors are and what they are doing
- Identifies opportunities to maximise profit
- Perceives opportunities for new business

Creativity

Positive indicators:

- Comes up with new ideas and workable alternatives
- Thinks flexibly, makes unusual links between issues
- Is prepared to use less conventional methods
- Generates imaginative ideas
- Is prepared to experiment

Decision making

Positive indicators:

- Is prepared to make decisions in unclear or ambiguous situations
- Accepts responsibility for decisions
- Makes decisions quickly
- Takes a calculated risk
- Does not exceed decision-making authority

Leadership

Positive indicators:

- Motivates others to reach goals
- Accepts responsibility for the actions of the team
- Encourages others to take responsibility
- Provides direction, focusing team members on goals
- Leads by example

Week Six

APPENDIX 1

Flexibility

Positive indicators:

- Reacts positively to change
- Enthusiastically drives through change
- Adapts own behaviour to suit different individuals and situations
- Is prepared to change own views
- Is open to new methods and technologies

Integrity

Positive indicators:

- Respects company values
- Is fair in dealings with others
- Maintains ethical standards
- Does what they say they would/will do
- Respects sensitive and confidential information

Relating to others

Positive indicators:

- Respects and shows consideration to others
- Acknowledges the ideas and contributions of others
- Actively helps and supports others
- Shows tolerance towards others
- Is sociable and approachable

Week Six

APPENDIX 1

Planning and organising

Positive indicators:

- Prepares in advance for short and medium term
- Creates effective schedules, sets and monitors objectives and time-scales
- Prioritises work accurately
- Meets deadlines
- Plans for changing circumstances

Persuasive communications

Positive indicators:

- Communicates clearly, both orally and in writing
- Speaks confidently on both a one-to-one and group level
- Utilises facts and information to influence others
- Promotes own ideas
- Convinces others and wins them round to own point of view

Quality driven

Positive indicators:

- Knows what standards need to be achieved
- Pays attention to quality issues
- Maintains quality standards
- Sets high standards
- Achieves high quality results

APPENDIX 1

Self-motivation and resilience

Positive indicators:

- Is calm and relaxed
- Remains upbeat, despite set-backs
- Is motivated by a challenge
- Is enthusiastic
- Shows drive and determination to get results

Strategic thinking

Positive indicators:

- Considers longer-term impact
- Perceives wider implications of actions
- Demonstrates a broad-based understanding of issues
- Is aware of broader market trends
- Links own and team's objectives to broader business goals

APPENDIX 2 — Week Six

STAR INTERVIEW TEMPLATE

For the Competency of . . .

What was the situation?

What tasks had to be done?

What actions did you take?

What was the result?

For information

on other

IN A **WEEK** titles

go to

www.inaweek.co.uk